FV_

St. Louis Community College

Forest Park
Florissant Valley
Meramec

Instructional Resources
St. Louis, Missouri

GAYLORD

IMAGES OF CONTEMPORARY ICELAND

IMAGES OF CONTEMPORARY ICELAND

EVERYDAY LIVES AND GLOBAL CONTEXTS

Edited by Gísli Pálsson and E. Paul Durrenberger

 University of Iowa Press

Iowa City

University of Iowa Press, Iowa City 52242
Printed in the United States of America

Design by Omega Clay

Printed on acid-free paper

Library of Congress Cataloging-in-Publication Data

Images of contemporary Iceland: everyday lives and global
  contexts / edited by Gísli Pálsson and E. Paul Durrenberger.
      p.   cm.
  Includes bibliographical references and index.
  ISBN 0-87745-528-7 (alk. paper)
    1. Ethnography—Iceland.   2. Iceland—Social life and
customs.   I. Gísli Pálsson, 1949–   .   II. Durrenberger, E. Paul,
1943–   .
DL331.I43   1996
306'.094912—dc20   95-35078
                                                           CIP

01 00 99 98 97 96 C 5 4 3 2 1

CONTENTS

PREFACE

In 1987 we organized a workshop to take stock of anthropological research on Iceland. We collected and published papers from that meeting in *The Anthropology of Iceland* (University of Iowa Press, 1989). This volume proved to be a success; in the next five years anthropological work on Iceland intensified as people continued various lines of inquiry and there were more people, both Icelanders and non-Icelanders, working in the area. We thought it an opportune time to reassess the state of this work and organized a second workshop held in Iowa City in 1993. This time we defined the subject more narrowly as ethnographic research on modern Iceland. We invited all those who had recently worked in Iceland, and many of them were able to participate in the workshop. Most of the contributions appear in the present volume, but some were committed elsewhere; the papers by Sigríður Dúna Kristmundsdóttir and Gísli Pálsson appeared in *Social Anthropology* and *Man*, respectively.

During the course of the lively discussions among the two dozen participants, it soon became apparent that a focus on images was emerging. This focus reflects a broader trend in anthropology, which we take up in the introduction. Thus, we could see the anthropology of Iceland as grappling with central issues of the discipline in the context and locale of a modern nation. Since the workshop we have worked with the authors to prepare a set of related essays addressed to similar questions about the many different contexts of modern life in Iceland. While most of the essays in this volume are revisions of work first presented at the workshop, others emerged as topics that first arose in the discussions there; the essays by Brydon and Pálsson and Helgason were prepared later with this volume in mind.

The workshop upon which this work is based could not have occurred without the support of the University of Iowa–University of Iceland Exchange Program. Both of our universities supported the workshop not only with words and in spirit but with money. For their support we thank President Hunter Rawlings of the University of Iowa and Rektor Sigmundur Guðbjarnason of the University of Iceland. The United States National Science Foundation and the Iceland–United States Educational Commission also funded the workshop.

We thank Shaun Hughes of the English Department and Myrdene Anderson of the Sociology and Anthropology Department at Purdue University for their lively and informed participation in our workshop. Hughes provided the fine-grained historical and literary detail from his familiarity with a diverse range of sources on Iceland, while Anderson provided her expansive view of anthropology and comprehensive understanding of issues. The contributors to this volume also benefited from comments and discussion by several other participants, including Sigríður Dúna Kristmundsdóttir, Hanna Ragnarsdóttir, and Hallfríður Þórarinsdóttir. Joe Bishop took care of the important details of the workshop, making everything from transportation to coffee breaks function smoothly. Agnar Helgason helped in the tedious details of the final preparation of the manuscript.

IMAGES OF CONTEMPORARY ICELAND

E. PAUL DURRENBERGER AND GÍSLI PÁLSSON

1

INTRODUCTION

If ever there was a bounded, self-contained society, it might be Iceland. It is a moderately large island in the middle of the North Atlantic with a small and relatively homogeneous population descended from ninth-century refugees from the unification of Norway. If ever there was an island of history, it, too, might be Iceland. The settlers had hardly disembarked when their descendants in the twelfth century began writing about their histories, family relationships, hardships, and victories. Iceland presents an image of a homogeneous island population with a long, well-recorded history—an apparently ideal subject for anthropologists looking for neat boundaries, self-contained cultures, and natural laboratories. In one way or another these dimensions have been the focus of much past work on Iceland by anthropologists, sociologists, historians, or others, Icelandic and foreign. The essays in this book challenge the notion of the cultural and historical island with reference to both Icelandic ethnography and anthropological theory, emphasizing the flow of cultural constructs in a holistic global world.

The process of inventing self and ethnicity entails claims to uniqueness. While one hears a lot about the past in connection with Iceland, this volume focuses on the ethnography of the present. Iceland is a modern nation and a site for the manufacture of nationalism; it is, to use Benedict Anderson's term (1991 [1983]), an "imagined community," composed of people who imagine themselves as such. Imagination works on images, and images of Iceland are the focus of the works in this book. We have divided the essays into three sections: Contested Images of Nature, Nation and Gender, and Nature and Nation. In this introduction we develop a framework for the work as a whole and suggest directions for a reorientation of anthropology. It draws heavily upon the writings of Arjun Appadurai (1990, 1991), Ulf Hannerz (1992, 1993), and Tim Ingold (1992, 1993), emphasizing the continuity of the human world and the relativity of viewpoints.

Ethnography, moving into different landscapes to see different perspectives, takes us between and among spaces, puts us in the experienced realities of people so we can see the diversity within boundaries and the consequences of ritualized images in everyday life. Rather than denying reality, it puts us into a confrontation with realities. Discovering realities on the ground, in the landscapes, is the job of ethnography. Collectively, the following essays emphasize the importance of moving from text to ethnography, assessing the lived experience of real people. This work points to a number of common themes which challenge the concept of culture itself as a theoretical construct in anthropology as well as the potential for understanding differences and similarities. The following discussion focuses on four dimensions of the process of imagining: the chaotic flow of images and identities in the global context, cultural constructions of gender and landscape, the politics of custom and history, and the plurality of voices.

The Landscape of Images

The dominant reality of modern ethnography is the inescapability of nations, apparent in anthropological writings wherever they engage them. We see nations as continually manufactured artefacts that emerge from contests among states and individuals in global flows of images, power, and commodities (Foster 1991). Like Akhil Gupta and James Ferguson, we are interested "less in establishing a dialogic relation between geographically distinct societies than in ex-

ploring the processes of *production* of difference in a world of culturally, socially, and economically interconnected and interdependent
spaces" (1992: 14).

Rather than search for isolated bounded groups that function in a
changeless ethnographic present, Appadurai (1990) points to the dis-
junctures between economy, culture, and politics in a global flow of
"ethnoscapes" of different moving groups of persons such as exiles,
guestworkers, tourists, immigrants, refugees, and others. He uses the
term "scape" to suggest that social understanding depends on the
observer's perspective as the view of landscape depends on where
the viewer stands. Besides ethnoscapes, he suggests, there are "tech-
noscapes" (of moving mechanical and informational technology that
knows no boundaries), "financescapes" (of stock markets, commodity markets, and currency markets), "mediascapes" (supplying the
materials for imagining lives), and, finally, "ideoscapes" (of state and
counterstate ideologies centered on images of rights, sovereignty, and
democracy). The interactions of these dimensions are disjunctive
and unpredictable, since each moves in terms of its own constraints
and incentives, but acts as a constraint and parameter for each of the
others. Though Appadurai does not use the term, this is an image of
a chaotic system.

Groups that see themselves as nations, sharing common imaginations, seek to become states and states seek to monopolize the moral
resources of community by claiming they are connected to nations or
by manufacturing national heritages. Catherine M. Cameron and
John B. Gatewood (1994) show how a community in Pennsylvania
has appropriated the nostalgia of authenticity as a marketable tourist
commodity to replace reliance on heavy industry to manufacture
steel as that enterprise has moved to other global locales. An industry
relocates and a town invents authenticity. Labor, finance, and technology are separated, each moving across the face of the globe in
swiftly changing currents. Therefore, states have to stay open to the
influences of travel, technology, and media. Ethnicity is no longer
local; it is a global force forming on the borders of states with the
chaotic fractiles of commerce, media, national policy, and consumer
fantasy.

Anthropology has played a role in these processes, feeding the
imaginations with visions of essentialized cultures, "attributional
identities" as Ingold (1993) calls them, based on characteristic patterns
or essences that define them. In Java and Bali, "the attention shown

to certain dance dramas and art forms by high-status foreign professors has led the Indonesians to privilege those forms within their own
culture" (Bruner 1993: 20). Anthropology—a discipline traditionally
focused on local bounded worlds, othering, and "cultural translation"
(Pálsson 1993b)—has found and defined the units of comparison,
given them contents and descriptions, and defined the direction of
translation to the centers of global power in Western and Eastern Europe, America, China, and Japan. The "cultural critique" school starts
with difference, peoples with separate histories, that anthropologists
bridge by using experience in one to comment on another. Thus anthropology has provided material for the construction of ideoscapes
of nationality and ethnoscapes of romantic harmony that inform mediascapes. Sometimes this involves fostering beliefs in holistic heal-
ing and ecological compatibility (Keesing 1989), the contradictions of
which have become increasingly apparent in Iceland, as Anne Brydon and Níels Einarsson point out in this volume.

In developing such portrayals, scholars have often described unity
where there was multiplicity, in binary opposition to their Western
self-imagining in a process that Edward Said (1978) has called "Orientalism." In India, a unitary view was useful to nationalists for the
construction of images of a shared nationality. The idea of cultural
relativity and bounded cultures led them to represent India as a vi-
brant and independent entity. The attribution of this entity also provided the basis for further Orientalist descriptions (Prakash 1990).
Thus essentialism, characterizing a people by enduring characteristics, is not unique to the "West." Indeed, to speak of Europe or the
"West" or Euro-America is to partake of the same essentialism; it is
less a geographical characteristic than a characteristic of nationalism.
Nationalism defines nations in essentialist terms whether they be East
or West, and then defines others in opposition (Macdonald 1993).
While the Orientalist process of definition in natural, uniform terms,
has taken place in Iceland, both by natives and by foreigners (Pálsson
1995), Iceland has not been uniform. Works in this volume indicate
that there have been significant differences of gender, as Julie Gurdin, Unnur Dís Skaptadóttir, and Inga Dóra Björnsdóttir show, and
class, as Paul Durrenberger and Gísli Pálsson and Agnar Helgason argue (all in this volume). These and other differences are frequently
denied in the imagining process of nation-making rhetoric.

In the search for people in contact with their ancestors, free of
the sadness of the tropics, as Claude Lévi-Strauss (1955) called the

condition of modernity, anthropologists have searched the deserts and oceans of the world. Often, however, the realities of everyday life we find on islands of romantic imagery do not match the images, and anthropologists are searching for new ways of understanding their ethnographic observations (Carrier 1992: 18). Roger Keesing and Margaret Jolly (1992: 239) see indigenous responses not as mechanical results of blueprints or grammars but as creative solutions informed by individual agency—an image Jean Lave, uncomfortable with the concept of culture, presents as the idea of cognition "seamlessly distributed across persons, activity and setting" (1988: 171), the idea of persons acting in settings to solve problems. Again, she sees mind, culture, and history as interrelated, mutually constituting each other, emphasizing the relational interdependency of "agent and world, activity, meaning, cognition, learning, and knowing" (Lave 1991: 67), of people in social relations engaged in activity in and with a practical world.

Anthropologists have thought of cultures as blueprints for action, as grammars of behavior, as rules, as meanings, but almost always as systems of some kind—systems that are internally coherent and have edges. The idea of these systems, Ingold (1993) argues, is the consequence of the idea of universal reason, which stands outside cultures and sees different views of the world. For the people to whom anthropologists attribute cultures, they are simply experiential reality. Do people, then, inhabit different worlds to the extent that they differ? If we are all alike, do we inhabit but one world? The questions only make sense if we think of the mind as separate from the body and culture as separate from nature. If we do not make these separations, people in the same situations see the same things—not different ones. Hence we can learn to see as others do by putting ourselves in their places. The sense of the questions derives from the dualism of mind and body—the worlds of nature and culture.

The idea of homogeneity has been subject to criticism and the concept of culture brought to the brink of extinction. In his book *Europe and the People without History*, Eric Wolf (1982) contests the notion of isolated worlds, emphasizing that if cultures are bounded entities like billiard balls they bounce across the table of history, colliding with each other with unequal effects. The reality of the larger world is not a new state of affairs. K. F. Olwig (1993) shows, for instance, how Afro-Caribbean identity in a West Indian community has been carved within a global context since the 1600s. Sidney Mintz (1985) similarly shows how the British working-class custom of drinking tea and the social relations of tea production on South Asian plantations and of sugar production in the Caribbean were all parts of a difference-generating historical process.

As Ulf Hannerz points out (1992, 1993), partly drawing upon Marshal McLuhan's concept of the "global village," recently the human world has become a "global ecumene" in a very real sense, "an area of persistent social interaction and cultural flow" (1993: 44). These global flows have been coming over the human horizons since we started walking, but they became exponentially faster first with boats and printing, then with airplanes and telegraphs, and now with electronic and fiber optic networks and computer technology. The conventional anthropological idea of cultural translation in the global mosaic of cultural islands, therefore, is no longer appropriate, if it ever was. Because of radical changes in means of communication— the introduction of space satellites, computer technology, E-mail, mobile telephones, FAX machines, cable television—cultural artefacts nowadays move across continents with the speed of light. This is likely to lead to a redefinition of the anthropological project:

> One necessary ingredient in making anthropology contribute realistically to an understanding of the contemporary world . . . might be to look not only in front of us, first, at whatever we take to be an "other" culture, and then over the shoulder, at an audience at home, but also sideways, at the various other people also situated at the interfaces between cultures and engaged in making the global ecumene. There are journalists and film-makers there, tourists and tour guides, social workers, jurists, business consultants. (Hannerz 1993: 48)

Several scholars have followed Hannerz's lead, focusing on the dynamics and the channels of cultural flow and the tension between homogenization and heterogenization, between cultural hegemony (usually attributed to the West) and local appropriations of cultural constructs.

Continuing the metaphor of the landscape, imagine, as Ingold (1993) invites us to, people in a continuous, unbounded, endlessly varied landscape. Each place we move is different from the others, surrounded by different horizons which dissolve into others as we move, but there are no lines to cross. We describe the view of each place from that place, how it looks from that viewpoint. Another place has another view of the same world. If we stand in the same place, we see the same view. The view of universal reason suggests that the landscape is uniform but the people viewing it are different—have different representations of it. Ingold, following G. H. Mead, suggests instead that people construct self-identities from their positions within a continuous field of ongoing relationships, each position defining a unique point of view within the process. Difference is a function of involvement with others in continuous processes. Community is continuous, so the category "we" expands indefinitely from the center where "I" stands (Ingold 1993: 228). If, however, instead of expanding to include others, we include only those who share the same vantage points, we create boundaries—at the same time claiming similarity for those within the boundary and attributing difference to those on the other side. Homogeneity and heterogeneity, therefore, are two sides of the same boundary. Ethnicities are not primordial, not original natural groups or identities like big families; rather they are consequences of an affiliation in which identity given by a position in a social field is replaced by identity defined by essential patterns of mental representation—cultures.

In this volume, Níels Einarsson situates Iceland not only in the warming waters of the Gulf Stream but in the international flow of images that wash over Iceland and the lives and thoughts of the inhabitants of coastal villages. He describes how fishers conceptualize their prey and how their economic uses of maritime resources inform their conceptualizations of them. Environmentalists contest such constructions with more distanced interpretations based on other positions in the landscape and other experiences in it. Moral, and sometimes romantic, constructions by foreigners thus become part of the cognitive and political environment of fishers as much as the fish in the sea they engage as part of their economic environment. Magnús Einarsson takes us on an ethnographic tour to show how Icelanders stage their ethnicity for an audience of visiting tourists during the summer season and how that foreign gaze shapes the staging of national identity at Christmas for a domestic audience of Icelanders as they remind themselves of who they are and rehearse for the summer.

Again, we see the island awash in a sea of global images, as well as the tourists who witness them and manufacture them, and how Icelanders respond to them. The ethnography of local tourism and of localities bidding for tourist attention shows the role of larger processes that define economic and cultural realities. Leisure migration in Europe, conditioned by a series of social and economic processes associated with the industrial revolution, now occurs on a massive scale: "Tourism relates to earlier forms of travel for pleasure in the same way as printing, especially mass-produced book printing, has been the industrial-capitalist equivalent of the manuscript" (Böröcz 1992: 736). Where islands of culture do not exist, they are manufactured for tourists, in Cajun country, Chinatowns, the French island of Québec City, and Little Germanys in the United Kingdom (Boniface and Fowler 1993: 17). We observe even a new "Iceland" in Gimli, Manitoba, in Canada (Durrenberger and Pálsson 1989b).

Constructions of Boundaries: Gender and Landscape

Nations, as Anderson suggests (1991 [1983]), are limited in the boundaries of the territories they claim. The boundaries become especially important when they are invisible, easy to invade and hard to defend, as in the case of a small island like Iceland that depends on the resources of the sea within the boundaries of the sea it claims. The boundaries delimit and define; they draw lines and specify who may be inside and who must be outside. The !Kung, archetype of the isolated primitive band, whose identity and name, Bushman/San, is a consequence of retribalization policies of colonial powers, are not isolated but form an underclass in a larger formation. Davydd J. Greenwood (1985) shows that Basque ethnicity is a product of specific circumstances, a geography and political economy, and has changed with changing circumstances and that Andalusian ethnicity is not more artificial but only more recent. The question is how these processes happened. The "primordial" categories become consequences rather than causes. Rather than asking why is it that people are willing to die and kill for ethnic notions such as nation, we might better ask how those categories and sentiments are generated—what are the economic and political realities and relationships that lead to ethnic cleansing, mass rape, and homicidal and suicidal terror and war? What are the alternatives for the people in those landscapes, what interests are contested, who defines the issues and alternatives and by what means, by what power, and what relationships stand behind and ratify that power? The questions are as relevant for Bosnia as for Bushmen.

It may be human to classify as Claude Lévi-Strauss (1972) suggests, but making boundaries and defining categories only become

obsessions under particular historical circumstances. One classificatory exercise is the attempt to define species in such measures as the
Endangered Species Act in the United States. Having drawn the lines
around species, having demonstrated their uniqueness from others
and their homogeneity within the boundaries, the state can protect
them to ensure the diversity of life forms on the planet with no
concern for human realities. The rhetoric of the debates has been
strongly dualistic—"we" and our side—environmentalists or fishers—are rational, scientific, and progressive and "they"—our opponents—are irrational, superstitious, and traditional or reactionary
(Durrenberger 1992b; see also Brydon, this volume). We see the same
rhetoric in Iceland as the movement becomes international, with the
environmentalists' concern for the welfare of whales and marine
mammals. Though Níels Einarsson and Anne Brydon (this volume)
do not assess the debates and controversies about whaling in the
same way, they both point out that the very issue—no matter how it
is formulated, no matter how it is interpreted, no matter how it is understood—places Iceland in a global context. Culturally, politically,
and economically Iceland is not an island.

Since the first government of the newly independent Republic of
Iceland initiated a development policy centered on industrial fishing
there has been no debate about the importance of fishing to Iceland's
economy and society. Anne Brydon discusses the ways in which media, government, and industry have framed understandings of the international whaling issue in order to emphasize the nationalist definitions of territory, property, and nature on which industrial fishing
is built. By situating her analysis in an examination of both the independence movement and strategizing within the International Whaling Commission, she demonstrates how protagonists within the whaling debate selectively represent their opponents in order to justify
their respective stands. Icelandic nationalist sentiment is thus mobi-
lized in defense of the whaling industry, which, ironically, contributed relatively little to the Icelandic economy.

Gísli Pálsson and Agnar Helgason (this volume) chronicle the
redefinition of space from inside Iceland as the state has reallocated
access to fish, the major economic resource, from all Icelanders to a
select few with a quota system. Economics has replaced marine biology as the hegemonic discipline as the accumulation of fishing rights
in fewer hands challenges previously salient images of equity. In this,
as in the redefinition of fishing boundaries, Iceland has led the way

along with a few other countries. Other nations are watching the experiment with individual transferable quotas (ITQs) as the state has blessed some with ownership of this new form of property and damned others to work for the new owners. Pálsson and Helgason show the development of inequality as a consequence of the quota system, demonstrating how it is being contested in the process. Salient dimensions of the story are its international context, the way it is locally contested, and the role of the state and the flow of images in both.

The rhetorical identification of nature and nation, the creation of national landscapes, is frequently part of nationalist ideologies (K. R. Olwig 1993). Roots in the soil become especially important when one is a native of a nation. Thus nation, native, and nature all have much in common and in nationalistic images one can celebrate the purity or decry the pollution of all. Given such an identification, people who leave the homeland become anomalous. "West-Icelanders," emigrants from Iceland who left to go to the United States or Canada in the late nineteenth century, are one example. They became curiosities in Iceland (Durrenberger and Pálsson 1989b; Brydon 1987). Their images of Iceland were formed before those current today, causing some dissonance to both Icelanders and West-Icelanders when the older images are compared with the newer in visits to relatives. Hutu refugees who fled genocidal massacres of 1972 in Burundi to Tanzania provide another example (Malkki 1992). One group was settled in a rigorously organized isolated camp and other individuals were dispersed in working neighborhoods. Those who were apart in the camp constructed and passionately reconstructed their history as a people became concerned with matters of purity and developed a strong national identity, while those who integrated into an existing social order got on with their lives, sought ways to assimilate, and borrowed identities to develop creolized rhizomatic identities based on situation rather than essential and moral identities. The camp refugees saw their worldly cosmopolitanism as impure, beyond the boundaries—as Other.

One universal identifying element of the self is the nation, defined by boundary lines. National communities are presented as images rather than experiential realities, imagined as horizontal comradeship in spite of realities of hierarchy, inequality, and exploitation. National identities are shaped by what they are not (McDonald 1993), and nations seek to draw lines, define and enforce categories, and administer difference via segregation, censorship, and more brutal means. Nationality becomes a sign of personal identity—everyone in the world of nations has one. Everyone who does not have a national identity, such as refugees or immigrants worrying about whether their real identity lies with the old homeland or the new one or people in frontier and border areas who have not been administered sufficiently thoroughly to have been issued identity papers, are anomalous, without names. They do not fit.

The seemingly "natural" construct of gender, another universal of personal identity, is illustrated by nations' tendencies to represent themselves as chaste, dutiful, maternal, daughterly women. Few nationalisms, however, grant women and men equal access to resources. Nationalism legitimates male dominance over women and has a special affinity for male society, the passionate brotherhood that requires the identification, isolation, and containment of male homosexuality to protect its proper homosociality. The virile brotherhood's idealization of motherhood excludes nonconforming sexualities from the imagining of the nation (Parker, Russo, Sommer, and Yaeger 1992).

One reading of the Icelandic sagas, a favorite source for nationalist ideologues, emphasizes the strength and independence of Icelandic women. Modern literature stretches the image from Guðrún Ósvífursdóttir of *Laxdæla saga* to the heroine of one of Halldór Laxness's most popular novels, *Salka Valka*, written in the 1930s. Julie Gurdin (this volume) identifies independence as a key theme in the rhetoric of the nation and of individuals, pointing out that the discourse is unmistakably masculine because it excludes women. The state and motherhood are public and prized, but domestic violence of men against women is defined as private and thus not a matter for public policy. Gurdin shows how women in Iceland are contesting these constructions in their struggle to move domestic violence into the public discourse and motherhood into the private domain. Unnur Dís Skaptadóttir (this volume) challenges the naturalness of gender constructs and argues on local ethnographic evidence that they must be constructed of everyday experience of gender segregation and discrimination. These definitions have material consequences: they limit the range of economic opportunities for women in Iceland as well as their economic well-being, since they are connected to the occupational possibilities for women to their disadvantage. The images of brave and independent women carrying on with their households while their heroic husbands are away fishing contribute to disguising the sociological and economic realities of gender discrimination in Iceland.

Inga Dóra Björnsdóttir (this volume) continues the discussion of cultural constructions of gender in her analysis of the political stance of President Vigdís Finnbogadóttir, arguing that the masculine/political dimension is paired with an opposite maternal/cultural dimension and that the president has strengthened this dichotomization by playing the maternal, cultural role and not the political one that could potentially alter, if not transform, the realities of gender relationships—realities chronicled in the papers by Skaptadóttir and Gurdin.

The Politics of Custom and History

Franz Boas stressed the history and autonomy of cultures. Modern anthropology, however, has made the culture of history problematic and reemphasized the dynamics of history, broadening the scope from the local to a global scale. Anthropologists such as Sidney Mintz (1985), Robert Murphy and Julian Steward (1956), Elman Service (1955), and Eric Wolf (1957) confronted history when their studies of peasants in the face-to-face relationships of the little community of ethnographic observation had to be placed in historical context to comprehend their institutional forms. Maurice Freedman (1963) pointed out how anthropologists buried in the details of local village cultures in China were forced, by their expulsion after 1949, to conceive of China as an entity, as a transvillage polity they had to understand when access to the locales of their research was cut off. Students of European villages and folk are facing a similar reorientation today (Macdonald 1993). Many others have felt compelled to reconceptualize their object of study to include large, complex, and constantly changing national polities and international relations. Anthropology's intersection with history is not especially new (see Comaroff and Comaroff 1992), but it is current as anthropologists continue to rediscover that local communities are situated in the dynamics of nations and time.

The confrontation with history, the very sense of dynamism and change, has challenged some of anthropology's organizing concepts from classical works of British social anthropologists. If social structure is the systems of classification and rules—blueprints, grammars—and social organization is how people use them in everyday life, there can be deviance from rules, but there is nevertheless no way to change the rules themselves. There is no relationship, as Maurice Bloch points out (1977), between nonconforming behavior and the ordering system of rules and categories. Assigning motive force to material or economic infrastructure external to rules and conceptual structures may solve the problem of accounting for change. If, however, one assumes that the actors fail to comprehend their own infrastructures, it becomes impossible to theorize how people in a system can develop alternative views or critiques of any aspect of their own system—as for instance, Gurdin argues Icelandic women do. There is no agency. If concepts are determined by social realities, there is no escape from the prison of culture, and no way to understand change. Bloch suggests that in exoticizing the foreign some British anthropologists have extracted what they call social structures from local ritual expressions which vary from place to place. These social anthropologists did not focus on invariant universal dimensions of human cognition, he argues, and therefore they described cultures as so many billiard balls, each changeless and bounded and isolated.

Bloch (1977) reasons that awareness of their own infrastructures is the basis for peoples' critiques of their own social structure, depicted to themselves in ritual, and thus the source of changes of ideas (cf. Scott 1985). Ideas based on realities of everyday life in the present are the basis for challenges to concepts of timelessness represented in ritual. The greater the inequality in a social order, the greater the amount of ritual versus mundane communication, and the greater the sense of the past in the present to ratify the ritual and justify the hierarchy. Cognitive images of hierarchy, "social structures," Bloch argues, are mental models of social relations in which inequality appears to be an inevitable part of an ordered system divorced from everyday realities in which nature and society are mystified, presented to people as ritual.

Appadurai (1990) challenges Bloch's view that ritual is entirely shared and that everything that is not ritual is pragmatics, suggesting (following Leach) that ritual is a language of argument and that the important question concerning that argument is how it is organized within local frameworks. He suggests four universals of argumentation: consensus on sources and their credibility (authority), linkage of current cases with sources of authority (continuity), the relative values of different periods in the past (depth), and interdependence of any past with others to be credible. Saga scholars' reception of anthropological analyses of medieval Icelandic literature that violate their textual assumptions provide an apt Icelandic example. Thus, for instance, because Knut Odner (1974) developed an understanding from anthropological theory and comparative examples, his analysis of the sagas was roundly rejected by the community of saga scholars. This analysis failed on every one of Appadurai's universals of argumentation and was therefore not credible to saga scholars of that time. Magnús Stefánsson (1974), a native scholar, refused to acknowledge the contribution of anthropology to source criticism, the use of anthropological theory, or comparative studies and accused Odner of breaking with the tradition of literary scholarship, concluding, for that reason alone, that Odner was not to be believed.

The contemplation of nations raises the politics of history to as important a level as the history of politics, because all nations create themselves and their images of themselves through the manipulations of their histories (Keesing 1989). History, Lévi-Strauss suggests, often plays the organizing role for nations that totemic systems do for peoples who do not conceive of themselves as nations. As Appadurai (1990) points out, *contra* Bloch, nationalist discourse shapes the politics of the representation of history in a nonritualistic rhetoric. In Iceland, Paul Durrenberger suggests (this volume), as a whole generation since independence in 1944 has grown up embroiled in industrial fishing and fish processing, a new historiography is emerging, challenging the orthodox view of the independence movement and romantic nationalists that centered on farms and farming. In South Asia the politics of the past center on linear accounts of events organized around written texts including colonial legal and administrative documents. When the pasts of contending groups are mutually credible, conflict may be muted. But, where one vision of the past does not match that of another, the past is contested. In Ethiopia different groups appeal to different dimensions of history as they challenge the dominant nationalism (Sorenson 1992).

The romantic historiography and folklore of Iceland were the products of a nationalist movement and served its purposes. As David Scott (1992) points out for Sri Lanka, it is important not simply to receive such established wisdom but to attempt to understand it as socially created. We can see this outlook as largely ritualistic, in Bloch's terms, but if it mystified at all in the Icelandic context, it may have mystified scholars who construct images of the country at least as much as the people who live there (Jónsson 1989). In Sri Lanka agriculture has been reoriented from domestic to commodity production and relationships of reciprocity and mutual aid have been supplanted by wage relationships, but ritualistic presentations of nationalist rhetoric make the nostalgic image of farming villagers central in its ethnoscape for local consumption (Brow 1990). In Ethiopia and much of Africa local elites developed national identities around dimensions of peasant culture while they were studying abroad in London, Paris, and New York (Donham 1992). Icelandic nationalism has in common with other nationalisms the creation of images of nationhood and self as enduring and constant subjects of history, an emphasis on deep historical roots, and continuity with a remote past, all guaranteed by stories vouchsafed from ages long ago.

If we define ritual or the symbolic as action that is not directed toward empirical ends—following Edmund R. Leach (1954), Roy Rappaport (1971), or Dan Sperber (1975)—then all the panoply of symbolism and action surrounding nationalism is ritual. A focus on this dimension of life in modern nations can yield a picture of great local variation from one nation to another as each invents traditions, languages, customs, costumes, dances, and usages (Macdonald 1993; Hobsbawm and Ranger 1983). Focusing on the exotic, anthropologists focus on this variation and not on similarities. Thus anthropology can become part of the phenomenon, ratifying the sense of ritual separation, providing evidence for uniqueness, contributing to nationalist discourse and ritual statements (Keesing 1989; Prakash 1990). For this reason folklore studies have an important place and role in the creation of nationalist rhetoric. If ritual is all the nonempirical actions that generate messages and images, we might better understand why people in refugee camps and university campuses in foreign lands indulge in the creation of the rituals and myths of nationalism to such a great extent. In such contexts the pragmatic, the practical world of work, is reduced to almost nothing and the only reality left is symbolic. It is no mistake that many nationalisms, including Iceland's, were created at foreign universities and others, such as those of Hutu and Palestinians, were built in camps.

In their review of the literature on ritual, structure, and history, John D. Kelley and Martha Kaplan (1990) challenge the idea of an ongoing structure or system-informing practice, suggesting that there are no templates that produce rituals, through which anthropologists can infer the blueprints for cultures. Rather, rituals are acts of power that build structures. This seems to agree with Leach's point that it is rituals that make gods, kings, presidents, and property rights by ratifying the authority of actors, whether it is rooted in some kind of *mana* or a constitution. Ritual confers authority. And, as Keesing (1989) points out for *mana*, academic authority may define ritual because it was anthropologists who spread the concept throughout the Pacific. Again, our minds are focused on the exotic, but Kelley and Kaplan direct our attention to practice, emphasizing that ritual is a vehicle for authority. In this volume Björnsdóttir points out how the ritual actions of the president of Iceland ratify cultural practices of gender inequality.

The cultural constructs of nationalism are focal in the last section of the book. Daniel Vasey discusses the image of miserable conditions and compensatory high fertility in premodern Iceland as mythical. Partly using information from censuses and church records, preserved on microfilm in Mormon archives in Utah to propitiate the ancestors of Icelandic converts to that religion, Vasey constructs demographic data to show that the processes that characterize Iceland were common to Europe. He does not deny the reality of misery, but points out that the image of unique and almost unbearable misery, endured and survived in the unique island of "fire and ice," is an exaggerated construct of the nationalist ideology of independence. That idea, as Magnús Einarsson shows, has been reinforced by the tourist industry of recent years.

Paul Durrenberger continues this theme in his discussion of the ideology of the individual and shows that the privileging of this concept at the expense of the social is apparent in constructions of language use and understandings of the fishery. This privileging of self is central to the denial of difference by class as well as gender. He recommends that anthropologists move from texts to real life and ethnography, as Beverly A. Sizemore and Christopher H. Walker (this volume) do. The latter show that in the nationalist ideology of independence there was a powerful image of literacy, saga reading, and continuity of medieval language into modern times. Loftur Guttormsson (1989), Vésteinn Ólason (1989), and Richard Bauman (1992) have outlined the role and realities of readership in the past. The ethnographic work of Sizemore and Walker adds to our understanding by showing how the current nationalist image projected to the outside fails to capture the everyday realities of Icelanders in the global context of electronic media, pointing to the disjunction between images of literacy—the textualism of Icelanders (Pálsson 1995)—and realities of literacy practice in contemporary Iceland.

Contested Voices

David Scott (1992) argues persuasively that because knowledge is embedded in networks of assumptions shaped by power relations we must interrogate rather than simply receive it. He leaves unanswered, however, the question of who interrogates the interrogator, or what gives him or her the right to privilege this interrogation over any other? As with postmodern discourse, it is "turtles all the way down" (Geertz 1973: 29), interrogations of interrogations with only egoistic claims for attention. Akhil Gupta and James Ferguson (1992) rightly ask: Who are the "we" who interrogate? In raising the question, they draw attention to the rules for inclusion and exclusion, where the lines are laid and who draws them. Scott may, therefore, recreate, along with much anthropology in the writing-culture genre, one of the more recent "new ethnographies," the conditions he critiques. The one who interrogates the interrogator is the purveyor of the next "new" ethnography, always a fixture on the moving horizon of anthropology as we plow old fields and reinvent wheels. Perhaps we should revise our questions and vocabulary, asking how difference is produced rather than assuming it. Instead of looking for the next turtle, perhaps we should seek the ground.

Tim Ingold, Jean Lave, and some others advocate abandoning the idea of culture and cultures—the assumption of difference and boundaries. But culture is the business of anthropology and we may wonder if it is not heretical—or worse, will we not do ourselves out of business—if we deny the salience or the existence of culture and cultures? We think not. We think it can help bring us out of an absorption with romantic images to a more authentic understanding of human life. We advocate *old* ethnography, attention to local detail; if we pay attention, we see the links to the global. Imagine yourself on that paradigmatic beach with Bronislaw Malinowski in the opening of *Argonauts of the Western Pacific*, but now put the pearl traders, the ship's captain and crew, the missionaries, and the colonial administrators into the ethnographic picture instead of filtering them out. Then proceed as he advised. We do not chastise realist ethnography for describing realities. We ask for it. Without it, we fall into the other traps of the new "new ethnography," passing responsibility for reality claims to the readers or the people we write about, evading responsibility ourselves, pretending we are not part of the process, and misrepresenting relationships. There is nothing very new, for instance, about the multiple processes of the modern world—the supposedly "new" economic forms of fractured capitalism are only new to those who ignore ethnographic description (Smith 1991). Attuned to ethnography rather than literary images and posturing, we should ask how these very forms that some anthropologists think new have survived so long in many places. To go even further, there is even less new or European about empires and states. Consider China, Ethiopia, the Inka, the Aztec, Japan, Thailand, Burma, and their incorporation of others into their empires and states.

We know it is impossible to know reality in any final way, but rather than withdraw into the images provided by the states of the world, ready-made fantasies we are invited to share and perpetuate, we advocate attempts to know reality as best we can. We can conceive of anthropologists not as objective culture-free observers moving local knowledges from their exotic locales into the world ecumene for edification, entertainment, or exchange values, but as people among people who move from place to place in the landscapes of the planet to see the variety of viewpoints and understand how they are produced and how their production affects the daily lives of the people of those places. We can try to understand the production of difference as a historical process and see the attribution of differences, ethnicities, and boundaries as consequences rather than causes of the way they have been integrated into the modern world, a continuous and connected space traversed by economic and political relations of inequality. This needs more than a sympathetic hearing and good writing to represent the voices of others, and ratify the image of otherness in so doing; it requires a willingness to question the very divisions and how they came to be and why they persist (Gupta and Ferguson 1992).

If the nation is an imagined community connected to a state, it provides other images and conditions our imaginations in other ways besides community. The most obvious is the preoccupation with images. Nations without states are striving to build them, and whatever their rhetoric, as Donald Donham (1992) shows, they strengthen states. The state is such a part of our landscapes that it comes to be wherever we look. Its logic is one of classification and definition of categories—gender, ethnicities, peoples, cultures, and species. We see state landscapes in the canyons of Reykjavík, the capital city of Iceland, defined by the distances between the buildings that house different agencies of government. State landscapes fade as we travel away from capital cities with their smooth cement and asphalt roads. The gravel roads of the countryside resemble the lava of the Icelandic landscape they cut through but are more intrusive than the cairns people of previous centuries built to find their way through the darkness and fog on horses and on foot. The builders of the cairns affected the landscape more than those who stayed home, who never had passports to identify themselves in the international language of states—national and ethnic categories.

States draw borders around and between peoples and things, so we ask, with our state imaginations, how everyone defines and draws borders whether they do or not. Ingold argues (1992) that in practice categories are fleeting and contingent on our purposes and the affordances of landscapes—what they offer us; different purposes and landscapes give us different affordances. Because purposes even in a single landscape are varied, there is no consensus (Wallace 1961). Just because people can make categories does not mean that they obsessively categorize the world. Some of the ethnoscience literature attributed systems of categories where there demonstrably were none (Durrenberger and Morrison 1979). Anthropological discourse, then, has reflected the state's demand for homogeneity within boundaries. Robbins Burling (1964) addresses the issue of classification and cognition by raising the question of god's truth versus hocus pocus in connection with the new ethnography of that day, componential analysis. What guarantees, he asks, that the one of many possible analyses of categories that an anthropologist presents is the one people actually use? Is the tidy system a representation of a reality, god's truth, or is it an artefact of the systematizing gaze of the analyst, hocus pocus? Burling does not entertain the possibility that it could be neither—that all people do not actually use a single classificatory system for all purposes at all times—that people in different rhetorical, political, or work situations may appeal to different principles of classification and creatively invent new ones. If cognitive anthropology bored itself to death, as Keesing (1972) suggests in a somewhat premature obituary notice, it may be because it resolutely refused to situate itself in the world of action and experience.

Ethnic groups and boundaries are not realities to be mapped but flowing lines defined by peoples' purposes, created and defined and made real by human action. We affect landscapes by our actions and impress realities on them and move and live in landscapes created by our predecessors. In the created landscapes and their affordances, the past shapes our actions in the present and thus conditions the future. We only escape, as both Ingold (1992) and Lave (1988, 1991) suggest, by getting into radically different landscapes—fieldwork. The process of engagement of different landscapes produces the tension Ingold (1993) discusses between the formal findings we publish and teach and discuss at meetings and our experiential responses chronicled in the confessional literature that some try to bring together in reflexivism, the haunting concern for self and autobiography which seems indulgent until we understand the impossibility of communicating the basic insight via formal means. Ingold describes the process as substitution of universal reason for diverse reasons in practice. The formal findings are equivalent to objects for the state, defined in the dichotomizing logical space of the state which seeks consensus of science. In the experience of different viewpoints, there is no search for consensus, but the views of different landscapes.

One notion of science to which some anthropologists appeal is the one we inherit from the last century based on the notion of matching deductive reason to experience in the experiment. We know reality through the testing of our deductions that inform predictions our experiments corroborate. For some anthropologists, the intuition of the inadequacy of the match between the experience of fieldwork and its formal representations has led to a rejection of science, the logic of the Enlightenment, and Cartesian dualisms—maybe even reason itself and the search for something else that is a more adequate framework for representing to others the experience of different landscapes. Some anthropologists advocate thick description to represent the view of other landscapes, artfully to put readers into them. Geertz (1973) opens his exemplary, much assigned, and often cited piece on the cockfight with a police raid to situate his reader in the space he wants to describe and goes on to entangle the reader in the thicket of thickness. William Roseberry (1989) challenges this approach by asking a different set of questions he finds more relevant to the project of anthropology, about the relations of power that created that landscape and the relations among the people in it. Geertz inscribes a text, as he says, and makes the landscape stand still for a moment, emphasizing the importance of literature. In textualizing anthropology, in importing literary models, we do not escape the appeal to universal reason. It makes no difference whether the universals appealed to are literary or scientific.

If one response to the disjunction between the formal and experiential in fieldwork is to reject science, another is to seek a new kind of science. Thus chaos theory admits of nonlinear relationships, the importance of history in the critical specification of initial conditions, and the impossibility of prediction as a way to knowledge. Chaos theory may surface and begin to seem reasonable now because it reflects new realities in experienced landscapes. We do not just observe the changing fractiles of space, we experience them in our everyday lives and, like other people, attempt to craft intellectual artefacts to help us understand them. Renato Rosaldo argues that, in the absence of Ilongot rules and plans in everyday life, "zones of indeterminacy . . . promote a human capacity for improvisation in response to the unexpected" (1993: 256). This suggests the unpredictability of actions unfolding in coordination with those of other people. We advocate an understanding of creativity, agency, response, and impromptu invention, an image of Lévi-Strauss's bricoleur swimming in the chaotic currents of the global ecumene rather than the attribution of imprisoning rules, guiding blueprints, and determining grammars enduring in bounded cultures.

Like many of the people whose work we have cited, we are calling for a reorientation of anthropology. Anthropologists did not have to worry about change as long as they did not confront history. Likewise, they do not have to confront the problems associated with the concept of culture as long as they refuse to attend to the realities that surround them. Those are the realities of a contingent world that moves lightning fast and changes our perspectives with a touch of the remote control of a television or the switch of a personal computer or the lifting of a wireless telephone to hear a voice half a world away. The seamless landscape Ingold invites us to imagine is one we increasingly experience. In bringing together these currents of the realities of a chaotic planet with the concrete dimensions of persons in action on an island in the middle of the North Atlantic, we hear the multiple voices of age, gender, class, and locale, constructing various viewpoints as they move through the landscapes of fisheries quotas, domestic violence, environmentalists, nationalists, tourists, fish-processing plants, presidential politics, and electronic media. Iceland ceases to be the isolated natural laboratory and becomes one vantage point in ever shifting streams of events and images. If the ideal of the cultural billiard ball is like this, what of those with less secure boundaries?

Acknowledgments

We thank Hjörleifur Rafn Jónsson (Cornell University) for his thoughtful comments on an earlier version of this introduction.

PART I CONTESTED IMAGES OF NATURE

ANNE BRYDON

2

WHALE-SITING:
SPATIALITY IN ICELANDIC NATIONALISM

In Iceland, the dominant perception of the international whaling
    issue—that whaling practices have fallen victim to manipulative
environmentalists motivated by greed and/or sentimentality—relies
on particular intuitions and understandings of nature, human identity, and the moral value of community. In turn, these intuitions and
understandings derive from discursive practices which are linked to
the nation-state formation and figure in expressions of nationalist
sentiment. While elaborating on the dynamics of the whale issue, this
essay analyzes the cultural production of national boundaries and the
ways in which transnational actions both perpetuate and challenge
ideas of sovereignty and national identity.

A second purpose underscores the following discussion. Rather
than being tangential to the topic of nationalism, I argue, focus on an
issue provoking profound nationalist sentiment also raises central
questions about the politics of representation within anthropological
practice. Given that current anthropological inquiry in part studies
the connections between political and cultural ideologies, it has be-

come imperative to examine how producing ethnographic accounts is embedded in such ideologies and risks remaining blind to its own role in perpetuating them. The connection between power and knowledge in both ethnographic writing and the practice of advocacy remains a predicament requiring careful scrutiny in order that anthropologists may better respond to the realities of the contemporary world.

Discussing national boundaries entails understanding the production of space, through which the nation is constituted in relation to the space of other nations, and the place—or homeland—of the national citizen. Space is not a backdrop against which everyday life unfolds, but is rather a dialectically formed apprehension of the world of which we are part. Recent writers (Foucault 1986; Harvey 1982; Lefebvre 1991; Noyes 1992; Smith 1984) have argued that spatiality is a concept which helps us to understand the interrelationships of representation, experience, and social form.

The depth of human attachment to constructed space is not an exclusive feature of nationalism; it is, however, integral to the legitimation of the division of societal space into discontinuous realms of experience and action. The space of the nation-state is parceled out through the discursive activities of territory, property, and nature, in a manner I elaborate upon below. The whaling issue, as it has come to be defined in Iceland since 1978, has evoked an emotionally charged nationalist reaction by its direct challenge to the boundaries of sovereign Icelandic territory and the presumed natural right of Icelanders to decide what are or are not to be used as productive resources.[1]

The Icelandic government advocates returning to commercial whaling as part of what it terms the rational management of the ocean ecosystem, despite international pressure to stop whale hunting enacted through environmental groups (most notably Greenpeace International) and the International Whaling Commission (IWC). Support in Iceland for a pro-whaling policy is high: surveys in 1989 placed that support around 75% of the adult population, although that proportion may have changed somewhat in response to debates over relations with the European Community, as well as to the economy, worsened by lower cod quotas and global recession.

In itself, whaling has not been a significant aspect of the Icelandic economy, which derives about 75% of its foreign export earnings from fish and fish products, and—until recently—only about 1.3%

from the sale of whale meat. Nor is whaling defended as a traditional activity, since it originated in this century. A single land-based capitalist enterprise, founded after World War II, hunted the large fin and sei whales using specialized catcher boats until 1989. Also, scattered along the north coast are—or were until 1986—ten families who combined seasonal hunting for the small minke whale with cod-fishing as part of localized petty commodity production.[2] In premodern Iceland, locals considered the occasional stranded whale a god-send, and on the west coast whale drives similar to those of the Faeroe Islands took place very sporadically when conditions allowed. Whales were not a mainstay of Icelandic subsistence, and the large-scale whaling of the nineteenth and early twentieth centuries in the waters surrounding the island was conducted by Norwegians.

Yet the majority of Icelanders defend the resumption of whaling. For them, this stand makes sense for at least three reasons: (1) principles of national sovereignty should prevail to protect the fishing industry as a whole, (2) government officials state that the majority of international scientists agree that regulated whaling will not result in the extinction of whales, and (3) whales should be viewed as a food resource just like cows or pigs. Other reasons have been given, but these are the ones I most frequently heard voiced.

These views do not exist in a vacuum, but are responses to what the Icelandic public knows of the arguments marshaled against whaling and of the politics surrounding the International Whaling Commission. Most of their knowledge is based on media accounts, which in turn rely heavily on government interpretations, including those of the chief whaling scientist: (1) Icelanders are unjustifiably accused of cynically bending or breaking international laws for the sake of profit, (2) most whaling scientists, who are reasonable and rational, are being held ransom by a minority of ideologically motivated anti-whaling scientists, and (3) the dominant motivation of antiwhalers, distanced as they are from nature, is a sentimentally premised or misconstrued view of edible and inedible resources.

This latter image, of rationality opposed to romanticism, is frequently picked up in anthropological commentary and used as an aspect of analysis (Anderson 1991 [1983]; Einarsson 1993a; Freeman 1990; Kalland 1993). This usage fails to note that the science/sentimentality dichotomy is a trope found in the rhetoric of prowhaling forces, a dichotomy which obscures rather than clarifies the local, national, and transnational political practices surrounding the issue.

Antiwhaling rhetorics employ a similar discursive strategy, juxtaposing their rational concern for the environment with the "underhanded greed" of whalers. In this way, each side in the debate strives to set up "jurisdictions of knowledge" by making truth claims through selective representations of their opponents. In the following section, I suggest that examining the practice of making truth claims to establish legitimacy illuminates the identity processes inherent in the whaling issue.

The Whale as Floating Signifier

When the annual meeting of the International Whaling Commission (IWC) convenes, the envoys of nations and nongovernmental organizations (NGOs), whalers, diplomats, natural and social scientists, environmentalists, and assorted advisers and media engage in an intense, polarized battle over knowledge and control of whales and whaling. In this environment, the whale has become a floating signifier in a choppy sea of legal, scientific, moral, and economic discourses. Rival claimants manipulate the IWC's moribund set of institutional rules to promote their own legitimacy in a setting where even science is exposed as partisan. Both pro- and antiwhalers complain of the shortcomings of the commission's mandate and procedures, which date back to its founding in 1946 under the International Convention for the Regulation of Whaling. To quote from its mandate, the convention is "to provide for the proper conservation of whale stocks and thus make possible the orderly development of the whaling industry." The IWC, once known colloquially as the International Whalers' Club, at its annual meetings was, until the 1960s and 1970s, primarily devoted to the divvying up of whale quotas in Antarctic waters. The commission paid belated attention to questions of whale biology and management techniques, and, as opponents to whaling point out, early management regimes gave priority to managing whaling by dictating quotas, rather than managing whale populations and their habitat.

Although it is the site for debating whaling policy, I argue that the IWC is also a location for the generation of Icelandic nationalist identity. Recent studies of nationalism emphasize the nation's contingent and contextual qualities and show how national identification is a process of positioning and reflexively monitoring the "imagined community" (Anderson 1991 [1983]; Kapferer 1988). Fredrik Barth (1969) identifies self-ascription and ascription by others, arising in interaction, as critical to identity formation. Ethnicity and nationalism are boundary-maintaining mechanisms which act to codify differences between groups and generate identities. It follows that the pro- and antiwhaling positions which currently define the IWC are relational, that is, dependent on their Others to articulate the grounds for their claims to legitimacy. Interest groups have cultures too, and their common cultures, like those of nations, are the outcome of social group organization rather than any reified traits or characteristics (e.g., rationality, sentimentality). Significantly, given modern telecommunications, groups need not be in physical contact for boundary-maintaining mechanisms to operate.

We need to think beyond the view that social groups interact directly and recognize how mediated these interactions actually are. An illustration of this point may be found in Einarsson (this volume). A minke whaler states that "there is nothing more inhumane about whaling than the killing of other animals." I have heard this sentiment expressed many times in Iceland, and not just among minke whalers. It may be read as a simple statement of fact if one ignores the discursive context in which it was spoken. More to the point, I think, the speaker is defining an aspect of his identity ("I am not inhumane, or at least no more inhumane than anyone else who kills animals") by refuting what he sees as the stand of antiwhalers. His statement takes a further twist, since it implicitly accepts the representation made of the antiwhaling movement by the Icelandic government and disseminated by the media: that antiwhalers treat whales as special-case, nearly human animals.

Another example typifies the mediation of interaction, in this case between the Icelandic public and Greenpeace. In 1989 Greenpeace ran an advertisement in the British press urging the public to boycott Icelandic fish. A stark black-and-white image of a whaling boat with harpoon underscored the headline "Would you buy fish from a butcher?" Use of the word "butcher" played on its double sense, a neutral reference to a person who cuts and sells meat (but not fish), and a pejorative reference to the cold-blooded motivations of a killer. This ad, translated and reprinted with commentary in Icelandic newspapers, offended those who felt that the moral stance of the Icelandic people was being questioned while its economic security was being threatened.

By linking the "butcher" image to the boycott of any Icelandic seafoods, Greenpeace demonstrated its at times inconsistent (some say hypocritical) handling of its Iceland campaign. Greenpeace states that it criticizes only the Icelandic whaling industry and its government supporters. Yet the British advertisement diffused this claim by targeting the products of the *nation's* most important economic resource. In my interview with the head of Greenpeace Sweden, I questioned whether the ad was not too strongly worded and likely to alienate support within Iceland. He responded that he thought the ad would gain respect in Iceland, since Icelanders prefer blunt speech and direct challenge. One might question his reasoning, yet clearly such an instance of mutual (mis)interpretation is part of the boundary-making process.

Whereas differences between social groups are grounded in knowledge and action in the world, they can become more rigid, codified, and partisan as conflicts escalate. In the case of the whaling issue, the rules and structure of the Whaling Commission have fostered polarization between pro- and antiwhaling stands and created allegiances amongst those with only moderately differing views. At its inception, the authors of the convention made allowances for handling disagreements in order to ensure continuing cooperation among whaling states. For example, it is possible for any state to object to an IWC decision and continue hunting a particular species of whale despite a majority vote in the IWC against such whaling. Norway and Japan objected to the moratorium, granting them legal right to hunt whales. Whaling for scientific rather than commercial purposes provides another means of avoiding any of the commission's resolutions. Issuing scientific permits has been a well-established strategy used by various nations over the years to avoid decisions they do not like. In 1985 Iceland's government, having already abided by the Alþing's decision to accept the moratorium, chose to conduct a four-year research program and sell half of the whalemeat to Japan to cover its costs. Both of these so-called loopholes have recently allowed Japan, Iceland, and Norway to continue hunting and minimize the impact of a moratorium on commercial whaling (more accurately, a zero catch quota) which took effect in 1985/86.

The hotly contested moratorium was intended to resolve uncertainties in scientific analyses and to determine more precisely the status of various whale stocks. These analyses took longer than anticipated, and the moratorium was not lifted in 1990 as originally planned. For Japan, Norway, and Iceland—the only member countries interested in continued commercial whaling—this was proof of their opponents' insincerity. They argued that the IWC had become a protectionist organization which hid its emotional motives behind scientific rhetoric in order to destroy the whaling industry. In response, Iceland quit the IWC in 1992, and Norway and Japan threatened to follow suit.

The impetus behind the moratorium resulted from another of the IWC's structural "flaws." Since the 1946 signatories never envisioned an antiwhaling movement, they opened membership to any nation willing to pay annual dues. The antiwhaling movement grew throughout the 1970s and attempted to affect whaling activities by means of direct action pickets and interference with hunting activities. Although the IWC had adopted its first scientifically based management scheme in 1975, by 1979 it was acknowledged by biologists to be significantly flawed. The antiwhaling movement employed a new tactic by persuading nonwhaling nations to adopt antiwhaling policies (some states, such as Australia and New Zealand, already had these in place) and to join the IWC. In order to succeed at placing ecological goals on the political agenda, environmentalists are often compelled to work through state-defined institutions and international organizations, or else to subvert state power by means of direct action. Since all commission decisions are made by 3/4 majority, the potential for environmentalists to affect international whaling policy increased dramatically through this new strategy.

With all the protagonists together within the same institutional framework, the conditions were set for the debate to be carried out in terms of science, since the Regulating Convention deems scientifically based knowledge to be the best source of "objective" measure. In the process, the IWC has also come to be a forum for negotiating issues of ocean management and conducting state diplomacy regarding sovereignty and coastal rights (Hoel 1985). For their part, environmentalists are using the IWC to institute a new principle of environmental protection: that *first* consideration should be given to the resource's well-being, and not that of the resource users, and that users must prove that their actions will not damage the environment. In other words, the benefit of the doubt should be given, in this case, to the whale.

The Scientific Committee advising the commission has also taken on larger dimensions. Japan, Iceland, and Norway, all of whom engaged in scientific whaling (a.k.a. "scientific whaling"; the quotations mark the phrase as, in the words of one antiwhaler, a euphemism for "business as usual") during the moratorium in order to keep their boats operating and continue exerting political pressure, increased the number of their scientific advisers. In the same mode, scientists with antiwhaling agendas found other institutional routes, whether through observer organizations or sympathetic nations, to participate in the committee. As the fisheries biologist D. S. Butterworth, a technical adviser on the committee, commented: "The scientists who serve on these committees are delegates of the countries that are members . . . and are often employees of their governments. . . . On occasion these scientists are under instructions to argue in support of a position adopted by their government for reasons other than science alone . . ." (1992: 533). Both in private conversation and in public comment, some scientists are willing to admit to the occasionally partisan nature of members of the committee, but usually as a means of undercutting their opponents' position. Thus Jóhann Sigurjónsson, Iceland's chief whale biologist, claimed that "there are some forces working within the Committee which are not purely scientific and these forces are producing a lot of delays . . ." (Icelandic press conference, 1992, Glasgow). For his part, fisheries biologist Sidney Holt has written about the "pseudo-scientific myths" which scientists of whaling nations have put forth to obfuscate real issues (1985: 117). Media accounts tend to lump all scientists together, insofar as their scholarly practices are concerned. While their national origins are given ("Japanese" or "American" scientist being a shorthand guide to interpretation), their expertise in management biology, mathematical modelling, or statistics is rarely mentioned. Thus a crucial element to understanding the *culture* of the scientists, their assumptions and emphases, is lost. "Science" becomes rhetorically another term for a monolithic "Truth."

The Scientific Committee has fought over data—stock boundaries, age mortality, reproduction rates—as well as the legitimacy of computer modeling and various strategies for collecting biological and ecological information. The committee meetings are closed to observers, but in interviews some points of controversy were voiced to me. One topic of debate was the status of the data produced by Iceland's scientific whaling. The Icelandic team argued that their findings were legitimate and necessary to a whale management regime. Their opponents argued that the data were redundant and unnecessary for the production of a computer model and that dealing with

Iceland's scientific reports had delayed the development of the final report to the commission. Finally, at the 1992 meeting, the Scientific Committee submitted for adoption to the political representatives in the commission the Revised Management System (RMS). The RMS is likely the most advanced quota-setting mechanism ever devised for any type of fisheries, in terms of its ability to "take direct account of concerns about ever-present uncertainty" (Cherfas 1992).

A mechanism had been established and accepted which could probably ensure that whale hunting of selected species would not lead to their extinction and that conservation would be favored over profit. Yet at the same time that the commission accepted the RMS the antiwhaling nations asked for additional features to be added concerning "minimum standards for data, guidelines for conducting useful sighting surveys and an effective inspection scheme to verify and police catches" (Cherfas 1992). Thus another year's delay in granting a quota to Japan and Norway (Iceland having left the IWC) was incurred. For the whalers, this was added evidence for their assertion that science had been a smokescreen for animal welfare issues and that members were using the commission to enhance "green" profiles at home. When Norwegians returned to minke whaling in 1993, they used an older formula for generating quotas since they could not access the new algorithms and necessary data, which remain under the control of two "antiwhaling" scientists who devised the computer model.

Great Britain and New Zealand openly admit that they are opposed to any commercial whaling. Other countries, although not interested in whaling, appear willing to let others do so providing that adequate safeguards are in place. Environmental groups vary according to their stated attitudes toward the future possibility of resumed whaling. Some argue that whale hunting is cruel and unnecessary, while other argue that, based on their past records, the whalers cannot be trusted to stay within set limits when profit is at stake. They cite Japan's earlier financing of whaling stations in Peru and Chile (then nonmembers of the IWC) to circumvent IWC-established limitations on catches. They also argue that Iceland's attitudes to whale science prior to its adoption of scientific whaling were indifferent and evidence of the country's current attitudes. Statistics were only haphazardly submitted to the IWC, even when required to be more thorough in documentation of its hunting activities. Further, Greenpeace points out that when the IWC made the blue whale a protected stock in the late 1950s the Icelandic government objected for five years before it stopped hunting.

The Icelandic government favors the creation of what it calls a more viable organization than the Whaling Commission. It has collaborated with Norway, Greenland, and the Faeroe Islands to design a new organization to manage the hunting of seals and small cetaceans. Known as the North Atlantic Marine Mammal Conservation Organisation (NAMMCO), the new group limits membership to only those countries hunting marine mammals, a proviso of which environmentalists are suspicious. Despite statements that Iceland will return to whaling, the future remains uncertain. Decreasing cod quotas and economic uncertainty have prompted many Icelanders to call for the resumption of controlled whaling. But any decision must measure domestic concerns against the risk to foreign markets of boycotts, although whaling received a boost when the American government failed to protest Norway's return to hunting.[3] Iceland must also wait until the Whaling Commission finally collapses before it starts to hunt any whales. According to IWC rules, Japan, Iceland's only foreign market, is barred from buying whalemeat from non-IWC countries.

Each side in the whaling debate lays claim to reasonableness, rationality, and fact, and it is difficult on the basis of limited reading to appreciate how strategic and selective seemingly innocuous statements in published accounts can be. Yet limited reports constitute what the general public is exposed to through the media, in Iceland and elsewhere. Outside of the IWC there exists no one forum where differing viewpoints are aired together. Academic journals and conferences, fund-raising literature, and magazine articles constitute divided domains which in practice do not readily allow any juxtaposition of interpretations. For their part, some anthropologists adopt the voice of seemingly detached social science to discuss the antiwhalers' point of view, while clearly aligning themselves with the whalers. The results, while presuming to be commentary, in fact provide further strategic ploys in the war of words cloaked in the guise of academic remove.

The image of all-powerful and greedy environmental groups bankrolled by gullible urbanites that I encountered in Iceland differs radically, not surprisingly, from the self-perceptions of those same environmental organizations. The prowhaling, anti-Greenpeace rhetoric in Iceland speaks of the risk and danger to the entire nation should some environmental groups have their way. Many Icelanders have come to define themselves in relation to groups such as Greenpeace and the International Fund for Animal Welfare, and antiwhaling nations such as Great Britain, the United States, Australia, New Zealand, Sweden, and the Netherlands, as muted, marginal, and powerless. Ironically, the image of the nation under siege resonates powerfully with nationalist sentiment. It connects with the national citizenry's moral obligation to struggle and sacrifice for the sake of the nation. As Ernest Renan remarks, "where national memories are concerned, griefs are of more value than triumphs, for they impose duties, and require a common effort" (1990 [1882]: 19).

Iceland and Nationalism

The lack of consensus regarding whaling provides fertile ground for radically divergent means of strategically defining the issue to emerge. In Iceland, several events conspired to transform the hitherto little-known whaling industry into a rallying point for the defense of the nation from those who would deprive it of its livelihood (Brydon 1990). These events were the 1986 sinking by the Sea Shepherd Conservation Society of two of the four catcher boats as they lay at berth in Reykjavík harbor; the threat by the American government to block purchases of Icelandic fish; a Greenpeace-organized boycott of Icelandic fish in Europe and the United States from 1988 to 1990; the national broadcast of an Icelandic-made documentary which portrayed antiwhalers as devious and greedy; and, finally, public demonstrations abroad proclaiming in front of Icelandic news cameras that Icelanders were cruel and barbarous butchers.

As significant as these events were and are, they cannot in themselves explain why the majority of Icelanders came to think of the whaling issue as central to the well-being of their entire nation rather than simply some of its citizens. Certainly Iceland's homogeneity and small population might allow for a high degree of consensus to be achieved, yet even a cursory glance at its political life shows a country accustomed to disagreement and controversy. It is necessary, therefore, to look beyond immediate circumstances to examine underlying motivations and constraints.

Giving national significance to the protests and rebuttals against whaling and antiwhalers relies on a prior construction which constitutes the nation and its borders in relation to foreign forces and conditions. In Iceland, this construction is a legacy of its independence movement and the rhetorics which nationalist leaders used to mobilize the population against Danish rule. Along with the effects of the modern reorganization of society and production, nationalist discourse has provided the context for the interpretation and narration of the whaling issue.

This returns us to the topic raised earlier: the production of space, through which the nation is constituted in relation to the space of other nations and the place—or homeland—of the national citizen. Space and place are central to explaining the link between nationalist discourse and the identity of the national citizen. Nationalism is one of a variety of ways humans organize knowledge about the world in the ongoing process of defining, articulating, and making solid and real who they are as a unified collective. The responses to the anti-whaling forces, issued by the Icelandic government and taken up by the majority of Icelanders, are constructed in terms of the privileged truth of sovereignty (territory), capitalist production (property), and a supposed special affinity between Icelanders and the harsh northern sea which endows them with a rational, sensible, but still respectful attitude to *nature*. These are not new ideas in the Icelandic context. On the contrary, it is their resonance with long-standing understandings of being Icelandic, pride in independence, hard work, and a paradoxical landscape, at once hauntingly beautiful and hideously desolate, which makes them so compelling. Place and nature are thus concepts which inform nationalism, intertwined as they are with the related concepts of history and identity.

Anthony Giddens (1985) maintains that the nation is an abstract system which situates individuals in the disembedded dimensions of modern time and space, dimensions which have become detached from local traditions and religious cosmology. But as experienced by the national citizen, abstract systems—I consider environmentalism to be another relevant example—achieve actual effects when they penetrate local actions. For Icelanders, notions of independence and uniqueness are tropes rendering the complexity of modern transnational systems (e.g., global capitalism) into experiential symbols for identification. In this way, nationalism serves as a vehicle for communicating or obscuring more complex messages regarding social, political, or economic issues and for evaluating new information thought to pertain to the nation, but which cannot be fully conceptualized. Tropes of national "destiny" and "progress" (understood in terms of rational and technological change) generate direction and purpose for social groups. When, in 1979, the Icelandic government arrested the captain and crew of the Greenpeace protest ship the *Rainbow Warrior*, the principles of sovereignty, direct action, and social justice became realities affecting Icelandic views of whales and whaling. Thus, disembedded systems which transect national borders may nonetheless reinforce those borders.

The historical production of the nation-state relies on the juxtaposition of territories and the imagining of boundaries. According to Giddens, modern understanding of territories as enclosed by borders rather than circumscribed by blurred frontiers is characteristic of absolutist nation-states. Modern territories have specific locations demarcated by boundary lines, although, of course, states can and do come into conflict over the exact placement of these lines. Although Iceland's geographical isolation would seem an obvious enough enduring boundary, it would be wrong to dismiss too quickly the changing formation of its territory. For example, the ongoing dispute between Iceland and Great Britain over ownership of Rockall, a crumbling edge of rock jutting above the ocean surface, is over the extent and location of Iceland's outer edge. Such a conflict would have been inconceivable when, two hundred years ago, Iceland had a primarily pastoral subsistence economy. The relational character of modern territories—the fact that states must come to agreement about their own existence—is evidence of the discursive element to the production of demarcated spaces.

With the rise of the state in Europe, sovereignty became a way of imagining first the monarch's and then the people's relationship to the territory. Overarching means of juridical, legislative, and military control established internal coherency to territorial units. Icelandic territorial boundaries, while instituted by the Danish state during its trade monopoly between 1602 and 1787, were "nationalized" by the nineteenth-century independence movement. Nationalist leaders sought to remove the exercise of centralized power over Icelandic territory from the hands of the Danish state and to place it under the purview of a wholly Icelandic state apparatus. Once having achieved its independence in 1944, Iceland engaged virtually immediately in juridical altercations with other states of northern Europe—notably Great Britain—regarding the expansion of territorial waters. Through the series of so-called cod wars with Britain, sovereignty and independence have been reinforced in Icelandic imagining as moral as well as political principles. The presence of American troops on a NATO base on Icelandic territory has provided an additional focus for defining, and disputing, the character of Icelandic sovereignty.[4]

Property as spatializing discourse is not exclusively bound up with the geographical partitioning of land, over which an individual or society can lay claims to ownership. In contemporary juridical discourse, property refers to capital and the ownership of the means of production. Property is a system of agreed-upon rights and obligations which exist between people and situate the individual's identity—his or her status or role—within systems of production. Capitalist societies are nation-states, and property relations are a means of legitimating their division into discontinuous realms of experience and action. Segments of the nonhuman world—whether animal or plant, land or sea—are brought into the logic of property relations in terms of their productive or nonproductive value determined by the technical capacity of industry, which categorizes them as "natural resources." Once dead whales could be defined as resources, the idea of turning them into living spectacles for whale-watchers has caused some Icelandic commentators to respond with derision. And the idea of leaving whales alone, not using them for profit, is even more antithetical to the primacy of property and production.

The movement for independence during the nineteenth century was expressed in Iceland through control over capital and production. The development of industrialized fishing rapidly transformed the country and laid the economic basis for national independence. The shift from subsistence pastoralist farming to fishing, together with population increase and the administrative demands of a national capitalist economy, has radically reorganized demographic distribution such that most people live in urban centers and over half of the country's 260,000 people are found in the capital city of Reykjavík and its immediate environs.[5] Now that Iceland has become an industrialized, capitalist social formation, divisions according to class, place of residence, gender, and productive sectors have appeared (see Skaptadóttir, this volume; Pálsson and Helgason, this volume), although a strong ideological resistance to perceiving inequality links egalitarianism to individualism and independence (cf. Durrenberger, this volume; Broddason and Webb 1975). Interestingly, the right-wing Independence Party, which usually receives the highest proportion of electoral votes, champions free-market economics as the best expression of individual industry and achievement, a powerful platform for an "independent people."

The discursive construction of nature is less apparent than that of property or territory, because, by definition, nature is that which operates and persists outside of culture, beyond that which is humanly made. This view of nature makes it difficult to grasp that nature is not, in fact, an already-constructed object of our perception, but is generated through our actions and understandings. Nature is used to situate human identities as a means to think about the human condition, a phenomenon which has been at the heart of feminist debate (Moore 1988).

Nature in Icelandic nationalist imagining brings together notions of place and history, on the one hand, and blood and kinship, on the other. German romanticism of the nineteenth century, of which Icelandic nationalism is one expression, claims that a nation is a collective unity, made up of people who, by virtue of a distinct language, shared origins, and an innate attachment to a mother earth or homeland, are distinct and separate from other nations. Although not all nationalisms in the world attempt to adhere to this formulation, the Icelandic instance is deeply embedded in the metaphors of organic unity.

Icelandic nationalism relies on various constructions of the natural world. National identity is naturalized through biological notions of "race" (expressed through notions of purity), geographical determinism (Icelandic character as shaped directly by the "fire and ice" of volcanoes and glaciers), and the demarcation of certain sites deemed significant to the nation and produced as symbolic landscapes. Nature is venerated as an object of beauty and a means of spiritual renewal, as well as a harsh and unforgiving foe in the battle for survival. In the discourse of nature, certain sites, monuments, and landscapes become symbols of the nation, preserved and exhibited in the form of national parks or protected areas. Nature, history, and nation call forth strong feelings of attachment. This trinity—the Christian term is not anomalous here—has a particular force in Iceland, where so much of history and imagining is linked not to buildings or artefacts, but to landmarks and farms. Since Iceland's settlement in the ninth century, the landscape has accumulated names denoting people, superhuman beings, or events, names which bear witness to the historic bond between people and their locale. Farms, too, have names which endure through the centuries. Farms are listed separately in the telephone book and continue to have histories written and told about them and the people and animals they sustain.

Writers such as Benedict Anderson (1991 [1983]) and David Schneider (1977) suggest that parallels to nationalism are to be found in the operations of kinship and religion and that at a certain level kinship, religion, and nationality are strikingly similar. These forms of social knowledge derive their power from notions of blood and belonging, of death and immortality. In short, the nation is understood through the metaphors of life and in this way is equated to the immediacy of human existence. Biological metaphors and notions of shared blood or pure "race" are one means of naturalizing the idea of the national self which have found resonance in Iceland. Memorials to drowned fishers found throughout the island are Iceland's equivalent to the unknown soldier, which Anderson suggests is integral to nationalist imagining. Through the image of the fisher/soldier (doing battle with the sea), the nation can imagine itself in a struggle for survival, transcending death to achieve immortality in national memory.

Nationalist discourse reembeds the self in place, by rearticulating its relationship to the experienced world using the symbolic landscapes of the past, present, and future. The discourses of the natural sciences have rationalized the operations of nature so that the forces of the earth appear law-governed rather than deity-shaped. In this context, nationalism as discourse about nature resacralizes nature by renaming the bond between people and their land as "homeland," "motherland," or "fatherland." The nation does not erase preexisting notions of place. Instead, it overlays them, posits itself as a larger context into which local attachments to place are assembled and defined in relation to each other. Foucault (1986) uses the spatial metaphor "domain" to discuss knowledge and how discourses circumscribe (in)appropriate knowledge. He notes that defining social space is necessarily strategic. In this way, the formation of discourses fundamental to the existence of the nation-state can be analyzed as tactics and strategies of power. As the following discussion shows, the discourses of the nation—territory, property, and nature—figure strongly in the arguments used by the Icelandic government to defend its whaling industry.

Making a Nationalist Issue

As mentioned earlier, two of the strongest and most resolutely pursued arguments put forth by the Icelandic government concern the sovereign right of the state to govern resources within its territorial waters and the right of Icelandic citizens to define for themselves what does or does not constitute an exploitable natural resource.

Pursuing at all costs a prowhaling position became a matter of the proper conduct of an independent foreign policy. Government officials hold the view that it is inappropriate to succumb to what they see as unfair pressure, issuing primarily from the U.S. government through its own domestic legislation. They argue that it is particularly necessary for a small nation-state to take a strong stand regarding its sovereignty and not to appear easily manipulable. If they were to compromise on an issue *un*important to the Americans, they reason, then they would set a bad precedent for the future.

In Iceland, whaling is classified as part of the fisheries and is thus bound up with notions of property and resources. Whale is considered by most Icelanders to be an appropriate source for protein (although they prefer to eat other meats). Whales are also seen as competitors for resources and/or hazards to boats and equipment engaged in fishing, although the accuracy of this view is debatable. The popular image of foreign antiwhalers says something about how many Icelanders imagine their relationship to nature: in a popular representation, Icelanders know the realities of food production and the need to struggle for existence against a harsh, competitive nature. Foreign urban dwellers, the argument continues, have become so removed from the realities of life and death that they would unwittingly allow the powerful forces of nature to assume mastery over the actions of fishers. Many Icelanders, because they see themselves living closer to nature, consider themselves more rational and pragmatic when interacting with nature, less prone to sentimentalizing animals.

For their part, the Icelandic media, dominated by the state-owned radio and television stations, failed to conduct systematically any independent investigative journalism and largely constructed events according to government rhetoric, using state officials as the definitive speakers for the issue both domestically and internationally. The five national newspapers varied in their reportage. For example, the conservative *Morgunblaðið* downplayed the issue since its editor felt it could damage Iceland's foreign image. Prowhaling *Tíminn*, the newspaper of former fisheries minister Halldór Ásgrímsson's party, sensationalized its coverage. Despite different policies regarding the issue, the media framed discussion in terms of domestic understandings and did not fully represent the full scope of foreign antiwhaling arguments.

The government strategizes as a sovereign body within the institutions of international law from the logic of capitalist production. The public, having varying degrees of knowledge about the strategies of law, must construct a narrative to explain the rhetorics surrounding whales and whaling. Information from the media, already selectively edited (consciously or unconsciously), is shaped by prior knowledge of the world grounded in the primacy of the nation. It is hardly surprising, then, that many Icelanders (but not all) find the idea of foreign forces with which the nation must do battle—more specifically, environmentalists—compelling.

Anthropology and the Politics of Representation

Anthropologists frequently adopt the role of advocate or defender of comparatively powerless peoples whose livelihoods are likely to be adversely affected by environmentalists' efforts to end, for example, fur trapping, sealing, the ivory trade, or the by-catch of tuna. Their research strategy may entail disproving elements from the arguments of environmentalists with ethnographic data. In addition, their writings may also involve "exposing" hidden agendas, underhanded practices, or faulty reasoning on the part of environmental groups.

Such uses of anthropology are laudable and important when the ethnographic data are thorough and well grounded, yet, as I have seen in the context of the whaling issue, some writers rely on cynical reason rather than methodological empathy when discussing environmentalists' views. Cynical reason permeates the rhetoric within and around the IWC. Opponents cannot listen to one another without reveling in the gulf between stated principles and actual actions. Anthropologists who align themselves with the whalers (I found no antiwhaling anthropologists) adopt the "rational management versus sentimental naiveté" framework which underpins Icelandic, Norwegian, and Japanese arguments. Inevitably, by establishing "jurisdictions of knowledge," their work becomes part of, rather than analysis of, the practice of making truth claims. This tendency is more pronounced when anthropologists participate in research commissioned directly by the IWC through its Management Committee.

Although it would be impossible in a short space to summarize all of the ways in which information circulates at IWC meetings, it is useful to recognize certain features and recognize that these meetings are ethnographic locales and rituals of truth-making. Since commission meetings are held *in camera*, lobbyists and the media use coffee and lunch breaks as opportunities to "debrief" commissioners and argue their causes. The press room, where anthropologists like myself and other observers camp out, provides one node in communication links. Tables are stacked with news briefs, press releases, photocopied articles (the Japanese-hired lobbyist circulated a piece from *Forbes* magazine which criticized former Greenpeace head David McTaggart), and more, which are then scanned and very selectively used by the media.

At the IWC, rumor, whether spoken or written in the two in-house gossip sheets published nightly by both pro- and anti-forces, provides another means of persuasion. In 1992, "Caribgate"—the supposed funding of four Caribbean nations by Japan in return for sympathetic votes—was a possibly well-founded rumor put forth by antiwhalers in "ECO" which made it into some British media coverage. In retaliation, the authors of *International Harpoon* hinted about a mysterious Mr. X with bags full of illegal money who supposedly helped David McTaggart buy other national votes back in the early 1980s.

I mention these two examples not as statements of fact, but as indicators of strategic discourses which flow behind the scenes and set up a mood of cynicism and distrust. I would argue on the basis of my own interviews that the stacks of brochures sitting on the press room table dealing with the cruelty of the whale hunt do not represent the entire body of antiwhaling opinion. Yet they inevitably dominate ethnographic descriptions, casting antiwhalers as romantics, sentimentalists, and/or religious fanatics. Interestingly, the gossip paper *International Harpoon*, which picked up a deliberate provocation at a rally during the 1992 IWC meeting in Glasgow as indicative of antiwhaling prejudice, did not reprint another statement from that rally made by a representative of a conservation group. She challenged the "economic necessity" claim advanced by the whalers, saying that Iceland, Japan, and Norway are among the wealthiest countries in the world, particularly when compared to Third World antiwhaling countries. Clearly her challenge could not be cast within the "rationality vs. romanticism" trope, and it was selectively ignored.

I do not wish to leave the impression that antiwhaling forces do not use cynical reason, strategic manipulation of information, and so forth, since they do. Rather, I want to draw the attention of the reader to the ways in which truth claims are made and how they permeate the worlds anthropologists study and the ethnographies they write. Reproducing the views of one or the other side only flattens the complexity of the issue, portraying it as a simple moral choice between two extremes. I am not claiming that truth is unknowable. Rather, I plead for greater scrutiny of what constitutes truth claims and a recognition of the crippling effects of pejorative understandings. The aim, ultimately and perhaps idealistically, is to transcend the limits of one's own discourse to achieve dialogic understanding.

Discussion

Examining issues and doing ethnography at points of conflict are a potential means of operationalizing criticisms of anthropology's colonialist past. It is in points of conflict—in those moments of danger—that the operations of power and the constituting of identities are exposed. Yet doing such research inevitably entails complications for the anthropologist which need to be brought forth in ethnographic writing. In a situation where everyone is seen to have some agenda, any claims to neutral observance are going to be questioned or simply disbelieved. While attending the IWC meeting, I acknowledged to my interlocutors my interest in analyzing the rhetorics of whales and whaling as a means of understanding Icelandic nationalism. To some, I sounded like someone claiming objectivity when they would argue against the possibility of objective positions. So my identity—a Canadian anthropologist studying Iceland—said it all: the Canadian observers at the IWC are prowhaling, Iceland is prowhaling, and some Canadian anthropologists (including Milton Freeman) actively work on behalf of whalers, whether Japanese or Inuit. Therefore, I had to be harboring prowhaling sympathies, and I was talked to accordingly. Not only was I attempting to position myself, but others attempted to position me for their own purposes.

The pull toward discursive closure, to create realms of truth, is powerful and fraught with hazards and requires new strategies of thinking, analyzing, and writing on the part of anthropologists. The representation of the whaling issue in this essay is necessarily partial since no representation of reality can ever be complete. It, too, is a strategy, one in favor of situated research, reading, and writing.

Notes

This paper is based on my Ph.D. dissertation (Brydon 1992). Field research was conducted over a 24-month period between 1988 and 1990. A return visit to Iceland in 1992 together with attendance at that year's IWC meeting in Glasgow provided additional materials. Funding for the project was gratefully received from the Social Science and Humanities Research Council of Canada, the Wenner-Gren Foundation, McGill University, University of Winnipeg, and the Canada-Iceland Foundation.

1. Further background on the whaling issue can be found in *Ambio* 12(6) (1983), *Arctic* 46(2) (1993), and *North Atlantic Studies* 2(1/2) (1990).

2. During the 1970s, Icelandic and Norwegian minke whalers increased the size of their catches, within the confines of IWC quotas, in response to a developing market for minke meat in Japan.

3. The Packwood/Magnuson Act and the Pelley Amendment allow the American government to enact trade sanctions against nation-states who transgress U.S. fisheries and whaling policies.

4. It is only recently, with the collapse of the Soviet Union and the lessening of the base's importance for monitoring submarine traffic, that public attitudes have shifted in favor of the base: the economic downturn of the early 1990s has rendered it a resource to be protected.

5. This was not a smooth transition but one marked by labor strife and protest (cf. Magnússon 1985).

3

A SEA OF IMAGES:
FISHERS, WHALERS, AND ENVIRONMENTALISTS

The present moratorium on whaling is leading to the perception of whales as pests. Icelandic fishers do not share the common feeling of what has been called "sentimental anthropomorphism" to the extent observed in urban Western culture (see Jasper and Nelkin 1992)—they do not believe whales are especially intelligent or otherwise endowed and therefore should be spared from hunting. They draw the moral circle fairly narrowly around humans. Outside of that circle come animals with very different moral rules attached to them. This is seen as self-evident and a part of a lifestyle that involves fishers in direct confrontation with animals.

These differences in the perception of whales are obviously not the intention of whale conservationists, but may become the actual consequences of total protection. Icelandic small-scale fishers have an intimate, practically based experience with the resources from which they gain their livelihood. Their attitudes toward sea animals are shaped by this fact. They are another example of how people construct their moral universe to fit their convenience. Fishers maintain that they have the right to hunt or otherwise manage animals in the ecosystem in which they participate. It is a matter of principle. To question that principle is to question what fishers feel is their self-evident right to survive. By referring to the fact that they work in close contact with the natural environment they exploit, they make claims on a truer version of reality and therefore a license to speak of nature "as it really is."

In this essay I discuss environmental perceptions among small-scale fishers and whalers in Iceland and what shapes their thinking about the marine resources they utilize for their living. I describe the everyday encounters fishers have with animals and how they explain to themselves and others what they think is their self-evident traditional right to use what they see as resources, arguing that the self-evidence is shaped by subsistence realities. However, fishers are also, whether they like it or not, enmeshed in the workings of the global village, which implies a growing homogeneity and interrelatedness in the world: "The way people think now, in much of the world, is shaped by books, postcards, telenovels, and the evening news, as well as by the words and gesture of their immediate surroundings" (Hannerz 1986: 366). The actions of Western environmentalists, as portrayed in the media, have evoked and informed a discussion of ethical assumptions about the rights of animals and people in conflicts over conservation (see Brydon, this volume), a discussion which has strengthened fishers' claims to resource use in accordance with their world view.

I should also make it clear from the beginning that this essay is based on research on Icelandic small-scale fishers and whalers and I do not wish to generalize about Icelandic culture in general. Here the minke whalers are subsumed under the category of fishers because whaling was mostly a seasonal activity of the nine enterprises that continued to whale until the moratorium on whaling in 1986. For some of them, however, the whaling ban meant a loss of over half of the total income (see Einarsson 1993a).

Images: Fishers and Environmentalists

To Icelandic artisanal fishers, the prime examples of alienated Westerners are whale and seal conservationists, who are seen as dangerous extremists. Conservationists are seen as a threat to fishers' basic economic and cultural survival, which is already under attack because of diminishing catch quotas (see Pálsson and Helgason, this volume). Fishers hold that such people should not be taken seriously because they have no understanding of how nature works or how to survive in it.

Contemporary literature on whales often takes for granted that a universal emotion of awe and wonder is invoked in humans by the sight and sound of whales. To quote whale conservationist Paul Spong:

> I really do think that the reason we love to watch whales is because they . . . take us away from ourselves, from our problems and anxieties, for the brief moment we are with them. I know we always return to the reality of our own world, but having been in the company of whales makes us a little more able to deal with it, for we have seen the possibility of living in harmony with our fellows. And, in these days when we are searching for solutions to the conflicts that surround us on every side, it is very important for us to know that there can be a future in which we live in harmony with one another. In a word, the whales give us hope. (1992: 25)

While whale watching has become a major industry and an ever more popular pastime among Western nations, it has gained little ground in Iceland in spite of some potential (see Lindquist and Tryggvadóttir 1990). Unlike whale watchers, Icelandic fishers do not return to reality after having enjoyed the company of whales—whales are an integral part of their everyday reality.

In their everyday work artisanal fishers encounter marine animals in a range of situations. Being out at sea in a small boat often means that fishers come into close contact with animals under conditions that they have not chosen. In contrast, most urbanized Westerners leave their cities not to engage in productive activity, to use the environment or natural resources for livelihood, but rather for the sake of recreation involving aesthetic uses of nature.

Whereas the visiting urbanite may seek out wildlife to look at and admire, fishers are primarily engaged in hunting (the Icelandic *veiða* translates into English as both "to hunt" and "to fish," acknowledging no terminological distinction) and find little reason for coming close to animals for other purposes. Sometimes contact with animals can indeed be too close for comfort, as in the case of breaching whales. In the village where I worked one story about whales tells how a fairly big boat was nearly capsized at night when a whale threw itself against its stern. Had it been a smaller open boat, fishers say, there would have been little hope for survival, as it would have been crushed. In Arctic waters a person can only survive for a few minutes. The fishers did not know what kind of creature "attacked" the boat involved but considered it likely to have been a minke whale. The minke is also known, especially by older fishers, as the "jumper" (or *stökkull* in the vernacular), because of its breaching habits. In the mythology of Icelandic folktales "jumper" was a whale with "flaps of skin hanging down over the eyes and the only way it can lift the flaps and see what is going on is by leaping clear over the water. When in the air it can look out from under the flaps. It attempts to sink anything that it sees floating" (Pálsson 1991: 98–99). In the folktales there were other "wicked whales" (*illhveli*) such as the "horse-whale," which "was said to resemble a horse, to neigh like a horse, and to have a horse's tail which sent tremendous waves across the ocean and destroyed boats and men" (Pálsson 1991: 99).

When out at sea, one can sometimes hear minkes breaching with a sound like that of a canon being fired, when they hit the sea after a jump into the air. And when many of them do this at the same time, things can get very lively. On one occasion some fishers felt they had to leave the area where they were fishing with handlines because they were worried that the leaping whales might hit the boats. The conversation among the fishers on the radiotelephone indicated that they considered themselves forced to flee. There was much frustration and anger and one fisher claimed that a minke had tried to jump into his boat. Whales are seen as potentially dangerous and stories of whales causing deaths by sinking boats, especially in the old days, are well known. Older fishers also tell of taboos on saying the name of whales such as sperm whales, which could attract their attention and possibly endanger the lives of a boat's crew. When small boats were lost at sea without evidence of how this had taken place whales were often blamed.

The lesson fishers draw from whales is that whales are predators. In encounters with whales fishers fail to see these animals as inherently positive. They do, however, see whales eat herring and other fish. This does not mean that fishers are incapable of appreciating the beauty of nature. In fact, one of the reasons small-scale fishers often give for their choice of occupation is that it offers them the opportunity to experience the beauty of the fjords and the coastline where they fish, in total tranquillity and at their own pace. This is seen as one of the positive attributes of being a small-scale fisher. To use nature and animals does not mean to deny that nature can at the same time be of aesthetic value, although many environmentalists see these as mutually exclusive. They may never have seen a fisher take a large, fat cod with a smile of appreciation and describe it as particularly beautiful. The word used for a catch of big fish of high monetary value is indeed "beautiful fish" (*fallegur fiskur*).

However, in the eyes of Icelandic fishers, whales are becoming more and more malign animals. They are accused of eating millions of metric tons of fish which would otherwise be available to fishers, while fishers are facing decreasing quotas which pose a serious threat to their livelihood. Fishers' claims that whales consume great amounts of fish and must therefore be controlled have often been met with scorn by conservationists, who maintain that fishers always show a stingy attitude when it comes to possible coexistence with other species and that whales have an insignificant effect on the fishery. However, this is not the case, judging from calculations resource economists have made with respect to the economic effects of biological predation of minke whales in Norwegian waters (Flaaten and Stollery 1994). Focusing on the minke whale's predation on the Norwegian cod and herring fisheries Flaaten and Stollery conclude that "the cost of predation is large, a 10% increase in the 1989 minke whale stock causing estimated damage over seventeen million $US in value, 5.2 and 12.4 percent respectively of the total gross profits of the Norwegian cod and herring fisheries" (1994: 19). The average net annual predation cost per minke whale in the Norwegian fisheries in 1991–1992 is calculated as close to ten thousand U.S. dollars (1994: 22).

If we assume that the diet of the minkes in Icelandic coastal waters does not differ significantly from that of their Norwegian kin (to anthropomorphize a bit), we have at least fourteen thousand minkes undisturbed consuming a great deal of fish and other biomass (figures from *Skýrsla til sjávarútvegsráðherra* 1994). If we include all whales in Icelandic waters, preliminary research indicates that the annual consumption of marine animals could be 4.6 to 4.8 million metric tons (Sigurjónsson and Víkingsson 1992). This is happening at the same time as the Icelandic economy is hitting the lowest economic slump since World War II, with no increase in GNP per capita since 1987, when the quota for cod is 25% lower than in 1993 and 50% lower than the catch in 1990 (see Matthíasson 1994). This situation has led Icelandic companies, desperate for fish, to send their ships to troubled waters in the Barent Sea and around Svalbard, leading to clashes with

Norwegian coast guard vessels in the summer of 1994 and a toughening atmosphere in diplomatic relations.

More small-scale fishers are thus forced to give up fishing as what is left of their quotas does not suffice to keep their petty commodity units going. At the same time, they are told that scientists at the International Whaling Commission maintain that, given restricted and regulated quotas, the minke whale stocks formerly hunted by Icelandic and Norwegian fishers could be sustainably hunted. Fishers claim that there have never been as many whales as today and, as a consequence of the international whaling moratorium which has been in effect since 1985 (excluding whales taken for scientific purposes), the numbers are out of control, threatening the ecological balance in the sea. All this is transforming whales into vermin for fishers. Not only are fishers forbidden to hunt whales, but they also must accept that whales may literally be eating away their basis for subsistence.

The perception of whales by fishers is thus influenced by what is thought of as their role in the ecosystem, how they affect fish stocks and thereby fishers' livelihood. Interestingly enough, this was also the case in the beginning of the century when fishers in the eastern fjords of Iceland protested strongly against the Norwegian whaling off the east coast. In the folk ecology of fishers whales had a very useful role as sheep dogs, driving herring and cod into the fjords, where fishers could then make their catch. At this time, before the introduction of motorboats, the fishing for herring was almost solely done in the fjords, and the herring was also, as it still is today, the most important bait when fishing for cod. Fishers pointed out how the pollution from the whaling stations destroyed the fishing and gear in the fjords with grime from rotting whale carcasses scattered around the stations (Geirsson 1993). Fishers also complained about the great numbers of sharks attracted by whale carcasses along the coast and how they made it difficult to fish with longlines. An example of what fishers saw as hard evidence for the negative consequences of inshore whaling is an account from 1903 by a fisher in the local newspaper *Austri* based in the coastal town of Seyðisfjörður. He describes how his boat and many others had been enjoying a good catch, thanks to the herring they used as fresh bait, which had been gathered in a bay and held there by two whales. One day a whaling boat came and killed the whales. After this the herring disappeared and as the boats had no bait they had to quit fishing (in Geirsson 1993: 78–79).

There were also humanitarian arguments against whaling, and some argued whaling should be forbidden on such grounds. In 1902 the newspaper *Austri* thus described the killing of whales as so cruel that the death cries of the harpooned whales could be heard for many miles and said that these inhumane acts showed the ugly nature of the whalers (Geirsson 1993: 78). Moral arguments against whaling are not an invention of the modern Save the Whale movement; they existed in Iceland at the beginning of the twentieth century.

The idea that whales drove fish toward shore and into the fjords (called *hvalrekstrarkenningin* in Icelandic) was not restricted to Iceland; it also caused considerable controversy in northern Norway, mostly around Varanger fjord, where fishers managed, in 1881, to impose a total ban on whaling in the fjord and on whaling within one mile from shore in Finnmark, for a certain period of the year (Tonnesen and Johnsen 1982: 64). The fishers' theory of whales as sheep dog for capelin and herring, and the fact that they blamed whaling for the decrease of fish, meets little respect in the description of Norwegian whaling historians J. N. Tonnesen and A.O. Johnsen: "Old superstitions die hard; they remain immune to fact and science, which in this case showed that it was not the whale and the cod that drove the capelin towards the cast, but that they followed this small fish when, for natural reasons, it sought coastal waters in order to spawn" (1982: 63).

Fishers may have been wrong in their conclusions about the causality between whale and fish, but the knowledge of contemporary fishers about conditions and behavior of fish is often treated with similar scorn by marine biologists in a discourse that presents the fishers as irrational and emotional while scientists see themselves as rational and free of "superstition" (see Pálsson 1991: 151).

Seabirds may look innocent enough, but they are often the cause of much anger and frustration when fishers use longlines—a common type of fishing gear in small-scale fishing. When the longline is set, a buoy is tied to the first line, then several lines, each measuring some 750 meters, are let out at moderate speed to avoid the loss of bait, mostly herring, from the hooks. Seagulls, terns, and fulmar flock to the line, before it sinks below the surface, to feast on the bait. A desperate fisher may thus watch how bait is cleaned from the line, destroying any likelihood of catch. In addition some of the birds get caught on hooks and act as floats, preventing the line from sinking to the bottom. As any fisher can tell, there will be no fish on that part of the line. Yelling, screaming, and banging metal plates while setting the line helps very little, especially if the birds are hungry. Some fishers resort to setting longlines while it is still dark to help lessen the problem with birds. During the light Arctic months of summer, when small-scale fishing reaches its peak, there is no hiding place from the birds.

Fishers often talk about seals in negative terms, although this is a fairly recent change in attitude (see Einarsson 1990b). The reason for this is that the common seals and gray seals living on the coastline are said to scare away fish from inshore fishing spots and damage fish in nets, usually by eating the abdomen of the fish (a fish damaged in such a way is called "seal bitten fish" [*selbitinn fiskur*]). And, like the whales, they are said to consume a great deal of the fish on the inshore grounds, a statement supported by biological research. It has been estimated that the twelve thousand gray seals and the thirty thousand common seals take around forty-eight thousand metric tons of fish annually; if it were not for the seals, the total catch of cod could be increased by 30% and the total catch of some other valuable species such as halibut, lumpfish, and saithe could be more than doubled (Hauksson 1989). In addition, seals function as a link in the life cycle of the codworm, which matures in their guts and spreads with the feces. Fish become contaminated by codworm and the cleaning of the parasite from the fish is a costly process. The fish industry complains about the infested inshore fish and maintains that less should be paid for such catches. Fishers are fairly convinced that the best solution would be thoroughly to cull seals, a position supported by some but by no means all Icelandic biologists (see Helgadóttir et al. 1985). Because of protests against the hunting of seals in Canada, seals are no longer an alternative source of income to fishers.

Treatment of Fish and Attitudes to Cruelty

The effective protest of various environmental groups against the hunting of seals and whales is a well-known issue in Iceland. Many fishers and nonfishers alike worry, however, about the possibility that arguments about animal welfare might be stretched to include fishing. This is seen as perfectly possible. Such arguments fall on barren ground with fishers because, according to their view, fish do not really feel pain, being cold-blooded. As to the reality of how and whether fish actually experience pain this is probably not true. As the British Campaign for the Abolition of Angling puts it on one of its posters:

"Just because the fish don't scream doesn't mean it's not murder." But fishers certainly suppress the idea that they might be causing suffering to fish.

Some older fishers had the habit of spitting or blowing into the mouth of undersize fish they had caught before letting them go back into the sea. This somewhat magical life-giving ritual was said to increase the likelihood of the fish surviving and growing into a bigger fish which could be caught later. The welfare of the fish was thus justified in utilitarian terms, although I did sometimes notice a certain hint of sentimentality in the action when fishers talked about "letting the poor little thing go" (*láta litla greyið fara*).

There are some other inconsistencies in the attitudes toward the treatment of fish. One older fisher told me how he found it difficult to understand why people enjoy sport fishing, especially for salmon. "The longer it takes to land the fish, the longer it takes for the fish to reach exhaustion and die, the more enjoyable and exciting the fishing is. And it is just a sport. The foreigners even let the fish go, when they've had their fun." This was a man who had spent more than fifty years as a professional fisher. When I asked him whether he really could afford throwing stones with his background as a professional fish abuser he replied that it was not the same thing. He had never enjoyed killing fish.

However, there is indeed a tendency among fishers to stress that the killing of animals is done in the pursuit of making a living and should be done as quickly and cleanly as possible. In the words of a minke whaler:

> There is nothing more inhumane about whaling than the killing of
> other animals. At least these animals are free in nature until they
> are hunted. Most animals are shut up in cages all their life and
> never know freedom. I can't see that better in any way. As to when
> people say that even fish shouldn't be killed I'd like to point out that
> Jesus ate fish, and for that matter mutton. I think nature and fate
> always expected people to use animals for subsistence, not just grass
> [*gras*] and vegetables. And if you look around in nature you see that
> creatures live off each other. The whale lives by eating other ani-
> mals. That is how the chain is.

Fishers often refer to their occupation as a natural way of life: they are hunters and an integral part of the ecosystem. Their methods of fishing are small in scale and fishers claim they pose no threat to fish stocks or to the environment in general. They also use this as an argument against cutting down the quotas allotted to small-scale fishing. The environmental arguments for the continued existence of artisanal fishing are in fact becoming more and more important in the struggle against other sectors of the fishing industry (see Einarsson 1993b).

Fishers also like to juxtapose what they see as a natural way of living with the lives of "city dwellers" who, they claim, are becoming ever more removed from nature, living in crime ridden, inhumane surroundings and buying all their products from the supermarket, including nicely packaged meat. Fishers point to the inconsistencies in the treatment of animals by their critics, who may even call themselves "nations of animal lovers" while at the same time tolerating the mass suffering of factory-raised animals, which ordinary people never know and never see. This criticism fits in with the critical questions raised by animal rights philosophers such as Tom Regan, who asks "How would we fare psychologically if the walls of slaughter-houses were made of glass? What would we feel and do if we saw the death of so-called 'food animals'?" (cited in Garner 1993: 252).

The stigmatizing view fishers have of whale conservationists hardly does justice to the different people and causes of the Save the Whale movement. It is understandable, however, in terms of the organizations and individuals they see as representing the movement. Paul Watson, the leader and founder of Sea Shepherd, a marine mammal conservation group, is one of the militant "eco-warriors" (a term endorsed by the members) engaged in whale conservation and a firm believer that in the future people will be able to communicate with whales. Having attempted and partially succeeded in scuttling a minke whaling boat in a small fishing village in northern Norway on Boxing Day 1992, he sent what he called "a letter to the Norwegian people" which was published in a Norwegian newspaper. There he says: "Do you want your children to hear about what you did to the whales from the very same beings that you have helped to slaughter? It is a certainty that the whales will talk about you in the same vein as Jews now talk of Nazis. For in the eyes of whalekind, there is little difference between the behaviour of the monsters of the Reich and the monsters behind the harpoon" (quoted in *High North News*, p. 1). Such messages and actions only serve to reinforce the image of environmentalists as potentially dangerous extremists who are not to be taken seriously.

Conclusion

To understand the attitudes fishers have toward marine animals, we have to look at the interaction between fishers and their culturally perceived environment, which they hold to be unproblematically natural, during their subsistence activities. Fishers see these animals as competitors for scarce resources, which influences their perception of this part of the natural world. What is important is that fishers are *engaged* with the marine environment in their day-to-day experiences and their understandings, assumptions, and attitudes should be seen in terms of those relations. Tim Ingold, following J. von Uexküll and J. J. Gibson, has argued for an anticognitivistic approach to the understanding of how people perceive their environment, emphasizing that environmental knowledge cannot be separated from productive activity or how nature is used and that nature becomes, through human use, meaningful environment (Ingold 1992). Cultural classification, he argues, is an afterthought, an epilogue rather than a prelude to practical action.

I agree with Ingold's main thesis. I think this is a useful way of addressing the problem of environmental perceptions. I nevertheless have some doubts about the universality of the thesis. For example, it may be fairly straightforward to argue for a hands-on basis of environmental perceptions, including attitudes to animals, among subsistence producers such as fishers and reindeer herders. More problematic is the question of where the majority of people (e.g., urban Westerners) acquire their views of nature. In most cases this is not through productive activity but rather through other channels of experience such as nature and environmental programs on television and other forms of media. Some go whale-watching or visit national parks. Ingold's thesis may thus in practice apply to only a tiny minority of humankind. At least in the Western world, it is a minority which—by being subsistence producers in a decontextualized and disembedded modern world, to use Giddens's (1990) terminology—has become premodern by insisting on the relevance of local reality and experience versus the abstractness of nature in need of conservation.

The statements fishers make about the effects of a growing number of whales and other marine mammals in Icelandic waters and how this affects the fishing are part of a cognized model, an understanding of how things work in the ecosystem. In this case there seems to be a close relationship between representations and reality, at least if we are to believe what resource economists and whale biologists have to say about the predation cost of whale stocks. Folk models that guide the everyday behavior and understanding of people are seldom a perfect reflection of reality. I would, however, maintain in the case of Icelandic fishers and their use of marine resources that the knowledge of those who gain livelihood from the environment at hand is not a primitive representation to be regarded as inferior to scientific knowledge, but rather as different in kind and no less valid or relevant.

What I see as the contribution of studies such as this one and the possible role of anthropologists is the stress on the human aspect of conservation: the plans people have for the environment should be taken into consideration and respected. While there are many reasons to believe that small-scale fishing is preferable with regard to ecological sustainability, we should not forget that "conservation consciousness" is linked to realities on the ground. Ultimately the conservation of wildlife and natural resources depends on the cooperation and engagement of local resource users. Such engagement of the engaged may, however, be difficult to achieve if the animals involved are seen mainly as threats and competitors for scarce resources, instead of contributing to economic survival. This is of course an issue not only in Iceland but worldwide where local people are prohibited from using wildlife and where wildlife causes damage and even threatens people's lives.

In fact there are many parallels between the effects of the whaling moratorium and those of the widespread ban on elephant hunting in many African countries (Buckoke 1993). In Tanzania the Maasai have been driven out of their traditional lands, which have in many places been taken over for national wildlife parks for the exclusive use by tourists, who often resent seeing the Maasai in what has been advertised as pristine nature, free of people (Monbiot 1994). As people have been "alienated by conservation, they have shown few scruples in attacking the animals with which they once coexisted. The friends of nature have been turned, by conservationists, into its enemies" (1994: 31). There are some signs that the international environmental community is becoming more willing to acknowledge the problems involving unilateral bans on wildlife use and the need for more pragmatic conservation which does not exclude local people and thus alienate them from the often few resources available to them. As Martin Holdgate, director of the World Conservation Union

(IUCN), recently remarked: "Such denial, in turn, may erode conservation because it eliminates the economic value of the wildlife and hence the incentive to maintain it" (1993: 27).

The danger in the transformation of animals into "pests" is that there are even greater problems connected with the conservation of a stigmatized animal species. In most of Western culture rats, for example, are stigmatized in such a way and there are very few people who advocate "rat rights" or argue for the necessary and natural part rats play in ecological systems. My hypothesis is that when animals compete with people rather than being of benefit to people, especially if these people have an anthropocentric, utilitarian view of nature, then most likely those animals will be seen as pests and treated accordingly. In such situations, conflicts are often the result between local resource users and conservation forces, be it the government or environmental groups. It also seems quite likely that we will have a growing conflict between Icelandic fishers and conservation groups over the hunting of marine mammals in the very near future, as is already the case in Norway, in times when a drastic cut in fish quotas is being implemented and the forecasts about the state of fish stocks are very bleak indeed.

In campaigns against whaling, conservation groups often depict whalers as cruel brutes who engage in the killing of animals with dubious motives; one sometimes gets the feeling that whalers must be less than humane. But what alternatives are there for people like Icelandic fishers apart from a utilitarian, human-centered view of nature? Isn't species-ism and the exclusion of some animals from the moral community almost a necessary prerequisite for fishing? To Icelandic fishers the arguments of Western conservationists who see themselves as "standing in for" nature (Yearley 1993) are not valid because they are not based on the practitioner's way of knowing the realities of fishing. It is totally alien to fishers' anthropocentric cultural model of the Great Chain of Being when animals are given moral standing on a level with humans. I should stress that I am not arguing that fishers' discourse on resource use is mostly a passive reflection of a wider discourse of modernity (Giddens 1990), the local version of the global, but rather that it is the outcome of what are seen as important issues of local realities and economic and cultural survival. There is a tendency within postmodern anthropology to ignore the distinctiveness and autonomy of human groups and to see practices and beliefs as mostly refractions of dominant outsiders (see Lee 1994). I do not think such an approach would do the material at hand full justice.

Acknowledgments

Thanks are due to Darrell A. Posey, Mikhael Kurkiala, Robert Barnes, Kay Milton, and the editors. My research has been supported by the University of Uppsala, the Royal Swedish Academy of Sciences, the Swedish Institute, the Nordic Environmental Research Programme (NERP), the Nordic Committee for Social Science Research (NOS-S), and Gosta and Marta Moberg Fund (Stiftelsen Småland Museum).

4

THE POLITICS OF PRODUCTION:
ENCLOSURE, EQUITY, AND EFFICIENCY

This essay discusses changes in Icelandic fishing associated with the introduction of a new system of resource management, a quota system, focusing on contested notions of equity, nation, and productive efficiency. With this system, some Icelanders were granted the privilege to exploit the major fishing stocks in Icelandic waters. Moreover, as our analyses indicate, since the introduction of the system in 1984 quotas have become increasingly concentrated in the hands of owners and directors of the largest fishing companies. We show how the powerful rhetoric of economics has influenced the formation of fisheries policy and examine some of the basic assumptions of economic theorizing on production. Current Icelandic debates on fisheries management combine elements of a global discourse on property regimes with heavily loaded images and metaphors from the feudal agrarian discourse of the distant Icelandic past.

Indigenous production discourse has undergone a series of successive changes as Icelanders have assumed new kinds of relations in the course of appropriating marine resources (Pálsson 1991). To each phase in the development of Icelandic society corresponded a particular dominant "paradigm," an underlying framework of understandings and assumptions. One of the important changes in the past concerns the discursive shift from land to sea. During earlier centuries, Icelandic farmers and landowners occupied a central position and, consequently, fishing was regarded as merely a supplementary subsistence activity. Those in power presented the growing fishing communities of the nineteenth and early twentieth century as "devoid of culture" (*menningarsnauð*), the source of degeneration, alienation, and deficient language. Finnur Jónsson, a native ethnologist, once remarked with respect to a fishing village on the southwest coast that while it was always regarded "as one of the best fishing places in the south, . . . its culture was at a rather low stage of development" (1945: 159). In the nineteenth century new markets for Icelandic fish were developed, especially in Spain and England. Fishing villages grew, and an expanding market economy emerged. Fishing became a full-time occupation and a separate economic activity. As a result, the focus of discussions on economics and production shifted from the landed elite to the grass-roots of the fishing communities. Gradually fishers, particularly skippers, became the key figures of production discourse. In the process, agriculture was redefined as a burden to the national economy. Now, once again, the discursive pendulum has swung in the opposite direction—from sea to land. Fishing remains a major economic enterprise, but the central agents—the makers of economic value—are no longer skippers and fishers but the land-based owners of quotas, boats, and fishing plants and the holders of scientific, textual knowledge. This significant shift in the way in which Icelanders talk about the production process alerts us to fundamental changes in social relations. While discourse is embedded in social relations, it is precisely through social discourse that people redefine their relations to one another and their place in the world. Discourse and context are dialectically interlinked.

In the modern world, quota systems of the kind we discuss and similar market approaches are increasingly adopted in response to environmental problems. Their wider social and economic implications are hotly debated, however, as they raise central questions of ethics, politics, and social theory. Market approaches to resource management are often assumed to be incompatible with egalitarian sensibilities (see, for example, Young 1992) and communitarian notions of stewardship and responsibility. However, given the predominance of such approaches in modern life, it is imperative that social scientists—including anthropologists and economists—attempt to examine more closely what the rather loose reference to the "market" entails (Dilley 1992). Studies of quota systems in fisheries and their effects are still in their infancy (for some examples in the emerging literature, see Dewees 1989; McCay and Creed 1990; Boyd and Dewees 1992). In the following account we explore the social consequences of quota management and the ensuing rhetorical contests over the nature of fishing rights, the morality of exchange, and the changing character of a nation. Our analysis of the history of access to resources, based on ethnographic fieldwork, detailed interviews, and quantitative data on the distribution of fishing quotas, indicates radical changes in the Icelandic system of production.

The Contested Character of a Nation

At least from the thirteenth century onward, the pressure on pastures was subject to systematic collective control by the local "commune" (*hreppur*) to prevent overgrazing. The early laws of *Grágás* (compiled in the twelfth century) and later *Jónsbók* addressed the problem of overgrazing in common pastures (*afréttir*) in fairly modern terms. The users were advised "to find the maximum number of sheep that could use the pastures without affecting the average weight of the flock—'let them find that number, which in their judgement does not give fatter sheep if reduced but also fills the afréttur,' says *Grágás*" (Eggertsson 1992: 433). The ocean, by contrast, was generally regarded as a boundless common resource.[1] While the resources of the beach belonged to the owner of the land and the landowner was given privileged use-rights in relation to resources of so-called net areas (*netlög*, defined in terms of the depth at which a net of twenty meshes could be located), generally the ocean was defined as a "common" (*almenningur*). The commons began at the point where a flattened cod could no longer be seen from land, this being the criterion used to define the "fishing limits" (*fiskhelgi*). During most of Icelandic history, the principle of common use-rights has been applied to the resources of the sea.

Both during and after the nationalist campaign for independence, the articulation of the principle of common use-rights has frequently incorporated concerns for political autonomy (*sjálfstæði*) and national sovereignty. In 1926, for instance, one Icelander, commenting in the journal of the National Fisheries Association on the use of the national flag at sea, urged fishers to "relish the rights conveyed upon [them] by the Icelandic nation, above and beyond the citizens of foreign nations," emphasizing that within "Icelandic" waters they were "the rightful heirs to the national estate [*óðal*]": "The fishing territories are the common property of all Icelanders, to be jointly exploited by them without interference, according to the laws and regulations in force at each moment in time" (*Ægir* 1926: 53–54). A few years later, an Icelandic county-level official (*sýslumaður*) urged the Icelandic parliament to pass new legislation that would expel foreign fishing vessels from Icelandic coastal waters (at that time, within four miles): "When this has been accomplished, *then, at last, we Icelanders will have reclaimed for ourselves Iceland as a sovereign state*, and then, both on land and sea, we can begin to sing in a free and mighty voice 'Rejoice Iceland's millennium!'" (Havsteen 1930: 41–43).

The principle of common rights in fish has been an important dimension in Icelandic society—equivalent, perhaps, to the sentiments codified in the "public trust doctrine" in the United States (see McCay n.d.; Macinko 1993). In both cases, notions of common access to fishing space carry a heavy symbolic and ideological load, combining concerns for national sovereignty and political autonomy with those of equity and personal autonomy. During the so-called cod wars with Britain and West Germany in the 1970s, Iceland claimed national ownership of the fishing stocks in coastal waters, in an attempt to carve a territorial as well as a symbolic space for itself in the larger world (see Brydon, this volume). The culmination of these events was described by the Icelandic minister of fisheries at that time as the final stage of the Icelandic nation's struggle for independence. Significantly, the measures adopted internally, to organize Icelandic fishing, were designed not to exclude anyone from fishing but to affect producers equally (the first serious limitations on the fishing effort of Icelandic boats were temporary bans on fishing on particular grounds). In theory, the commoners had equal rights to national resources, including fish. While there was always some degree of inequality in these matters, limitations on access tended to resonate with the dominant ethos of the independence rhetoric of egalitarianism. A sociological study of Icelandic values points out—overemphasizing, no doubt, historical continuity, attributing egalitarianism to "the conditions of life that faced the Icelanders from the beginning"—that "equality could . . . be singled out as the most dominant value orientation" of Icelanders (Tomasson 1980: 195). Indeed, the idea that inequality is minimal and that opportunities are equal still prevails in modern Iceland (Pálsson and Durrenberger 1992; Durrenberger, this volume).

The reasons for the maintenance and extension of the national fisheries limits were, however, ecological as well as symbolic. With the development of the Icelandic market economy early in the twentieth century, Icelandic catches multiplied as boats and fishing gear became ever more efficient. Furthermore, the activities of foreign fleets intensified in the coastal waters around Iceland. After independence in 1944, at the end of World War II, the fishing sector expanded even further. As a result, some of the most important fishing stocks were heavily overexploited. Although the cod wars put an end to large-scale foreign fishing, the problem of overfishing was by no means resolved, since the Icelandic fleet continued to grow. By 1982 Icelandic politicians and interest groups were increasingly of the opinion that more radical measures would be needed to limit effort and prevent the "collapse" of the cod stock. At the annual conference of the Fisheries Association, most interest groups were rather unexpectedly in favor of an individual boat-quota system suggested by the Union of Boat Owners, a system that would divide a reduced catch within the industry itself on the basis of previous catches or "fishing history" (aflareynsla). The precise allocation of catches was debated; late in 1983 it was agreed that each boat was to be allocated an annual quota on the basis of its average catch over the past three years. To this effect all fishing vessels over ten tons that had previously been active in the demersal fisheries (the cod fisheries)—a total of 667 vessels—were allotted uneven quantified rights of access to the fishing stocks, quota "shares" as they were called (aflahlutdeild). This meant that some boats would get higher quotas than the rest of the fleet, a fundamental departure, as we have seen, from the egalitarian approach of traditional policy.

At first, the quota system was introduced as a temporary measure designed to limit the fishing effort of the fleet until the fishing stocks could recover from their bleak and diminished state. In theory, such an arrangement would be sufficient to ensure the biological objectives of fisheries management—the sustainable exploitation of the fishing stocks. Indeed, this was the line of argument used to sway fishers to accept temporary quota management. However, quota systems, originating from the field of economics, were also intended to promote economically efficient production. In order to achieve this goal, it was assumed, fishing rights had to emulate private property rights to the fullest extent possible (Neher et al. 1989; Scott 1989). To begin with, the quota system in the Icelandic cod fishery only partly conformed to these ideals. While quotas could be leased relatively freely, they could only be bought or sold *en masse* along with the fishing boat to which they were allotted; they were not divisible. Quotas did not, therefore, constitute full private property rights inasmuch as they were intended only as a temporary measure and the transferability of quotas was partially restricted.

As it turned out, much to the chagrin of fishers, the quota system was extended several times, for a few years in each case. Meanwhile, the emphasis in the discourse of policy makers gradually shifted from the protection of fishing stocks to the (perhaps more controversial) goal of productive efficiency. Eventually, in 1990, with productive efficiency as the primary goal on the managerial agenda, a few radical alterations were made to the quota system. In particular, the system was extended into the distant future, regardless of the future condition of the fishing stocks. Quotas, therefore, became less transient in nature and more akin to permanent property rights. Moreover, quotas became fully transferable and divisible. These changes marked the full institution of the individual transferable quota (ITQ) system in the Icelandic demersal fisheries—in effect, culminating the process of enclosure and privatization initiated in 1984.

There has always been firm opposition among both fishers and Icelanders in general to the idea of quotas being the private property of boat owners. A national survey in 1991 showed that 91% of Icelanders opposed changing the common property nature of the fisheries. However, there has continually been much confusion and debate about the kind of rights quotas confer on their holders. Paradoxically, while economists generally view individual transferable quotas as being synonymous with property rights (see, for example, Scott 1989; Neher et al. 1989), this fact is staunchly denied by policy makers in Iceland. Administrators point to the first article of the fisheries legislation, where it is categorically stated that the fishing stocks in Icelandic waters are the common property of the nation, emphasizing that quotas merely represent temporary use-rights that can under no circumstances be defined as the private property of individuals.

Nevertheless, it seems that boat owners have become the *de facto* owners of the fishing stocks. The tax authorities have confirmed this interpretation in their decision that quotas are to be reported as property on tax-forms and that the selling of quotas involves a type of income. Recently, the Supreme Court resolved, in a case between a fishing company and the minister of finance, that accumulated permanent quotas represented private property liable to taxation. It seems that policy makers have introduced the full ITQ system to the fisheries in several stages, to avoid potential confrontation. Privatization has thus been sneaked in through the back door, being conspicuously absent from descriptions presented by the authorities to fishers and the general public. This in turn has granted quotas the transitional and somewhat anomalous status of being the public property of the nation, in name, but, in effect the private property of boat owners. According to one Icelandic fisheries economist, such a gradual transition to the full privatization of marine resources was unavoidable to alleviate opposition based on "traditional values and vested interests rather than rational arguments" (Árnason 1993a: 206). However, the privatization process has not gone wholly uncontested in Iceland. Indeed, fishers have engaged public officials and boat owners in a rhetorical debate over the exact definition of fishing rights. In a popular phrase from recent political campaigns, the quota system represented the "biggest theft in Icelandic history." Current debates on the extent to which individual transferable quotas violate established notions of equity and public access draw attention to a larger concern—offering, to paraphrase Seth Macinko (1993), a commentary on the apparently changing character of a nation. Now, as a large part of the Icelandic commons had been reserved for the privileged use of a few boat owners, Icelanders no longer had comparable rights in fish. Some Icelanders had become more equal than others.

The Rhetoric of Productive Efficiency

While marine science restricted the scope of fishing operations, setting the limit of the total allowable catch for a fishing season on the basis of precise measurements and informed estimates of stock sizes and fish recruitment, the science of resource economics was to play an equally important role, providing the theoretical framework and the political rationale for a quota system. In many ways, in fact, resource economics has replaced marine biology as the hegemonic discourse on Icelandic fishing. While the original, formal demand for the quota system came from within the fishing industry, it would hardly have been instituted if it had not been advocated by influential Icelandic economists. Not only did they play a leading role within political parties as well as on a series of important committees that designed and modified the management regime, but their writings in newspapers, specialized magazines, and scholarly journals paved the way for the scientific discourse on efficiency and the rational management which the quota system represents. Some of the economists argued, with reference to the "tragedy of the commons," that overfishing was inevitable as long as the fishing grounds were defined as "common property" (i.e., where access was free for everyone) and that the only realistic alternative—euphemistically defined as "rights based" fishing (see Macinko 1993: 946)—was a system of individual transferable quotas. Assuming a sense of responsibility among the new "owners" of the resource (the quota-holders) and an unhindered transfer of quotas from less to more efficient producers, economists argued, a quota system would both encourage ecological stewardship and ensure maximum productive efficiency.

Given the significant role of economic discourse in modern life, it is perhaps not surprising that economists have come to dominate the field of fisheries management. From the economist's viewpoint, the goal of productive efficiency—leading to the maximum economic yield (MEY) of fishing stocks—is the crux of fisheries management. Characteristically, economists argue that only the "hidden" forces of the market can ensure both efficiency and the sustainable use of resources; for them, the "tragedy of the commons" is first and foremost one of rent dissipation. Other social issues such as equity and traditional rights are pushed to the periphery, perceived as mere distractions from the objective and essentially technical undertaking of promoting efficient production.

An analysis of some of the assumptions of economic theory is a prerequisite to understanding the ongoing contest in Iceland over the exploitation of the fishing stocks. More specifically, to comprehend the transformation of power relations within the Icelandic fishing industry in the wake of eleven years of quota management it is necessary to explore the rationale and rhetoric of privatization and market regulation. Of central importance in this context is the concept that, for many, lies at the heart of the vocation of economics: economic efficiency. Economists use the concept of efficiency in two different but interrelated contexts, although this difference is not always made explicit in economic texts. The first and more prestigious form employs an "engineering" perspective to gauge the productive efficiency of individual fishing operations and of the industry as a whole. To this effect economists measure fishing effort and capitalization against the value of the catch (see, for example, Árnason 1991). Those producers that create a substantial profit at low cost are considered to be efficient; if all fishing operations are conducted in this manner, then the industry is held to exhibit a high degree of productive efficiency. Here the "invisible hand" of the market plays a key role, because theoretically the perfect market will allocate quotas to producers in just proportion to their productive efficiency—thereby achieving competitive equilibrium.

The second form of economic efficiency, allocative efficiency, provides economists with an answer to questions regarding the fairness and appropriateness of specific distributions of resources. While conventionally only applied to the distribution of wealth and economic goods among consumers—the subject matter of welfare economics—the concept of allocative efficiency has increasingly been extended to economic analyses of production.[2] This is especially apparent in the field of resource economics, not least in the case of quota systems like the one used to manage the Icelandic fisheries. Indeed, a central question in such management regimes that must be addressed by economists is that of resource allocation—in other words, how quotas should be distributed among producers. In economic theory, the greatest level of allocative efficiency is achieved when resources are distributed among individuals in just proportion to their utility. Utility, in this context, refers to an individual's needs and wants, based on subjective preferences. Hence, in the context of the Icelandic fisheries, those that have the most "need" for quotas should receive the largest quota allotments. However, this raises the problem of utility measurement. In other words: how does one, for example, go about comparing the utility of a small operator at the point of bankruptcy to that of a large and profitable company? Which is in more need of an extra share of quotas? Economists have long since given up on *direct* individual utility comparisons, disregarding such practice as hopelessly subjective and tainted with ethical considerations (Sen 1987; England 1993). To resolve this problem, they have come up with a seemingly neutral solution, that of Pareto optimality, which professedly spares them the distress of setting foot in the messy and irrational world of subjective utility comparisons. According to this ideal, a distributional change will result in greater efficiency if someone is better off after the change, without anyone being worse off (for a more detailed account of Pareto optimality, see Sen 1973, 1987; LeGrand 1991; England 1993).

Given the assumption that individuals would like to increase their share rather than see it diminished, it follows that any *involuntary* redistribution of resources will result in non–Pareto optimality and therefore a loss of allocative efficiency (even when such measures are taken to rectify truly awful situations of starvation and poverty). According to orthodox economic theory, only free market exchange can achieve a Pareto superior state and thus increase allocative efficiency. Such exchange is by definition voluntary—else the market is not free—and if both parties behave in a rational and self-interested manner, it will only take place when both parties expect to benefit in some way. Consequently, the "invisible hand" of the market inevitably achieves a state of greater allocative efficiency, revealing that the states of allocative efficiency and productive efficiency are in fact one and the same, despite being derived from different assumptions. A corollary of this line of reasoning is that *any* distribution of resources arrived at through market regulation will be deemed efficient. In fact, economists assume that all distributional changes that are due to transactions in the market will lead to increases in allocative efficiency (Sen 1987; Nelson 1993; Rothschild 1993). Hence, the more activity on the market, the better the outcome will be. Thus, the concept of allocative efficiency imbues the "invisible hand" of the market with a sense of ethical respectability, based as it is on utilitarian ethical principles. And since no one seems to be losing anything, an implicit sense of fairness is intimated.

Although economists allegedly refrain from wrestling with subjective comparisons of utility, in an attempt to divorce their positivistic methodology from ethical issues, the juxtaposition of the two forms of efficiency discussed above reveals a tacit evaluation of utility, based on the capacity of producers to maximize economic rents from a specific resource, in this case quota allotments. The concept of allocative efficiency is therefore not quite as objective or ethically unproblematic as many economists suppose. Allocative efficiency does in fact incorporate a notion of equity, albeit one that many would find unattractive, where "greater value is placed on increases in the utility of the better-off than on similar increases for the worse-off" (LeGrand 1991: 33; see also Young 1992: 40). However, in spite of this unexpected excursion into the untidy world of ethical judgments, economists nevertheless envision their task to be objective and devoid of moral concerns. Significantly, Ragnar Árnason (1993b: 141), a leading Icelandic fisheries economist, seems to consider distributional equity to be an extraneous issue, of no real concern to economists, important only insofar as it does not cause social conflict and thereby threaten the continued existence of the ITQ system. In fact, efficiency seems generally to have been elevated to the point of becoming some sort of metavalue—what Daniel W. Bromley (1990) has called an "objective truth rule," located beyond the scope of ordinary values, the attainment of which is the unquestioned goal of most orthodox economic theory. Commenting on the status of economic efficiency in modern life, the editors of an important collection of economic texts warn that "economics is often at odds with popular feeling. Economic theory leads naturally to some basic propositions about the efficiency of markets, and in the real world markets often operate in a harsh and arbitrary fashion, and make the achievement of other socially desirable objectives such as a more equal distribution of income rather difficult to achieve" (Bleaney and Stewart 1991: 730).

The portrayal of the economic endeavour as objective, rational, harsh, and mathematically oriented, detached from distracting ethical issues, brings to mind images of masculinity (Ferber and Nelson 1993; England 1993). Extending this metaphor, Donald N. McCloskey has described neoclassicists as the motorcycle gang of economics (1993: 76). The masculine image stands in juxtaposition with the more effeminate representation of welfare economists, whose inquiries deal with the softer distributional issues that are thought to be tainted by subjectivity, being descriptive and often normative in nature (Nelson 1993). Although originally deemed to be an integral part of the economic enterprise, distributional issues have more or less been pushed to a peripheral and less prestigious place in the discipline of economics. Some prominent welfare economists feel severely restricted by the harsh and uncompromising analytical tools provided by neoclassical economic theory (see, for example, Sen 1973, 1987). These scholars propose instead a more sensitive ethical approach to the problems of resource allocation. However, as the masculine dominates the feminine, efficiency dominates the attainment of other socially desirable objectives. In economic discourse it is conventional to posit this relationship in the form of a tradeoff between the rational objective of efficiency and irrational moral issues such as justice and equitable distribution (Okun 1975; LeGrand 1991;

Gatewood 1993). Heeding social objectives other than efficiency is articulated in the terms of a *sacrifice* of efficiency. Thus, Árnason (1990: 69) cautions against forfeiting efficiency by restricting the transferability of quotas, a measure that has been proposed to promote a more equitable situation in the fishing industry.

The market approach of individual transferable quotas has captured the imagination of modern scholars and policy makers. The editors of *Rights-Based Fishing* suggest that "ITQs are a part of one of the great institutional changes of our times: the enclosure and privatization of the common resources of the ocean" (Neher et al. 1989: 3). By instituting transferable private property rights to the fishing stocks and letting the market regulate their distribution, both allocative and productive efficiency will theoretically be attained; or, as Árnason puts it: "the total quota will always be allocated to the most efficient fishing firms in the most efficient proportions," generating "micro (or allocative) efficiency in the fishery" (1991: 411). Badly run fishing operations will be forced to sell their permanent quotas and get out of the business, making way for more efficient producers to increase their share in the fishing stocks. According to economic theory, then, it is not important who the individual producers are, how many they are, or how they go about their business (see, for example, Einarsson and Árnason 1994); the market will ensure maximum productive and allocative efficiency at each time.

Several anthropologists and economists have raised doubts with respect to the neoclassical preconceptions of economic theory which the system of individual transferable quotas represents (see, for instance, McCay and Acheson 1987; Hanna 1990) as well as the general attempt to separate economics from politics, ethics, and culture, emphasizing the insufficient attention of orthodox economics to empirical realities, its individualistic biases, and its androcentric assumptions (McCloskey 1985; Gudeman 1986, 1992; Ferber and Nelson 1993). Some have argued for an expanded, "provisioning" definition of economics, a definition that considers humans in relation to the world. "Economics," Nelson suggests, "could be about how we live in our house, the earth" (1993: 33). The actual functioning and consequences of markets in real settings, however, are problems that are seldom tackled by economists (O'Brien 1991; Ormerod 1994).

Recently, some critics of privatization and quota management have developed the argument that multispecies coastal ecosystems are highly unpredictable, with constant fluctuations in interactions among species and between species and their habitat. James A. Wilson and his associates (Wilson et al. 1994) suggest, for instance, that the "numerical" approach of current resource economics and marine biology, emphasizing linear relationships and states of equilibrium, fails to account for the "chaotic" aspects of many fisheries. Their empirical work shows that, while fisheries are deterministic systems, because of their extreme sensitivity to "initial conditions" even simple fish communities have no equilibrium tendency. As a result, management faces forbidding problems when trying to explain the noise in ecological relationships, such as the relationship between recruitment and stock size, often a key issue for managers. The degree of accuracy of knowledge required for prediction, it seems, is far beyond any proficiency we might hope to achieve in a maritime environment. Therefore, it may be impossible to know the outcomes of management actions such as quotas. It does not mean that governance is impossible; it suggests, however, a finer spatial and temporal scale that only the skillful practitioner is able to apply.

Leaving aside the biological and "economic" rationale of the Icelandic quota system, it is important to examine its broader social implications, what it means to the "house." In particular, how are rights of access to the fisheries distributed, what changes in distribution have occurred over time, how do people talk about the new system, and how do they relate to one another in the process of production?

The Concentration of Quotas

In the following we attempt to explore some of the social consequences of the transferability of fishing rights in the Icelandic demersal fisheries, focusing on the changing distribution of quotas among boat owners. For this purpose, we have constructed a database (the "Quotabase") with detailed information on quota allocations from the beginning of the quota system, a period of a whole decade.[3]

One rather simple way of throwing light on the distribution of quotas is to examine the number of quota-holders in relation to the size of their quota shares. Arranging quota-holders into four discrete and ordinal groups based on the size of their quota share, we used the following somewhat arbitrary classification: the "giants" are the group with the largest quota-shares, holding more than 1% of the total quota each, the next group of "large" quota-holders have 0.3–1%, "small" quota-holders have 0.1–0.3%, and, finally, "dwarves" have less than 0.1%. Employing this classification, a simple and effective

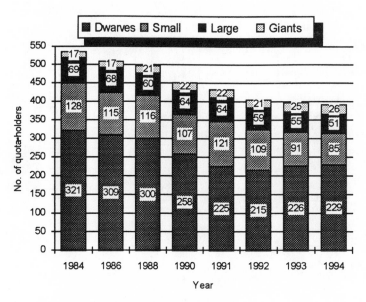

1 Number of quota-holders, 1984–1994.

way of discerning distributional changes of quota-shares among boat owners is to compare the number of quota-holders in each specific group for each consecutive year. Figure 1 shows the results of this exercise for an eleven-year period (excluding, for the sake of comparison, six- to ten-ton boats that were incorporated into the system in 1991). What is perhaps most striking is the steady decrease in the total number of quota-holders. Also notable is the gradual increase in the number of giants concurrent with a decrease in the numbers of the other three groups.

An even more telling way of elucidating distributional changes is to compare the aggregate permanent shares of these groups. Figure 2 indicates changes in the relative distribution of quotas for the same eleven-year period. Evidently, while the giants have grown in number through the years, they have been accumulating quotas to a disproportionate degree. At the same time, the shares of other groups have diminished in correspondence with their reduced numbers.

Another and more sophisticated method of exploring distributional changes over time is to use the Lorenz curve, a measure of inequality derived from welfare economics. This method conveys a graphical representation of distributional inequality and concentration. Operationally, this measure of inequality establishes the level of

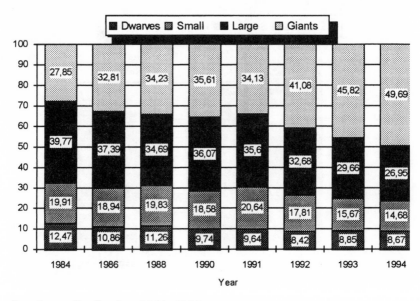

2   Quota distribution, 1984–1994.

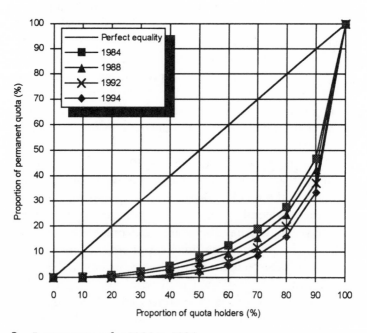

3   Lorenz curves for 1984 to 1994.

distributional inequality in a system as "the number or proportion of units that must be redistributed in order to create uniform shares" (Coulter 1989: 12)—in other words, the amount of quotas needed to be redistributed to create a condition of perfect equality. Moreover, this measure should reveal the concentration of quotas—for example, the extent to which the surplus is located at the largest one company, ten companies, or fifty companies.

Measuring inequality in the Icelandic fisheries is problematic due to the annual reduction in the number of small quota-holders. Most inequality measures react directly to such changes by indicating a greater degree of equality, since having fewer small holders means that less needs to be redistributed in order to attain perfect equality. One way of making measures sensitive to increased *inequality* caused by reduction in the number of quota-holders is to include those dispossessed as null components—in our case, former quota-holders. Such a procedure may have its drawbacks; the dropouts, it may be argued, are not necessarily dispossessed, they have simply sold their quotas. However, excluding them in our analyses would obviously distort the measurements. As Coulter points out in another context, "if nine equally large landowners seized the land of the remaining one hundred very small farm owners and divided it equally among themselves, many inequality measures would indicate a change from gross inequality to virtually perfect equality" (1989: 21). Using the procedure of including the dropouts as null components, the Lorenz curve provides an effective way of simultaneously displaying inequality and concentration in the distribution of quotas.

Lorenz curves plotted for four years of the whole period of quota management are shown in figure 3 (once again excluding six- to ten-ton boats). The horizontal axis (X-axis) shows quota-holders arrayed in ascending order; the first interval represents the smallest 10% of quota-holders, while the last interval represents the largest 10%. The vertical axis (Y-axis) shows the proportional share of quotas. Thus, for example, it can be inferred that 70% of the smallest quota-holders owned just under 20% of all quota shares in 1984, while the same proportion of quota-holders owned just under 10% in 1994. An increase in the area between the line of perfect equality and the Lorenz curves for each year represents a subsequent increase in the level of inequality. Moreover, the shape of this area represents the degree of concentration of quotas. Judging from figure 3, there is a continual increase in the level of inequality and a growing concentration of quotas at the top.[4]

The data, then, indicate a sizable increase in the level of inequality in the distribution of quotas from 1984. Many boat owners have been dropping out of the system in the past eleven years, and a large majority of these were the smallest operators. At the same time, quotas are becoming concentrated in the hands of fewer boat owners. The year 1991 seems to mark a turning point in this process. Prior to 1991 distributional changes mainly take the form of a reduction in the number of smaller quota-holders (see figure 1). However, after 1991 the reduction in the number of quota-holders seems to slow down, giving way to an accelerated concentration of quotas in the hands of larger companies (see figure 2). The reasons for this are somewhat complex, but may largely be explained by the extensive changes made to the fisheries management legislation in 1990. First, the restrictions on transactions with quota-shares were lifted, making them fully transferable and divisible property rights. Before 1991 boat owners who wanted to sell their quota-shares either had to sell a vessel with all its quota or to sell the quota and exclude the vessel from further activities in Icelandic waters. Assuming that the former quota-holder only owned one vessel, such transactions inevitably resulted in exclusion from the system. After the changes in 1991, operators could sell part of their quota-share, staying in business with a smaller share. Moreover, the incorporation of approximately 700 small-scale operators of six- to ten-ton boats into the quota system provided a fresh supply of quota-shares that have subsequently been swiftly bought up by larger operators. This has resulted in a drastic reduction in the numbers of these smaller quota-holders that is not shown in the data presented here (see Pálsson and Helgason 1995 for further details).

We need to keep in mind that some, if not all, of the giant companies are owned by a large number of share-holders. We could argue, therefore, that the concentration of quotas does in fact mask a more egalitarian distribution of access and ownership. But, for one thing, it is not unlikely that some individuals own shares in several different companies; thus the distribution of ownership of quotas may be even more unequal than the raw figures on distribution indicate. Also, the distribution of holdings within the biggest companies may be very uneven, with few individuals controlling the majority of the shares. Finally, even though share-holders turned out to be more numerous than before, in actual practice a small managerial group has immense powers. They are the ones who control access to the resource, how the resource is used, what happens to the products, and how the benefits are distributed. Currently, only twenty-six companies (the "giants") own about half of the national cod quota.

Feudal Metaphors: A Public Protest

It seems, then, that the privatization of the fishing stocks, followed by successive reductions to the annual total allowable catch, has provoked an increased consolidation within the fishing industry, with large vertically integrated firms buying out the supposedly less efficient small-scale operators. This growing inequality in the system has repeatedly engendered public protests. The editor of the Icelandic fishers' journal (*Víkingur*, literally, Viking), voicing these concerns for fishers in general, put it this way: "Before you know it the whole national fleet will be in the hands of 10 to 15 individuals, who will then also 'own' all the fish in the waters around Iceland. Thus a new aristocracy will have emerged, an aristocracy that decides where fishermen and employees of the fishing plants will live, what they earn and what rights they are to have" (Valdimarsson 1990: 5). In public discourse, the large firms that have been accumulating quota-shares are habitually referred to as "quota-kings" or "lords of the sea." Such metaphors have obvious feudal overtones. During interviews, many people expressed concern with increased inequality due to the concentration of quotas, echoing the Icelandic ethos of egalitarianism.

Large vertically integrated companies have long played an important role in Icelandic fishing. The small-scale operator, however, has never disappeared, often acting as a kind of shock absorber for the big companies and their processing facilities. With the advent of quota-leasing this situation has taken a new turn. Many of the small-scale operators still left in the quota system have helplessly watched their annual catch quotas plummet in size, with repeated cuts in the overall quota. One small-scale boat owner, for example, complained that while his quota-share originally had allowed him to fish 145 tons of cod, he was now down to 52 tons. Many small boat owners facing similar problems have taken the option of selling their shares and leaving the system for good. However, recently boat owners lacking quotas have been presented with another alternative—to lease quotas from, and fish for, larger quota-holders.

Originally, quota-leasing was proposed by policy makers as a way for boat owners to fine-tune their operation in order to meet short-term needs arising from bycatch problems and fluctuations in local and regional markets (for example, by trading haddock quotas for cod quotas). In time, however, some quota-holders came to discern that considerable profits could be made by temporarily leasing their quotas, particularly with many fishing operations suffering from reductions in total allowable catch after 1988. In some business transactions of this kind, commonly referred to as "fishing for others," the quota-kings offer to supply small-scale producers with additional quotas on the condition that they deliver the catch to the processing plants of the quota-kings, in return for approximately half of the market value of the catch. A director of one large company prominent in the business of quota-leasing describes his position in the following terms: "Our policy . . . is quite simple: 'You are fishermen, we are businessmen, we'll supply the quotas and you will do the fishing!'" Thus the small-scale operators manage to prolong their enterprise throughout the season, but receive only half the normal market value of their landings. To meet the resulting reduction in revenues, operators fishing for others normally cut back the crew's share in the value of the catch, accounting for this by informing the crew that they are participating in the renting of quotas to keep the vessel in operation and subsequently their jobs. This state of affairs, with large consolidated companies controlling most of the quota and profiting from leasing it to small-scale operators who actually do most of the fishing, has led many fishers to expand the feudal metaphors of the quota-kings and lords of the sea originally used to describe the concentration of quota-shares. Thus, quota-leasing is commonly referred to by fishers as part of a "tenancy" system; the quota-kings are likened to medieval landlords and, conversely, small-scale boat owners become "tenants" or "serfs" (*leiguliðar*). Furthermore, these references to images of exploitation and domination are augmented by a condemnation of what fishers call "quota-profiteering" (*kvótabrask*).

Many fishers claim that any kind of profit-oriented trade with quotas represents quota-profiteering. Resonating with Aristotelian notions of monetary exchange, fishers maintain that quotas that are not used by boat owners themselves should not be leased but should be returned and redistributed to other boat owners that have more need for them. To their minds quotas embody use-rights that should under no circumstances be traded between boat owners for profit.

Frustrated fishers look on as business owners prosper from trading these new fishing rights back and forth, picturing quota-kings spending hours in front of computer screens profiteering with quotas. One skipper, commenting on this situation, claimed: "For the chosen few who can lease quotas to others and buy more quotas for the profits, [the quota system] is like a snowball effect . . . There is no stockbroker in Reykjavík that can invest your money more effectively, that is, if you have any."

In addition to being the main source of national revenue, fishers say, quotas are the basis of their livelihood. Not only are boat owners making profits by selling that which is not really theirs, they are also selling fishers' jobs. In many fishing villages, almost everyone is dependent on one or two boat owners for work. In these cases, the issue of transferability of quotas is of great concern. By moving to a new location or selling his or her permanent quota-shares a boat owner can turn a thriving fishing village into a veritable ghost town. Fishers challenge the privileging of capital over labor represented by the quota system. This is sometimes expressed in a radical critique of the original notion of "fishing history" which defined quota allocations on the basis of previous catches. In the words of one fisher: "It's a shame that quotas were only allocated to boat owners. Originally, allocations were based on 'fishing history,' but that history has nothing to do with companies and boat ownership. It's the men on board the boats who have created the right to fish." Significantly, fishers went on a national strike in January 1994, protesting against the quota system, especially quota-profiteering, leading to a two-week standstill in the fishing industry (the government put an end to the strike by passing temporary laws to force the fishers back to work). Outside of the bargaining table, however, fishers and their unions appear to be willing to tolerate boat owners who merely lease quotas to keep their boats in action, even though this entails the participation of the crew in leasing quotas. Indeed, most fishers would rather suffer the wage-cuts involved in leasing catch-quotas to the boat than join the growing ranks of unemployed Icelandic workers. Nevertheless, in principle fishers state firm opposition to and condemnation of the quota system, which enables boat owners to sell rights to fish that have yet to be caught or even spawned.

Boat owners embrace a different strand of economic thought, deriving from Bernard de Mandeville and Adam Smith and culminating in neoclassical theory, that stresses the benevolent consequences of profit-oriented monetary exchange (Dumont 1977; Bloch and Parry 1988), justifying the current situation in the name of productive efficiency. One of the quota-kings described his position in the following terms: "Only those operators that can fish at the lowest price can fish my quota. It is solely a question of efficiency and so I say: 'any restrictions [on quota transactions] will just increase inefficiency in the industry.'" For the big quota-holders, quotas are equivalent to shares in the stock exchange. Their chief concern is the fluctuating market prices of different species, trading back and forth to maximize profits from the resource. Managers of fishing companies are responsible primarily to share-holders, then to fishers and fishworkers, and, finally, to the larger community. Some of those with a substantial quota at their disposal do express a concern with equity and fairness, much like fishers and the general public; thus, one skipper claimed that increased concentration was "totally unacceptable": "It scares me to think of the possibility that four or five companies might gain control of the entire national quota." Others embrace the rhetoric of productive efficiency, citing envy and irrationality as the main reason for the fishers' disquiet about quotas. In an interview a director of one of the largest fishing companies emphasized the argument of efficiency: "I don't mind if there are numerous boats without quota and many quota-holders living down in Majorka, if the Icelandic fishing industry becomes more efficient as a result."

In Icelandic fishing, quotas represent power; with both becoming concentrated in the hands of the largest companies, the discursive balance within the fishing industry has tipped heavily in their favor. Thus economic efficiency has become the overriding issue, while the more traditional egalitarian concerns, which still figure prominently in the minds of fishers and the public, have been pushed to the periphery of the discursive arena. Accounts of existing structural inequalities in Icelandic fishing were previously often formulated *implicitly* in euphemistic terms. Inequality was reproduced under the cover of an individualistic ideology which attributed differences to personal characteristics rather than to social structure or access to resources (Pálsson 1989b; Pálsson and Durrenberger 1992; Durrenberger, this volume). However, in reaction to the quota system these accounts have been radically transformed. Euphemisms seem to be things of the past, as fishers *explicitly* attempt to confront structural inequalities and differential access to the fishing stocks.

Conclusion

During most of the twentieth century Icelandic discourse on fishing has been developed from below, grounded in the practical knowledge and the grass-roots of Icelandic fishing communities. Recently, the pattern has been reversed. Discussions on fishing are increasingly textual and hegemonic, dominated by marine scientists, resource economists, state officials, and boat owners. These changes in the system of production and the ways in which Icelanders talk about it are not the results of local developments alone. To some extent, they have been informed by the prevailing fascination on the international scene with private property and productive efficiency, with the machinery of the market. The dispute between Icelandic fishers and boat owners, therefore, reflects a deeper conflict within Western society over the status of money and monetary exchange (see Bloch and Parry 1988).

Marine biologists, with their concern for the protection of spawning stocks, successful recruitment, and the constraining of aggregate catch of the fishing fleet below a certain critical level, figure prominently in Icelandic management discourse. Generally, marine scientists have presented the coastal ecosystem as a predictable, domesticated domain. While they may qualify their analyses and predictions with reference to some degree of uncertainty, the "margin of error," they often act as if that margin is immaterial. Fishers question their basic assumptions, arguing that knowledge of fish migrations is still very small. Knowledge of the ecosystem, they claim, is too imperfect to make reliable forecasts. "Erecting an ivory tower around themselves," one skipper argued, "biologists are somewhat removed from the field of action; they are too dependent on the book." Like their colleagues in other parts of the world, biologists have often focused on one species at a time, modeling recruitment, growth rates, and stock sizes, although recently they have paid increasing attention to analyses of interactions in "multispecies" fisheries. This means that fisheries policy is often literal and rigid in form, unable to respond to changes in the ecosystem.

The business of actually designing management schemes has primarily been left to economists, not biologists. The main stated objective of the quota system was to make fishing more efficient and economical as well as to control the total annual catch of the most important species (cod, in particular). While the cost side of the economic equation has been reduced for a small group of privileged producers, there has been little success as regards the ecological objective. According to biological estimates, the cod stock is still over-exploited and stock recruitment is poor year after year. During recent years some skippers have even had difficulties in catching what they have been entitled to, always considered too little. Sometimes they have given up mid-season because there have been "too few fish" relative to fishing effort. More importantly, given our present concern, the quota system has instituted a new level of social inequality. During most of the twentieth century the emphasis on equity, informed by the political agenda of the independence movement, has obscured real structural differences in wealth and access to resources (see Pálsson 1995). Currently, as we have seen, a forceful "feudal" rhetoric challenges established rules of access to fishing stocks, emphasizing the alienation and growing inequalities which they represent. Ironically, one of the strong arguments for quota systems is that they apparently obliterate the complex rhetoric and politicking required by traditional "manual" methods of dividing access, making it possible to circumvent local debates and everyday discourse, assuming that once the system has been instituted the machinery of the market will take care of "the rest."

The relative failure of the quota system and scientific management of recent years to deliver the goods they promised and the severe social and ethical problems of inequality they have raised suggest that it may be wise to look for alternative management schemes emphasizing the practical knowledge of the fishing industry, in particular the people who are directly engaged with the ecosystem. Skippers' extensive knowledge of the ecosystem is the result of years of practical enskillment, the collective product of a community of practice (Pálsson 1994). Formal schooling is essential for skippers, but they all seem to agree that most of their learning takes place "outdoors," in the course of fishing. This is emphasized by frequent remarks about the "bookish," "academic" learning of those who have never "had a pee in a salty sea" (*migið í saltan sjó*). Skippers discuss their own research strategy as a dynamic and holistic one, allowing for flexibility in time and space. Usually, their accounts emphasize constant experimentation in the flux and momentum of fishing, the role of "perpetual engagement" (*að vera í stanslausu sambandi*), and the importance of "hunches" (*stuð*), intuition, and tacit knowledge. If fisheries are chaotic systems (Wilson et al. 1994), those who are directly involved in resource-use on a daily basis are likely to have the most reliable information as to what goes on in the sea at any particular time. It may be essential, then, to pay attention to the practical knowledge of skippers, allowing for contingency and extreme fluctuations in the ecosystem. Some form of self-governance in fishing may be a practical necessity, strange as it may sound to those accustomed to the theory of the "tragedy of the commons."

Acknowledgments

The study on which this paper is based is part of two larger collaborative research projects—"Common Property and Environmental Policy in Comparative Perspective," funded by the Nordic Environmental Research Programme 1993–1997 (NERP), and "Property Rights and the Performance of Natural Systems," organized by the Beijer Institute of the Swedish Academy of Sciences. Our research has been supported by several other programs and institutions, including the Nordic Committee for Social Science Research (NOS-S), the University of Iceland, the Icelandic Science Foundation, and the Post-Graduate Research Fund of the Icelandic Ministry of Education. We thank Paul Durrenberger (University of Iowa), John Gatewood (Lehigh University), and Ralph Towsend (University of Maine, Orono) for their useful comments and critique on our arguments and an earlier draft of this paper. Einar Eyþórsson (Tromsö University) kindly made available one of his interviews with representatives of interest groups in Icelandic fishing.

Notes

1. While most of the seas were subject to the rule of common use rights, in early Icelandic history access to the sea was often controlled by ownership of sites in the bays where boats could land. Landing a rowboat on the coast was risky, especially during the winter season, and access to the ocean therefore depended upon the availability of good landing sites. Access to the fishing grounds was often controlled by inhibiting others from gaining access to landing sites.

2. See Young (1992) for a discussion of the use of allocative efficiency in resource economics and Árnason (1991) for an example of its application in fisheries economics.

3. We have computerized and standardized a series of extensive data sets in different formats for different years, to make them comparable for

our purposes. Most of the data were publicly available, provided by the Ministry of Fisheries. It is impossible, in the present context, to go into the details of our uses of the database. These have been presented elsewhere (Pálsson and Helgason 1995).

4. The so-called Gini-coefficient provides an accurate numerical expression of the degree of inequality presented by a Lorenz curve. This coefficient represents the ratio obtained by dividing the area between the line of perfect equality and the Lorenz curve of a specific year by the total area under the line of perfect equality. Hence, complete inequality gives a Gini-coefficient of 1, while perfect equality gives 0. The Gini-coefficients for the Lorenz curves depicted in figure 3 show a substantial increase for each consecutive year—going from 0.677 in 1984 to 0.715 in 1988, 0.769 in 1992, and, finally, 0.799 in 1994.

PART II NATION AND GENDER

5

HOUSEWORK AND WAGE WORK:
GENDER IN ICELANDIC FISHING COMMUNITIES

The concept of gender has focused our attention on the inequalities involved in the social construction and political realities of femininity and masculinity. So far, scholars have used the gender concept mostly to examine women's position and to make women more visible. Women have been the engendered subjects of their studies, not men. This focus reflects and is a response to definitions of men as "human" and women as the "Other," the context in which the feminine and the masculine are socially constructed. It is not that men do not have gender, but that they have been seen as the general and unmarked and women as that which differs from the general and is marked as divergent as S. de Beauvoir (1961) pointed out many years ago.

There have always been some disagreements among feminist theorists regarding whether to use the terms "gender" or "sexual difference" or simply talk about women. R. Briadotti (1992) has been critical of the gender concept and the clear division it makes between the social and the biological. She has pointed out how its use commonly lacks theoretical clarity and focus and that using gender instead of talking of feminist studies has led us away from the study of inequalities to the study of a more general social construction of how women and men are different from each other. Continuous critical evaluations are important, especially now, with an increased discussion of the masculine gender. It is, however, not necessary to give up the use of this concept as the solution; we do not need to use new words, but to make theoretical clarifications and hold on to the focus on the social construction of gender inequalities.

One such attempt is to be conscious of the fact that gender inequality is systematic and has interlinked domains. S. Harding (1986) has pointed out that gender not only refers to the level of ideas, or the symbolic, but consists of two other levels as well: the division of labor and gendered desires. We can approach the study of a particular past or present gender system from three different interlinked arenas. First is the domain of ideas, symbols, and dominant values—ideas regarding what women should be like and should strive to become. The second arena is the division of labor—the formal and informal institutions of society and social relations. Here we find the variations among women such as those based on class, race, or marital status. The third arena is individuals. Here we focus our attention on gendered identities, which often can be characterized by tensions because of the incompatibility or inconsistency between the first two or between the dominant ideas and women's different daily realities. Examining only one of these, such as the division of labor between men and women and their economic contribution, gives us only a limited picture and cannot in itself explain the differences in position. Perceived differences between the sexes affect the interpretation of the sexual division of labor as J. W. Scott (1988) points out, emphasizing that gender, a constitutive element in social relations, is based on perceived differences between the sexes. Y. Hirdman (1990) sees feminine and masculine categories as having distinct characteristics and particular activities that belong to the categories.

In recent years, with the interest in the multivocality of women, there has been a new emphasis on studying gendered identities and on people as active agents. Ignoring this domain of individual women may lead us to a view of women as mere victims of the societal structure. Women and men are molded by their culture, but it is a culture which is always in the process of change and which has many inconsistencies and allows for maneuvering. Moreover, they make decisions in their everyday life based on their knowledge of their social circumstances. Culture is neither a restrictive blueprint for thought nor a prison for action but a vocabulary of argument and action. In my analysis of women's position in Icelandic fishing villages, I thus consider these three domains: ideas, the division of labor, and gendered identities. I include women's own descriptions in an attempt at getting closer to their own subjective experiences and identities.[1]

There are two major approaches in anthropological studies of gender relations: emphasis on the symbolic analyses of women's subordinate status primarily focused on the level of ideas and emphasis on material conditions and historical context of women's and men's positions primarily focused on division of labor and control over resources. If we take the approach suggested above, we do not have to study either the symbolic or the division of labor as the more determinant but rather the three interlinked domains, none of which needs to be considered the prime mover.

Reproduction and Production

In the 1970s women's subordination was commonly explained in terms of their attachment to the domestic sphere, whereas men were seen as gaining higher status from being able to participate in the public sphere (Rosaldo and Lamphere 1974). The division into private and public spheres was also used to show women's informal influence in the household. The private/public framework was soon called into question by those who argued that many of women's activities, such as agricultural production and marketing, could not be seen as limited to the domestic sphere. In the 1980s many replaced the concept private/public with the concepts of production and reproduction as a more powerful analytical tool to account for the division of labor between men and women. As L. Beneria and G. Sen (1986: 151) point out: "Anthropologists dealing with gender roles have emphasized the role of reproduction as a determinant of women's work and the sexual division of labor. Using the concept of reproduction they are not only referring to biological reproduction and the daily maintenance, but to the social reproduction." The expanded concept of reproduction has advantages over the concept of the private sphere when it comes to clarifying the sexual division of labor, as it refers to several levels of women's participation in society: the biological reproduction of children, the social reproduction of labor power on daily and generational levels, and the reproduction of society. Moreover, we see the household not as a separated area but an important aspect of the economy as a whole: "It is linked to the market both by what it purchases and what it provides—the commodity labor power that is exchanged for a wage" (Beneria and Sen 1986: 151).

The concept of reproduction implies a research focus not only on sexual division of labor and difference in position but on the ideas that justify the inequalities. These concepts of production and reproduction imply that within each area there are relations which have to be analyzed: power differences and unequal access to resources (Meillassoux 1975). Reproduction refers not only to what occurs in the household, but also to many activities in the society and the reproduction of society as well. Within reproduction are the maintenance of kinship relations, which are commonly women's responsibility, and the care for other people, whether it takes place in the household or in institutions. Many of women's activities are defined as "relations" rather than work, but they take a great deal of time and energy and make it easier for men to engage in other activities.

If we want to gain a better understanding of women's position in the work force it is important to take into account the relation between production and reproduction. However, the use of the concept of reproduction can be problematic and the division between productive and reproductive work is not always clear. For example, should women's wage work be seen as reproductive work that has been extended out from the household to the public sector or should it be seen as productive work? I have found that Icelanders commonly describe women's work in freezing plants as requiring similar qualities as work in households and do not clearly distinguish work related to managing a boat owned by the household from housework. The concept of reproduction does not contribute to our understanding if it is taken to be coterminous with women's work and all the work women perform outside the household is viewed as defined by, and reflective of, the work they do in the household.

In looking at Icelandic ethnography we must not only consider how gender is extended from the area of reproduction to the area of production, but how it is constructed and reconstructed in the sphere of production. The gender construction may then also be seen as extending back into the household or the area of reproduction. In examining women's position in fish processing I not only show how their association with the reproductive sphere affects their lower status in the work place, but focus on the process involved in reinforcing women's lower status in terms of the interrelation between the two areas. In both areas, activities are defined as feminine and masculine as well as skilled or unskilled. However, before this examination of what I refer to as women-centered households and of gender construction in the freezing plant, let us take a brief look at the dominant ideas in Iceland regarding women in fishing communities.

Cultural Perception of Women in Maritime Society

It is sometimes said of women in fishing communities of the North Atlantic that they are unusually strong and independent and that they are more powerful than other women. This independence and strength is seen as deriving from their participation in production and from the fact that they take care of the household when their husbands are away fishing. But these women are also sometimes talked about as invisible army of reserve labor in the fishing industry. When we look at women in Icelandic fishing villages we see that there are some truths to be found in both of these views. Women are generally the center of households as well as being used as a reserve labor force. To understand how these different components of social identities come together, we need to consider the aspects of gender identities, division of labor, and dominant ideas.

In the identity connected to the fisheries in Iceland there are clearly contradictory images. Icelanders see themselves as a proud fishing nation, glorifying the risks and rewards of fishing, while simultaneously considering the fishing communities a burden. Images of gender in Icelandic culture, related to the fisheries, present a different but related set of contradictions. On the one hand, there are ideas about fishers' wives, who have strong characters and patiently wait for their men. On the other hand, there are rather negative views of the fish factory women. If we look at the fishers, we also find contradictory ideas. On land they are seen as drunk and rowdy, but at sea they are national heroes. Their heroic role—out at sea bringing wealth to the nation—is intensely romanticized in popular songs. The cultural perception of women in fishing villages is primarily linked to their roles as wives and girlfriends. The songs are about wives who are happy at the return of their husbands, of men missing their girlfriends, and of men who have a woman waiting in each harbor. Every Icelander knows many such songs. One of them is *Kátir voru karlar* (Men Were Happy):

Merry were the men on *Kútter Haraldur* [the name of a boat].
They went out to fish from Akranes.
And all of them returned and none of them died
Every woman laughs from happiness
She laughs, she laughs [repeated].

There is also the song about "fisherman's life, the dream of every man," who goes in the arms of *bára* (wave), who invites him into a wild dance. It goes on to say: "Fisherman's life, love and adventure, happiness in heart, and the sound of high waves and winds." The third and last part of this song is: "To the girls I say words of love, one two, three kisses and I jump on board." *Bára* in this song is not capitalized and therefore refers to the ocean waves, but it is also a woman's name.

The first verse of another fishing song is:

I am a cook on a boat from Sandur.
I get hit in the face every day.
And I don't feel better on land,
if I get into a fight with my wife.
She is double in strength, Tóta [her name],
especially if she is angry.
So I usually run,
because escape is my only solution.

This verse shows the unclear status of fishers on land as well as portraying a very strong and dominating fisher's wife. The wife is respected as such and her role is emphasized.

Songs or stories of women's productive activities are hard to find. The only exception is the herring girls of the 1950s and 1960s. They were and still are remembered as young and unmarried, dreaming about love and the nice clothes they would buy with their wages. Their "adventure" is so romanticized that the hardship involved has been well hidden. The fish factory women, by contrast, are seen as rough and tough, and their work is looked down on. Thus in general we find that the productive role of the fishers is romanticized whereas women's productive role remains invisible or debased. These images of both men and women in Iceland contain their own negations. The fisher is a hero when involved in production but a failure on land. The fisher's wife is respected; but fish-processing work is not.

Women-Centered Households

Fishers and their wives in Icelandic fishing villages have different daily experiences because men spend so much time away fishing. This is also true for many others in these communities; the work places are very gender-divided and work hours long. Instead of assuming that men's absence and women's importance in the running of the household in fishing communities lead automatically to more power, S. Cole (1991), in discussing women's lives in a Portuguese fishing village, describes maritime households as women-centered. This term can be applied to maritime households in Iceland. Households tend to be women-centered whether men are absent or present. Women run the household from day to day and are usually more involved in maintaining kinship relations and relations between households. The fact that the household is more women's domain does not, however, mean that they are limited to this sphere or not free to go wherever they want. Women's centrality does not necessarily imply power, nor that their households are characterized by equality.

Fishers' wives commonly act as heads of their households. This gives them a certain amount of autonomy and independence. However, it is necessary to make a distinction between wives of different kinds of fishers. Being a wife of a fisher on a large ship that goes far and stays out long is different from being married to a small boat owner who returns home every evening. In the former case the wife has to stay alone with the children for long periods, but in the latter the family life is closer to the Icelandic norm. The position of wives of small boat fishers is also different because they are commonly involved in managing the finances of the boat. Some wives are involved in baiting or hiring someone else to do it. They often have gained experience running a small business, even though they usually do not view their work as that of a manager of a small firm. Instead they usually talk about this work as helping the husband and as something that can easily be combined with housework. Most fishers' wives, whether married to small boat owners or trawler fishers, have the sole responsibility for the finances of the household and work for wages as well.

Kristín is a woman in her thirties who is married to a trawler fisher. They have four children. In the morning she works in the freezing plant, but she keeps the afternoons for housework and to be home when her children return from school. Kristín described what it is like being married to a trawler fisher:

> In the past they used to stay out ten days to two weeks, but now this has changed. Before, when we had to call them through the coastal radio station, I only called him when it was very urgent. You had to talk in a secret language if you did not want others to hear about your problems or financial situation. We take care of financial matters, since they do not have any time. If there is something that has to do with taking loans or talking to the bank manager we do that. . . . The children always miss him after a while and begin asking about him. In the past my husband did not come home as often; we were building the house so he never took time off and was always at sea. Then our son used to talk about him as "the man who visits mother," and he was a bit shy toward "the man who visits mother." The younger children do not see it this way since he comes home more often now. . . . When they come home and stop for a short period of time they don't do much. You are used to them as guests and turn around them, you just do everything. There is no reason to ask them to do anything if they do not suggest it themselves. But when they stay longer they do more.

I generally found that housework is women's responsibility, although men help to a varying degree. Age does not seem to be an important factor in this regard.

Guðrún, a woman in her early fifties, has been married twice to fishers. Her first husband fished with his brothers on a boat they owned together with their father until he drowned when fishing. They used to go on short trips, except in the winter season, when they fished from other areas. The second husband is alone on a small boat. Guðrún described how the fishery is related to the household.

> They used to go away for the winter season. They went in 1964 and then I went along with my seven-month-old child and worked as a housekeeper in the kitchen in the worker's quarters. My parents had my older children, two and three years old, in the meantime. I could not stand the thought of staying here again for the whole winter from January till May. In my first marriage I did not have to be involved in the fishery at all because they were so many brothers together. In the second marriage I have been more involved in the fishery, because my husband is alone on a boat, more for fun than

because I have to. It was just to make the knots and such, you just did this at home—it was before we bought this ready made.

When I asked her about the household finances she said:

It has always been my job to take care of the finances, since the fishers come to land after everything has been closed. It has always been my job to take care of and pay, that is, to take care of the finances and such things. Only I have taken care of this the whole time.

I asked her if she thought fishers' wives were therefore more independent than other women and she replied:

I think so. When I stood alone with all my children, I think I would not have been able to cope on my own if I had not been used to taking care of this. This is common in fishing villages. Some men joke and say, "We cannot even have our wallets." They just have to talk to their wife if they need something, since she takes care of this. My husband has sometimes no idea how much things cost. I have often said that it would be good for the men to get closer to these issues because they wonder where the money goes.

When I asked Ásta, a fisherman's wife in her early thirties, the same question she replied:

When I come to think of it, it is possible that they are. It is not only in the home, because they have to be more in contact with companies and institutions like the bank. Fishers' wives often have to tell their husbands not to accept something that is not fair or correct in silence and without protest, because the women know that it can be straightened out. I have often heard this and women will not be pushed around.

We can see from this that it is not easy to maintain that the position of women in fishing communities is determined by their limitation to the private sphere, because there are aspects in the public sphere which they consider themselves to be more able to deal with than their husbands. This responsibility gives them strength and a certain amount of independence. While many women see it as an advantage to have control over household finances, others see it as an added burden, especially if they continue to take care of this alone after the husband begins to work on land. The latter complain that the men are uninterested and that they must worry about the next payment alone. This can be a source of tension in relationships. Many women say that their husbands complain that they spend too much money, even though they are trying very hard to save money. Some women collect receipts to prove their thrift.

Women generally do not express much worry about their husbands out at sea. They commonly argue that it does not help talking about these things. They maintain that they do not worry about their husbands except in bad weather. A description of one man who is a son of a former fisher shows very well the attitude which still exists today. He said that as a child he used to stand on the pier and look at the boats coming in, waiting for his father:

> Therefore I often stood there in bad weather and waited. Women were not exactly worried about their husbands, but of course they were [worried] in bad weather. Maybe underneath they were somewhat worried, but they did not show this. I can remember when I was about ten or eleven years old and the weather was bad. My father was on a five-ton boat and it was four o'clock and he should have been here before noon because of the storm. Then I was out on the breakwater but ran home regularly. Then I noticed that my mother was always walking to the window which faced the ocean and going to the door, but she did not say anything. But you could feel she was looking for someone. Then they came. This was common for women, but they did not talk about or express their fear.

If we take only the division of labor and the independence that derives from it, but do not include the analysis of the dominant ideas or other relations related to the household, we could come to the same conclusions as P. Thompson (1985), maintaining that the position of women in maritime societies is better than elsewhere and that they are more powerful than other women. A closer look reveals that the fact that they take care of the household and household finances alone without their husbands does not give them higher status. Using the same argument, single mothers would have a high status as well, but they do not. The positive ideas we find about fishers' wives are only partly caused by the fact that they take care of running the households by themselves. More important is the fact that they are associated with the fishers who go out to sea in all weathers and bring wealth to the nation. They have to remain strong and not express their fear when their husbands are working under dangerous conditions. The fisher's wife gains her respect because of her role in reproduction, not in relation to her work outside of the household.

Gender Construction in the Work Place

There is a clear division of labor between women and men and Icelandic fishing communities. This division has become more clearly defined with industrialization (Skaptadóttir 1992). This can be seen in the freezing plant as well as in other jobs in these communities. One can almost say that there are men's work places and women's work places. Going to sea is a man's job, except for a few women who go as cooks. The majority of women have at least a part-time job outside the home, with the exception of a few women with young children. The children commonly know where the mother works and can walk to her if something comes up. Moreover, everyone goes home for lunch and some even go home for the coffee break. Those with young children go to work when school is out and leave their children in the care of girls of ten to thirteen years old. From a young age children begin to earn money in a very gender-divided labor market. Girls, for example, commonly baby-sit until they are old enough to work in the freezing plant and sons of fishers go to sea with their fathers from the age of fifteen or so.

Although fish processing is commonly thought of as a woman's job, we find both men and women in the freezing plant. Men and women work in the same place, but there is a clear segregation in the sexual division of labor. Men and women rarely intermingle either during work or during breaks. In the breaks men and women usually sit at separate tables, often on separate sides of the room. Moreover, the jobs performed by women are described as feminine and the jobs performed by men are described in masculine terms. There are fewer jobs within the plant which are defined as women's jobs than as men's jobs. Women cut, clean out worms, and pack the fish, and a few are floor managers, although fewer than men. The work on the pier— driving forklifts and unloading the fish from the ship—is a man's job, although there are some very rare exceptions to this. Men work in the freezing room—they are commonly floor managers and only men do machine maintenance work. Old men sharpen the knives for the women who cut; before the conveyer belt came in the 1980s, young boys would bring in the fish and take it out. Men more commonly operate machines, although this is changing now, as discussed below. The jobs women perform are generally more monotonous and have become even more monotonous in the last few years with the conveyor belt. They stand at the same place almost all day long performing the same job. Men have jobs that allow them to move around more, which allows them more control over the work process itself. For example, they can more easily control the speed of their work. They also have more possibilities to talk to others in their jobs.

Until the early 1960s men's and women's jobs were differently paid, with men getting a higher salary. It is often said that the harder-working women would take on men's jobs in order to raise their wages. Men's jobs were and still are considered more arduous. Alda, a woman who in the last two decades has done almost every job in the freezing plant, including most men's jobs, described men's jobs:

> Working on the machines is generally a man's job, because it is work that goes on later into the evening. They are freezing and it is also hard work. Men have almost all the jobs that require strength. Men's work is almost always limited to the forklift and to jobs involved in transferring the fish from the ship to the factory—then they have to use physical strength lifting up heavy boxes of fish.

It is not possible to maintain that it is the job per se which is manly or womanly because its characterization can change depending on whether a man or a woman generally performs it. Consequently if a woman performs a job defined as a manly job, then she becomes defined as having manly characteristics. If she is not strong physically she may be described as talking men's talk. However, if the same job increasingly comes to be defined as a woman's job it loses its masculine characterization and begins to be considered feminine.

It is too simple to argue that women's work in the freezing plant has more similarities to housework than other work and that it is devalued because it is an extension of the work performed in the household. There is more involved in this process. Women of course become good at performing a job that they have been trained to do from a young age; thus they are in fact better at cutting the fish than those who had no training. This is a job that requires a skill and training to be done well and efficiently. Moreover, it is possible that "feminine" characteristics such as patience are more likely to be acquired by women since they are valued and reinforced in women.

Thus the ideas regarding what is feminine and what is masculine at a particular time affect the gender division of labor, which reflects upon the definition of the feminine and the masculine. This reproduction of the gender division of labor is based on power differences. This can be seen when the pattern is broken, as in the pride women evince when they perform men's jobs either in the freezing plant or at sea. By contrast, when men perform work defined as women's, they talk about it as a humiliating experience. Difference in salaries can not explain this difference in job status, as men and women in the freezing plant have the same hourly wages. This is therefore not just a question of wage differences but rather of status differences. Clearly it is not the job itself that matters but who performs it. When I asked men why there were no men in cutting and packing they would usually answer that men did not have the ability or the patience this job requires. Some said they were too clumsy. However, more said, especially in informal discussion, that it would be humiliating for them to do women's work and that they would rather be unemployed than do women's work in the freezing plant. Anna, a woman in her early forties, was born and raised in a fishing village and has worked with fish from an early age. She explained:

> The work women perform requires more patience, which is something men lack. Men on the other hand do jobs that require more physical strength—they do not have enough patience to cut or pack fish. In the past only men used to operate the machines, but today many women have begun to do this work. It is just a fact that because of their compassion [*hugulsemi*] women are able to run the machines longer without repair.

An example of a manly job is baiting, and the baiting huts are associated with men and male talk. Salting the herring and packing it into barrels is an example of a woman's job. Alda said that the salting of herring used to be much better paid in the past:

> In the herring years you could get good money over the summer if you could salt herring. It was far better paid than it is today. Also if you consider that if you were salting herring you had to put each herring down in the correct manner. In those years you had to follow particular rules about how to go about putting the herring into the barrel. At that time [in the 1960s] it was possible to get as much money for salting one barrel as baiting one bucket, but today salting of one barrel is valued less than half of what one can get for baiting

a bucket. This is woman's work and naturally and usually it is men
who are doing the baiting.

Edda described her experience when she decided to cross the
borderline to go baiting with her husband:

> I and my husband baited for E. G. for a while. I did four buckets
> and he did four. One puts hooks on the line and then the bait.
> When I began baiting it was seen as awful. To leave the freezing
> plant to go baiting! My brothers were very shocked. But I have
> since often teased them, saying this is not at all harder than the
> work in the freezing plant. I think I would ten times more like to
> bait than work in the freezing plant.

In response to my question "Why do they think it is harder?" she
replied: "Because they have never worked in the freezing plant.
They think it is harder because men are used to doing this work,
but this is changing and now there are more women than before in
baiting."

Today all the workers in a freezing plant have the same wage.
However, it is noticeable that the men who work at the freezing plant
are commonly either old or young; there are not many men who are
middle-aged. The men who are over twenty-five and under sixty-five
usually work either in managerial jobs or as repairmen and thus have
higher incomes. Alda discussed this fact:

> The women who work here are of different ages, from youth to, in
> some cases, over seventy years old. But a certain age group of men
> is not to be found here, it seems to me, unless they have some edu-
> cation. And therefore men repair machines, are managers or electri-
> cians, or if not, then they are young boys or older men. From the
> ages twenty to fifty they seem to be doing something else, like go-
> ing to sea or something else where they can earn more money. If
> men are going to be providers and get a roof over their heads, it
> cannot be done with this kind of work, for that you have to go to
> sea or do something that brings more money. But some of these
> men return later when they have given up on the sea. . . . The fact
> is that among those laborers who are least educated like us there is
> least inequality in the wages between men and women. . . . In fact
> this is maybe understandable because we are just selling pure labor
> power, and women are absolutely indispensable in the cutting and
> packing of fish. Men have tried to do this and it just does not work

out; they just don't have the patience that this work requires. Maybe they see it as an old woman's job [*kellingadjobb*] and too degrading to do. At least it has been shown that it is not possible to have men do this and therefore women are necessary. . . . I work full time, that is, from eight to five, and naturally, as everyone knows, we are always saving some important valuables from ruin. We are always processing fish that would otherwise be ruined.

Anna summed up her view on work in the fisheries as follows:

There was a time when people did not view the fisheries as good enough work places. It was seen as nothing at all. . . . The freezing plant! No! But there is no shame working in a freezing plant. It is more honorable working in fish processing than merely working in an office, because you are providing for the whole nation. . . . There are women my age who have never set their foot in the factory. "Work in fish? Ugh. I'd rather be unemployed!" they say. I have done everything related to fish except catching it.

The pride that many women who work in fish processing take in the fishery has to do with being part of the activity most important for the Icelandic economy. Even when evaluating men's work as more important than their own, women still see their own work as important for the national economy. They see it as a major aspect of the entire fishing industry, and many of them are very interested in other aspects of the fishery such as the fishing and marketing. Ólöf, a young woman, told me that when she took the fish processor course she was most interested in the marketing aspect, while many of the others said that they found the part on interpersonal relations and quality control most interesting. Ólöf said:

In the course I liked to learn about quality control. But I think a great deal about where the fish goes, so I liked to learn about the market in the course. . . . We all follow day by day where the trawlers are and how much they are getting, even when you are not working in fish at that particular time and you ask about them. It is as if one has become part of it all. I heard an interview in the radio recently with a woman who works in a large freezing plant in Reykjavík and she said that with the conveyor belt she felt like a part of the machine. Here it is different because here everything revolves around fish. But still working in fish processing is seen as a second-class job, as elsewhere in Iceland including Reykjavík. I don't

know why it is. Maybe society has made it this way but the mentality is just like this.

The view expressed by the fish processors above contradicts
H. Bradley's argument that by moving into modern factories women
have "lost all sense of connection with the mainstream of fishing activity, and all sense of involvement in the skills and traditions of one
of humankind's oldest occupations" (1989: 103). Women are conscious of their work being looked down upon, but they feel that the
fishery of which they are a part is important for the economy and the
continuous existence of the nation. By doing their work well they are
saving resources that would otherwise be damaged and making quality products for the market.

The fishery is not peripheral to the economy as in many other
countries in the North Atlantic. It is central to any discussion of the
Icelandic economic situation and a part of the modern national identity. Moreover, and maybe more importantly, women do not see their
identity as just fish processors. There is not a very clear line between
their identity as fish processors and as members of fishing communities or families or households which include fishers. They see themselves as a significant part of the fishing community; often when I
asked women about when something happened, they would answer
that they were not exactly sure, but they were sure that it was the
year before or after a particular trawler had been bought into the village. Thus their identity as fish processors cannot be clearly separated
from their identity as members of their fishing community or as members of families which include husbands, brothers, or sons who are
fishers. "We are all on the same boat," as the saying goes. The stronger
division felt is between "us," fisherfolk who produce the wealth on
which society builds, on the one hand, and "them," the city dwellers,
on the other hand, who spend it and see fishing villages as a burden
but depend on them without realizing it.

Whether women are fishers' wives or not they generally express
a strong "attachment" to their role in reproduction. Most of the
women interviewed emphasized that work in a freezing plant can be
easily adjusted to household responsibilities because of the flexibility
and possibility to take time off when their child is sick or their husband is home from the sea. Although women's work in the freezing
plant has become more stable and not as seasonal as it used to be, it
can still be argued that women are used as a reserve army of labor.

Many of them are hired under conditions that allow them to work when they want to, although they feel responsible to work when there is a large quantity of fish. It is only in the last decade that women have been guaranteed employment in fish processing. Prior to that, workers could be sent home with very short notice, and women are still usually sent home first when there are few fish. Thus these women can be called upon when there are many fish and sent home when there are few. Having the advantages of flexible working time can make it hard for women to leave when they need to while there are many fish to be processed. One woman said, referring to occasions when she needed to leave work, "They made me feel like a traitor to the nation, to leave all these valuables to be damaged."

Women are generally not upset about the fact that men are higher paid than they are. Men are perceived as the main providers, and fishers are seen as working in a dangerous and tough situation. The main reasons women give for working in the freezing plant besides earning a living and having their own income are to get out of the home and to be in the company of other women. Women still define themselves as both workers and housewives. The women who have been most involved in the labor unions complain that it is hard to fight for better pay when women do not see themselves as providers. Women in freezing plants of fishing villages, like over 90% of Icelandic workers, are unionized into local unions for each village. The attitudes I have described above, they argue, have hindered the achievement of economic equality. However, they do not put all the blame on the women themselves and are also critical of the labor union leadership.

Conclusion

I have discussed some of the aspects at work in the social construction of gender in Icelandic fishing communities, examining women's central position in the household, on the one hand, and their work in the freezing plant, on the other. I have focused on the division of labor and how gender differences are created and recreated in production and reproduction. Gender construction is extended from the reproductive sphere to the area of production, as we have seen by examining the construction and reconstruction of gender in the freezing plant.

Applying the theoretical perspective suggested in this essay with its three arenas of analysis—dominant ideas, division of labor, and gendered identities—can help us understand why women's centrality in the household and their contribution to the fishing economy have not led to gender equality. Men are dominant and their activities at sea are considered more important than the activities performed by women on land. Control over their own and their husbands' income, as well as acting as heads of households in daily life, does give women some independence. Women, however, gain status primarily from being associated with men as fishers' wives. By showing their strength and not expressing their fear when their husbands are at sea, these women participate in their heroic activities. At the same time the emphasis on their role in the reproductive sphere helps justify their low wage because they are not considered providers. Women who go out of the household to engage in wage labor are still primarily responsible for the work in the household and thus carry a double workload.

By examining the work in a freezing plant we have been able to gain insight into the process involved in the construction of gender and the maintenance of gender inequalities in the sphere of production. We have seen that a strict gender division of labor is maintained between jobs which are seen as appropriate for women and those seen as appropriate for men. In spite of very high participation in the labor market, women find themselves in a highly divided market in which men's jobs are more highly valued. Women do not gain respect from their economic activities in the fisheries, where they are a reserve army of labor. Even though they are aware of their work being looked down upon and may talk of themselves as "only" working in the fishery, they take pride in being part of the fishing economy. Thus the images of Icelandic women are stratified by gender and class and age as well as by region—between urban areas and fishing villages. Rather than there being a single Icelandic cultural image of women or fishers' wives or factory women, there are multiple images, as there are multiple experiences, from which various individuals can draw to construct rhetorics and personal identities.

Acknowledgments

I would like to express my appreciation to the Joint Committee on Western Europe of the American Council of Learned Societies, the Social Science Research Council, the Ford Foundation, and the William and Flora Hewlett Foundation; the National Science Foundation (USA) and the Icelandic Research Council.

Note

1. The material presented in this essay is based on fieldwork in two Icelandic fishing villages in 1989 to 1990. The quotations from seven different women and one man were chosen from interviews conducted during this period. Names have been changed and some facts about the individual women altered to hide their identity.

INGA DÓRA BJÖRNSDÓTTIR

6

THE MOUNTAIN WOMAN AND THE PRESIDENCY

> *... subjects are not in possession of the totality of*
> *the meaning of their behavior as an immediate*
> *datum of consciousness and their actions always*
> *encompass more meaning than they know or wish.*
>
> —*Pierre Bourdieu and Loic J. D. Wacquant,*
> An Invitation to Reflexive Sociology

Soon after the former president of Iceland, Kristján Eldjárn, announced that he would step down after twelve years in office, several Icelanders expressed the view that the next president of Iceland should be a woman.[1] In early June 1980 their wish came true; Icelanders elected the first woman president, Vigdís Finnbogadóttir, a high school teacher and a former director of the City Theater of Reykjavík. Besides Finnbogadóttir, three men ran for the office. Finnbogadóttir won with a slim margin, acquiring 33.8% of the vote, while her closest competitor received 32.3% of the vote. However, soon the majority of the Icelandic population took great pride in having Finnbogadóttir as their president; when her presidency was challenged in 1989, she got 92.7% of the vote. In Iceland it is a popular belief that Finnbogadóttir's election reflects Icelanders' age-old liberal attitudes toward women and that as president she has been an exemplary advocate of women's liberation in Iceland. The purpose of this essay is to evaluate both of these popular beliefs.

Age-Old Ideas about Icelandic Women's Strength and Liberty

The historian Ólafía Einarsdóttir (1984) suggests that Vigdís Finnbogadóttir's election in 1980 is a reflection of the high regard Icelandic
women enjoyed during the early settlement of Iceland. She does not
attempt to explain how these ideas survived throughout the centuries or why they suddenly reemerged in 1980, when she states that
"not long ago, Icelandic farmers and fishermen demanded that a
woman should become a President. Could it not have been the old
ideas [i.e., about women's strength and liberty] in the national consciousness that made the Icelandic nation elect a woman as a President, the first nation in the world to do so?" (Einarsdóttir 1984: 25).
Several Icelandic historians have argued that, in spite of some strong
female characters in the Icelandic sagas, Icelandic women did not enjoy better legal or social standing than women in other European
countries (Karlsson 1986; see also Hákonardóttir 1992). My own research also indicates that the processes that led to Finnbogadóttir's
election cannot be traced as far back in Icelandic history as Einarsdóttir suggests but are more recent.

Three processes contributed to Finnbogadóttir's election as the
first female president of Iceland: first, the Icelandic presidency was
from the outset, in 1944, constructed as an androgynous role, with
both political/masculine and cultural/maternal dimensions; second,
the first two presidents represented primarily the political/masculine
dimension of the presidency, while the third primarily cultivated its
cultural/maternal dimension, which facilitated women's access to the
presidency; and, finally, radicalized views of women's potential were
introduced by the Icelandic women's movement, the Red Stockings,
during the 1970s.

Nature and the Nation

At the turn of the nineteenth century, when the Icelandic nationalist
movement emerged, Iceland was a small underdeveloped Danish
colony with less than one hundred thousand inhabitants. It lacked all
the means by which other Western nations had been establishing
their national selfhood: an independent economic and political base
and a military force.

To become legitimate citizens of society, and thus fully human,
people had to suppress their selfish desires and the longing of the

flesh and reach instead a state of pure spirituality and selflessness, through participation in politics and warfare. Politics was regarded as peoples' and nations' pursuit of freedom from natural necessities and the body (Brown 1988; Di Stefano 1991). War represented the ultimate mark and test of the capacity to transcend self-interest, as it was the ultimate offense to natural feelings of self-love and love of one's own (Lloyd 1987: 65). In Western political discourse, the king usually represented the epitome of manhood. He was the political and military leader who had succeeded in totally conquering and suppressing the forces of nature and the feminine within himself. He was closer to God, the father, than any secular being was (Galey 1990).

The writings of the German nationalist Johann Gottfried von Herder came to have profound impact on the thinking of Icelandic nationalists (Óskarsdóttir 1982: 78–79). Herder was critical of the vision that humans and nature were opposed to each other and that humans could create themselves and political units through their own will. Humankind, he argued, was an inherent part of nature, and human life, spirit, and consciousness rested within nature, the "maternal" body. It was not human will but the supreme power of nature that ultimately decided character and fate (Herder 1968: 4, 79). Nature also created nations. The natural contours on earth were nowhere exactly the same, and thus the forces of nature in each and every region on earth were unique. The country's unique natural characteristics set their inalienable mark on the language, culture, and history, which were, according to Herder, organic forces rooted in nature, and in that way played a key role in the construction of the national spirit, *das Volkgeist* (Herder, in Ergang 1931: 90). Since no two countries had the same natural features, no two countries could generate the same kind of national spirit. Accordingly, there was no universal mind or universal human, only a national mind and a national human. As nations were natural entities created by the unique forces of nature and governed by their own natural laws, peoples could legitimately demand their political independence and sovereign status regardless of their size, political, economic, or social advancement.

The Mountain Woman: A Countersymbol to the Danish King

By considering the historical and political circumstances in eighteenth- and nineteenth-century Iceland, one can better understand the appeal of Herder's ideas to the Icelandic nationalists. While Icelanders lacked a strong economic and political base and had no military force, the more traditional means to assert national selfhood and political power, they could argue for a distinctive history and cultural heritage. Icelanders possessed a language, culture, and history that, as they claimed, were rooted in and shaped by a natural environment.

In the nationalist discourse these forces were believed to be controlled by the "mother," who played a key role in making Icelanders into humans. These ideas are manifest primarily in poetic texts, which were widely read and recited by the public during the nineteenth and early twentieth century. These forces also provided Icelanders with a distinct identity that separated them from the Danes and served as a rhetorical base for demanding their freedom and political independence. In Iceland's independence movement one of the crucial arguments for sovereignty was that they were born and shaped by a different "mother" than the Danes (see Björnsdóttir 1992, 1994).

The centrality of the mother/feminine in the Icelandic nationalist discourse manifested itself in the Mountain Woman trope (see figure 1) that became, and remains, one of the central symbols in Icelandic nationalist discourse. The Mountain Woman was constructed as a countersymbol to the Danish king, the "father," but in nationalist discourse Icelanders referred to the Danish king as their "father" (see, e.g., Jónsson 1942: 40–41). She was an independent mother, royalty in her own right and the embodiment and the possessor of the land. The Mountain Woman had two separate but intimately related dimensions: the cultural/maternal and the political/masculine. The cultural/maternal dimension included Icelandic language, culture, and history, which were believed to be rooted in her body and actively controlled by the mother. Her political/masculine dimension included Iceland's political power and sovereignty. The Mountain Woman was the source of these, but she did not actively control the country's political power. Instead she delegated her powers to her sons. But the sons were still tied to and dependent on their "mother"; if the tie with the mother was cut, they would cease to exist as free men (Björnsdóttir 1992).

The Mountain Woman and the Presidency

In 1944, when Iceland became a republic, the president replaced the Danish king as the head of the Icelandic state. A comparison of the meaning of the Mountain Woman and the Icelandic presidency reveals that there are some fundamental similarities between the two. Like the Mountain Woman, the president represents Iceland's

Frumdregin af J.B.Zwecker, að fyrirsögn Eiríks Magnússonar. Þessi ávekkaði eftirdráttr gjör Helga Magnússon.

FJALLKONAN

1 The Mountain Woman.

sovereignty and national unity. The president's unitary role is reflected in the fact that she or he may not take a public stand on particular issues and cannot be a member of parliament. Neither may the president represent a particular company or public institution (Constitution, Art. 9). Like the Mountain Woman, the president represents the supreme political power of the nation. But, like the Mountain Woman, the president is "sedentary" and "immobile," "sitting on a throne," and delegates her or his political power to the ministers (Constitution, Art. 13). The ministers are tied to and dependent on the president, as it is the president who ultimately guarantees the national order and unity. Laws passed by the parliament have to be signed by the president to go into effect. If the president considers the new laws to be unjust or to pose a threat to the national unity or independence, she or he can refuse to sign them into law. The laws still come into effect temporarily, but as soon as possible a national referendum has to be held to decide whether the laws come into full effect (Constitution, Art. 26).

Like the Mountain Woman, the president represents what all Icelanders have in common: their country, their language, their culture, and their history. It is the president's duty to keep the national spirit alive and to cultivate Icelanders' love for their country, language, and history. Traditionally, presidents have given public speeches to accomplish this goal. The most important speech is the one on the National Radio on New Year's Day.

Sveinn Björnsson, the First President

Iceland remained part of the Danish kingdom until June 17, 1944, when Iceland became a republic. On that day, Sveinn Björnsson, a former ambassador to Denmark and the governor of Iceland, was unanimously elected as the first president in a ceremonial session of the Icelandic parliament at Þingvellir. The installation of an Icelandic president signified the final separation from the "father," the Danish king, and the recognition of Iceland's independence.

The election of Sveinn Björnsson was an honor bestowed upon a man who had served his nation well: he had played a crucial role negotiating Iceland's final separation from Denmark (Björnsson 1957). As president he was no longer a politician, but he remained a statesman and a pragmatist. During his presidency he did not hesitate to influence the activities of Icelandic politicians and of parliament. His New Year speeches were devoid of nationalistic sentimentality, but were devoted to political and economic issues. He had great faith in Iceland's economic progress and the role technology was to play in it. For example, his New Year speech in 1950 was entitled "Better Cultivation on the Basis of Science" (Björnsson 1950).

Ásgeir Ásgeirsson, the Man of the People

In 1952 Sveinn Björnsson retired from the presidency. At the outset the leaders of the two largest political parties, the Independence Party (the conservative party) and the Progressive Party (the center party), hoped that the parliament would unite unanimously behind one candidate, as in 1944, so that popular elections would not have to take place (Gröndal 1992), but the members of the parliament could not agree on any one candidate. When it became clear that popular elections would have to be held, the leaders of these two parties decided to unite behind one candidate, hoping that, since together their parties had the support of the majority of the Icelandic electorate, their presidential candidate would easily win. During these elections, as during presidential elections ever since, the Icelandic public expressed its desire to show its independence *vis-à-vis* the political establishment. The president was not to be hand-picked by the power elite, but chosen by the Icelandic public. This time the Icelandic public elected Ásgeir Ásgeirsson, the representative of the smallest political party, which is (pointedly) called Alþýðuflokkurinn or the People's Party (the social democratic party).

Ásgeir Ásgeirsson was a theologian who had devoted his whole adult life to politics. He had been a member of parliament for thirty years, first as the representative of the Progressive Party. As such he had served as the speaker, as finance minister for one year, and as prime minister for two years. He was a political maverick, and after some internal fights within the Progressive Party he left it to become an independent candidate until he joined the Alþýðuflokkurinn. His unruliness may have helped him during the elections; he was considered the man of the people, and not of the power establishment (Gröndal 1992).

Ásgeir Ásgeirsson regarded the presidency as a good way to retire from the turmoil of politics, but when he saw fit he did not hesitate to direct his words to politicians and advise them or scold them. For example, after the parliamentary elections in 1953 it took a long time for the parties to form a new government. The drawn-out process became the main theme of Ásgeirsson's New Year's speech in 1954, when he criticized the politicians for not acting swiftly and decidedly. The title of his speech was "Without Responsible Governments Democracy May Fail" (Ásgeirsson 1954: 2). Still, his speeches were much less politically oriented than those of his predecessor. The political dimension was not absent, however, as he frequently drew the public's attention to the crucial connection between Icelandic history, culture, and language and Iceland's political and economic independence. Only through hard work and dedication to their mother, the Mountain Woman, would the new nation survive and thrive (Ásgeirsson 1959: 11).

From the Political to the Cultural

When Ásgeir Ásgeirsson was elected president, he represented the antiestablishment. However, when he retired sixteen years later, in 1968, he and his family were seen as being at the center of the power elite. His son-in-law, Gunnar Thoroddsen, a law professor and a prominent member of the Independence Party, was the first person to announce his presidential candidacy.

Gunnar Thoroddsen had been a member of parliament for over fifteen years, a popular mayor of Reykjavík from 1947 to 1959, and the minister of finance from 1959 to 1965. He had been planning his presidential candidacy for several years. In order to distance himself from his strong association with the Independence Party, he had become Iceland's ambassador to Denmark for four years prior to the elections. To further his nonpolitical credentials he had devoted his time in Copenhagen to completing his Ph.D. dissertation in law, "Fjölmæli" (Defamation), which he defended at the University of Iceland in early 1968 (Ragnarsson 1981). His efforts to distance himself from his political background did not have the desired effects, however. In the eyes of the Icelandic public he had a strong political profile and was deeply entrenched within the power elite.

In the 1952 presidential elections, experience in politics was regarded as important for the future president. In 1968, however, a close association with any of the political parties (especially the Independence Party and the Socialist Party) had become a drawback for any potential presidential candidate and Icelanders chose a challenger to Thoroddsen's candidacy from outside the ranks of politicians.

It is beyond the scope of this essay to provide a detailed historical analysis of the political events in Iceland during the late 1960s, but one important reason for this turn of events was related to the U.S.

involvement in the Vietnam war. At one level the debate centered around whether or not the American military presence in Vietnam was justified. At another level Iceland's relationship with the United States became a highly controversial issue. Historically the two countries had close ties. During World War II Iceland was occupied by British military forces, which were soon replaced by American troops. The original agreement between Iceland and the United States had stipulated that American troops were to leave Iceland at the end of the war. But as it turned out they have been stationed there almost ever since. In 1947 the Icelandic and American governments reached an agreement allowing U.S. troops to return to Iceland and about the same time Iceland became a beneficiary of the Marshall Plan. In 1949 Iceland became a founding member of NATO. These events divided the nation into two camps, for or against membership in NATO, a division that remained until the end of the cold war (see Whitehead 1980, 1985).

The American involvement in Vietnam polarized the Icelandic public around these issues. Among the critics of close association with the United States were individuals who were primarily concerned about the purity of Icelandic culture and language. The more vocal and visible opponents based their criticism on socialist ideology. Thus, I argue, the political rifts were too deep and marked for Icelanders to seek a challenger to Gunnar Thoroddsen's presidential candidacy among politicians; the president, after all, represented the nation's unity and independence.

In the light of the nature of the Icelandic presidency, with its political/masculine dimension and its cultural/maternal dimension, it is not surprising that at this time the political/masculine dimension became deemphasized while the cultural/maternal dimension came to the foreground. Kristján Eldjárn, the candidate who was chosen as Thoroddsen's challenger, had devoted his life not to politics but to Icelandic culture. As the director of the National Museum of Iceland, he had cultivated and protected the historical and cultural treasures of Iceland, much like a "mother."

Kristján Eldjárn, a Nationalist

Kristján Eldjárn was a farmer's son, and farmers were idealized in the Icelandic nationalist discourse as the cultivators and protectors of pure Icelandic language and culture. He studied English and Latin at the University of Copenhagen for a while, but soon changed his subject to archaeology. He became the director of the National Museum in 1947 and ten years later, in 1957, he defended his Ph.D. thesis, on burial customs during the pre-Christian era in Iceland, at the University of Iceland.

Eldjárn was an ardent nationalist. During his career he had twice been politically involved, in both cases in relation to the American "threat" to Iceland's cultural and political independence. In 1946 he was one of the founders of *þjóðvörn*, literally, "nation defense," an association of people of different political orientations who opposed the agreement made between the Icelandic and the American governments allowing the U.S. military to stay.

In 1965 Eldjárn again became involved in protesting against American influence on Icelandic culture and society when he, along with fifty-nine other men and women, signed a petition demanding that the TV station at the U.S. base in Keflavík limit its broadcasting to the territory of the base (an increasing number of Icelanders were watching the American TV). The petition had the intended effect, and the American TV was kept from the Icelandic audience. In spite of some efforts to denigrate Kristján Eldjárn's actions during the presidential campaign, it turned out that they worked in his favor (Gröndal 1991).

Kristján Eldjárn's presidential speeches clearly showed that a humanist, scholar, and nationalist was speaking, not a politician. His speeches lacked some of the confidence and the optimism of his predecessors. He was greatly concerned about the bad economic and political state of the world and often expressed his concern about world hunger, pollution, and the buildup of atomic weapons. But the predominant theme in his speeches was the country itself. While Iceland has throughout the centuries been harsh and demanding, it is, he constantly repeated, a beautiful country, with many valuable resources that can be used to improve Icelanders' economic life and sense of well-being, through the application of modern science and technology. Like nineteenth-century nationalists, he was tireless in reminding Icelanders that nature had played a central role in creating and maintaining a distinct culture and national identity. Only Icelanders' faith and love of the country would keep their national identity alive and thriving (Eldjárn 1969–1980).

"We Want Vigdís!"

During Kristján Eldjárn's years in office the public had come to regard the president primarily as the representative and guardian of Icelandic culture. Early in 1980, when he announced that he was going to resign, it soon became clear that the majority of Icelanders wanted the next president to follow in his footsteps (Arnórsson 1980).

Initially, three candidates announced their candidacy in the 1980 presidential elections. One was Albert Guðmundsson, a former star soccer player, wealthy businessman, veteran populist politician, controversial member of parliament, and later minister of finance for the Independence Party. In his campaign, he tried (unsuccessfully) to distance himself from his political career, presenting himself instead as the "man of the people" (Matthíasson 1980: 26). He emphasized the fact that he was a self-made man, who was born poor but had climbed to society's highest ranks through his hard work and perseverance. Another candidate, Pétur Thorsteinsson, was also affiliated with the Independence Party. He was a member of the elite diplomatic core, had lived abroad almost all his adult life, and was little known to the majority of the Icelandic public. The third candidate was Guðlaugur Þorvaldsson, a former professor of economics and the former chancellor of the University of Iceland.

Of the three candidates Guðlaugur resembled Kristján Eldjárn the most. He was a man of learning and had no background in politics, and initially the polls showed that he would be the winner of the presidential elections. However, as an economist Þorvaldsson had not been directly involved in cultural affairs and thus lacked a distinct cultural and nationalistic profile. It seems that the Icelandic public was not satisfied with the three candidates and started "looking for" the fourth candidate to enter the race, which turned out to be Vigdís Finnbogadóttir (Guttormsson 1980).

Vigdís Finnbogadóttir's Unusual Career

As she tells it, Finnbogadóttir was herself from early age steeped in Icelandic culture (Sigurðardóttir 1988: 7–10). She was raised in a highly educated, ambitious family that was greatly concerned about the progress and the welfare of the new nation. Her father, one of Iceland's first engineers, originally worked for the Lighthouse Administration, but later he became a professor of engineering at the University of Iceland. Her mother was among the first Icelandic women to receive a degree in nursing and devoted her life to the advancement of nurses as well as to the improvement of the social rights of women. Her parents made great demands on her and had high expectations. She completed university entrance exams in 1949, not common among Icelandic women at the time, and went to France to study French and literature, first in Grenoble and later at the Sorbonne in Paris. Later she completed a B.A. degree in French and English from the University of Iceland and for years taught French at two of Reykjavík's high schools and at the University of Iceland. In 1970–1971 she had her own program on National Television, teaching French, which made her well known and very popular with the public (Friðriksson and Elísson 1980: 73). During her stay in France Finnbogadóttir had also developed a great interest in the theater. In 1972 she became the director of the City Theater of Reykjavík, the first woman to hold that position. She devoted her summers to guiding tourists around Iceland. She also became involved in promoting tourism and thus was frequently in the public limelight.

Finnbogadóttir was well educated, had traveled widely, spoke several languages, and had considerable experience in socializing with people of various nationalities and professions. But she also took great pride in her country's history, culture, and language. Like Kristján Eldjárn, she was a pacifist and a nationalist and as such she was officially against the American military presence. Finally, she was, like the Mountain Woman, an independent mother. As a young woman, Finnbogadóttir had been briefly married to a medical doctor and had lived for several years in Denmark and Sweden, where her husband completed his medical training. Finnbogadóttir divorced her husband and did not remarry. In her late thirties she adopted a daughter, but continued to work outside the home (Sigurðardóttir 1988).

Until the late 1960s the majority of Icelandic women worked within the home. Unlike most Icelandic women at this time, Finnbogadóttir had public standing and her own independent identity as a professional woman. Thus her nondomestic career made her better qualified than most other women of her generation to assume the role of the national mother.

Why a Female President at This Time?

It was not merely coincidence that some Icelanders were open to the idea of having a woman as a presidential candidate in 1980. With the election of Kristján Eldjárn the cultural/maternal dimension of the presidency had come to the foreground. It still demanded some changes in Icelanders' consciousness to perceive that a woman could actually fill this predominantly maternal role.

In 1970 a small group of women, many of whom had previously been active on the radical left, established a women's liberation movement. Inspired by the burgeoning Western women's movements, they followed European tradition and named their organization Rauð-sokkahreyfinging or the Red Stocking Movement.

In accordance with the predominant views within the international women's movement at the time, the Red Stockings regarded the domestic and maternal role as having been the major contributor to women's oppression. They demanded critical reevaluation and a total reconstruction of women's roles and capacities. The division of labor along gender lines was to be abolished both within the home and in the public sphere. Men were to share the caring for children and domestic chores equally with women. Similarly, women were to shoulder the responsibilities of the public sphere to the same extent as men (Kristmundsdóttir 1990).

Icelandic women (as well as the "general public") reacted to the Red Stockings' message in an ambiguous way. They were, in general, sympathetic toward the Red Stockings' demands for increasing women's equality and raising women's salaries and toward their demands for improved child care. They also agreed that women's realm of activities should be expanded. Still, there was a strong and persistent resistance to what was perceived as being the Red Stockings' antimaternal message. As I have argued elsewhere (Björnsdóttir 1992), the central configuration of the mother in nationalist discourse empowered women and helped them win some crucial political and social rights. Icelandic women were at this time neither ready nor willing to denounce or seriously reconsider these ideas, which, to them, were still important and empowering.

Icelanders' openness to the idea that women's fields of activities could be expanded and their refusal of the idea that women should become like "men" help explain why at this time the public so quickly or "easily" saw it as a viable option that a woman should become the next president. This reflected an underlying awareness that the presidency had now become primarily a cultural/maternal role. Thus neither radical rethinking of the fundamental nature of the presidency nor rethinking of the nature of women was needed to envision a woman as president.

This in turn helps explain the fact that, once the idea had been introduced that Finnbogadóttir might become a presidential candidate, fishers and farmers, traditionally some of the more conservative groups, were among the first officially to endorse her candidacy. Men were also in the majority of those who first signed a public petition for her presidential candidacy (fifty-three men and thirty-one women signed this petition; see *Þjóðin kýs*, 1–4 [1980]: 1). For many of them, Finnbogadóttir was not to be like a man, even though all the presidents of Iceland so far had been men. Instead, she was to embody all the best *feminine virtues*.

It is also highly significant that while the Red Stockings played an important role for Finnbogadóttir's presidency, she did not run her campaign on a feminist agenda. Instead, from the outset of her campaign Finnbogadóttir disassociated herself from the Red Stockings and their radical image. It is also telling that for some of the founders of the Women's Alliance, a political party specifically for women established in 1982, Finnbogadóttir's election was a great inspiration (Kristmundsdóttir 1990). The Women's Alliance emerged as an alternative to the Red Stockings and was strongly opposed to the Red Stockings' notion of equality. In contrast to the Red Stockings' idea that women should strive to become the same as and equal to men, the Women's Alliance argued that women were to be granted equality on their own terms, not on men's terms. These terms were to be rooted and based on women's own culture and traditions (*Hugmyndafræðilegur grundvöllur Kvennaframboðsins*, quoted in Kristmundsdóttir 1990: 273).

The support and admiration of Finnbogadóttir on the part of many members of the Women's Alliance again reflected an underlying awareness that by becoming president Finnbogadóttir was not becoming a "social man," even though the presidents of Iceland had all been men. Instead, as president, she was entering a maternal role, embodying women's difference from men.

Vigdís Finnbogadóttir: The Mother of the Nation

Finnbogadóttir's presidential speeches show that she is deeply entrenched in the hegemonic nationalist/maternal discourse (see Finnbogadóttir 1981–1993). Her presidential activities also reflect that from the outset she sensed the cultural/maternal nature of the presidency. Her speeches center around the country itself; its culture, language, and children. She harbors no doubts about the unique qualities of Icelandic nature and culture and how fortunate Icelanders are to be born into a society with such a distinguished historical and cultural background. But at the same time she is greatly concerned about the undesirable polluting effect that foreign influence is having on Icelandic culture, especially on the language. This influence, she repeatedly claims, is likely to rupture Icelanders' holy trinity: the nation, the country, and the tongue. This is a recurrent theme of her New Year speeches (see, e.g., Finnbogadóttir 1985: 28–29, 1989: 26–27).

Her main focus is on children. They are most open and vulnerable to foreign influences, but they are also Iceland's future. They are to inherit the country, and only if they are raised as true Icelanders will the nation remain true to itself. In contrast to her predecessors, Finnbogadóttir has not limited her concerns about the purity of Icelandic culture and language to speeches. She has instead taken an active approach and launched a campaign to keep the "mother tongue" pure and free from foreign slang. During her public appearances and visits around the country she is tireless in telling children to eliminate such foreign greetings as *halló* from their vocabulary. Instead, she insists, children should use such good Icelandic expressions as *komdu sæl(l) og blessaður(-uð)*.

Finnbogadóttir has also dedicated herself to planting trees. The landscape has through the centuries become increasingly barren and the president has been tireless in her tree-planting, inspiring both individuals and organizations to join in her effort. When planting trees, Finnbogadóttir again emphasizes her maternal role. She always plants one tree for girls, another tree for boys, and still another for the future. In 1990, when she turned sixty, her friends and admirers published a collection of articles in her honor. The theme and the title of the book reflect the spirit of her presidency, *Yrkja* or Cultivation (Pálsson et al. 1990). Significantly, the proceeds of the book are to go to a fund to buy plants for children to plant all over Iceland (Finnbogadóttir 1991: 27).

Finnbogadóttir's identification with the maternal aspects of the presidency is not limited to her desires to keep the mother tongue pure and to adorn the country's maternal body; it also manifests itself in the way she herself dresses for official events. On festive occasions

2 President Finnbogadóttir: modern impersonation
of the Mountain Woman.

she impersonates the Mountain Woman by wearing *skaut*, a national
costume of the same kind the Mountain Woman wears when she appears on Iceland's national holiday, June 17 (see figure 2). At her in-
augurations her close association with the country has also been
vividly expressed. She has worn dresses in the same colors as the Icelandic flag: blue, the symbol of the sky and the ocean; red, the symbol of volcanoes and fires; and white, the symbol of snow-covered
mountains and glaciers.

The close association between Finnbogadóttir's body and the
country itself manifested itself clearly during the 1980 presidential
campaign. An anonymous woman knitted an outfit for her out of
lamb's wool in the natural colors, *sauðalitunum*. Icelanders have, from
the outset, been sheepherders and sheep are seen as an inherent part
and product of Icelandic nature. Finnbogadóttir received this present

3 President Finnbogadóttir in "natural" dress.

with great gratitude, but promised not to wear it until it had become clear that she had won the elections. When her victory had been declared, she greeted her supporters in her woolen outfit in front of her home in Reykjavík during the early morning hours of June 30 (see figure 3).

Finally, Finnabogadóttir's identification with the national mother is expressed in the symbol she chose for her presidency. Soon after she became president, Finnbogadóttir started collecting objects representing the mother/child relationship. When foreign dignitaries visit Iceland they are instructed to bring a present with this theme (Kristjánsdóttir and Björnsdóttir 1988: 20–23).

The President and Political Power

Laws passed by the parliament have to be signed by the president to go into effect. None of President Finnbogadóttir's predecessors ever saw a reason to refuse to sign new laws. However, in her twelve-year career, Finnbogadóttir has twice openly expressed her opposition to new laws before signing them. In both cases the laws had disadvantageous effects on women's professions (specifically, stewardesses and teachers).

In the fall of 1985 the stewardesses of Icelandair, Iceland's major airline company, went on strike. On October 25, International Women's Day, the government issued a law declaring the strike unlawful. Icelandic women were celebrating the tenth anniversary of the women's holiday by staging a rally in downtown Reykjavík. To commemorate that day, they had brought their country to a standstill by laying down their work for one day. Finnbogadóttir did not sign the law immediately, insisting that she needed some time to think it over (Finnbogadóttir 1985). This was the first time in history that the president refused to sign new laws right away, and the delay immediately became a cause of great controversy. It was rumored that the government put great pressures on the president to sign, which she eventually did before the end of International Women's Day.

Two years later the Teachers' Union in Iceland was granted a wage increase. However, before the pay raise went into effect the government issued a law annulling it. The president expressed her opposition to this law. Not only did the law do injustice to teachers, but it would affect the welfare of schoolchildren. In Finnbogadóttir's view both children and their caretakers deserve the best (Grímsdóttir 1993). As in the former case, she did not use the political leverage of the presidency, but complied with the demands of the government and signed the law.

It is debatable whether or not the president should have demanded a plebiscite to decide the lawfulness of the stewardesses' strike and the legitimacy of the teachers' salary freeze. This legislation was limited to a small portion of the population and the outcome did not pose a threat to the nation's unity or independence (Benediktsson 1993; Þórðarson 1993). More recently, the parliament passed laws that many believe pose a great threat to Iceland's political and cultural independence. In January 1993 the parliament voted for Iceland's entrance into the European Economic Area (EEA), which many Icelanders regard as a prelude for entrance into the EC. Before the vote in January, the three opposition parties, the Progressive Party, the Socialist Party, and the Women's Alliance, unsuccessfully demanded that a national referendum should decide whether Iceland should enter the EEA. When it became clear that the majority of the parliament would not vote for a national referendum, the supporters of the referendum realized that only the president would make a referendum possible by refusing to sign the new law on Iceland's entrance into EEA.

There is strong opposition to Iceland's entrance into the EC, and the president received petitions from people in all parts of the country of various political inclinations asking her not to sign the law. Many people had high expectations of her in this matter and thus became greatly disappointed when she not only signed the law but issued a declaration stating that, since no president so far had refused to sign laws passed by parliament, tradition had made the president's constitutional right to refuse to sign laws invalid and ineffective.

Needless to say, Finnbogadóttir's declaration became a cause of controversy. Critics pointed out that "tradition" alone could not eliminate laws written into the constitution (Þórarinsson 1993); instead, Finnbogadóttir's decision was to be regarded as her personal interpretation of the Constitution. Future presidents, the critics claimed, do not have to follow her lead; the president's declaration temporarily diminished the power not only of the presidency but also of the Icelandic nation. At the same time the power of the parliament, and especially the power of the government, was greatly increased (Benediktsson 1993; Þórðarson 1993).

Conclusion

One of the major points raised in this essay is that from the outset the Icelandic presidency had two different, but complementary, dimensions—a political/masculine one and a cultural/maternal one. As I showed, during the late 1960s the cultural/maternal dimension came to the foreground. Thus even *before* Finnbogadóttir became president there was an established maternal role for her to play.

One can unquestionably claim that President Finnbogadóttir has played the role of the national mother with excellence. For example, her involvement in tree planting has been very well received by the public. But the question still remains whether Finnbogadóttir's presidential activities have served in some way to advance women's cause in Iceland. The evidence of her activities in regard to the cultural/maternal dimension discussed above shows that she has not only adhered to the fundamental principles of the cultural/maternal dimension of the presidency, but as a woman has been able to realize the maternal aspects of the presidency more fully than any of her male predecessors. In this regard, it is not unfair to argue that President Finnbogadóttir has not challenged but *further strengthened* the national ideal of the mother, an ideal deeply rooted in the male-dominated nationalist discourse.

In regard to the political/masculine aspects of the presidency, Finnbogadóttir's actions have been more ambiguous and inconsistent. Her sympathies with women and their cause became clear when she protested the government's actions against the stewardesses and the Teachers' Union. She also became the first president to remind the public and the government alike of the political power of the president. It could not be taken for granted that the president would automatically sign all new laws into effect. Her protests, however, were of no political consequence: in both cases she signed the new laws and the will of the government prevailed. Furthermore, by signing the declaration discussed above President Finnbogadóttir took the unprecedented step of completely undermining the political power of the presidency. At the same time the power of the male-dominated political establishment in Iceland has been further solidified.

Acknowledgments

I would like to express my special thanks to Helga Kress, Sigríður Dúna Kristmundsdóttir, and Guðný Guðbjörnsdóttir, all at the University of Iceland, and Björn Birnir at the University of California, Santa Barbara, for their valuable comments on this paper. I also thank Guðrún Eggertsdóttir at the National Archives of Iceland for her assistance.

Note

1. In August 1976 Þórður Valdimarsson wrote an article in the newspaper *Vísir* titled "Next Time We Should Elect a Woman as the President" (see Ólafsson 1993: 5). Laufey Jakobsdóttir was the first person officially to suggest that Finnbogadóttir should be the next president of Iceland (see *Vísir*, "Lesendabréf," January 15, 1980). During the 1952 presidential campaign, in a letter to the editor of a small magazine called *Reykvíkingur* (May 9), one reader suggested that the nation should elect a woman as the next president, naming a well-known opera singer and a well-known actress as possible choices.

JULIE E. GURDIN

7

MOTHERHOOD, PATRIARCHY, AND THE NATION: DOMESTIC VIOLENCE IN ICELAND

Patriarchy is both larger than and located within families, but it can be separated analytically to examine the relationship between the family and the state, the private and the public. In this essay I address how domestic violence involves the interface between public and private patriarchies and public and private motherhood. Icelandic women who left their abusive partners drew upon the state-supported resources available to them for support, but these agencies often subjected them to other kinds of power. In Iceland fighting and resisting domestic violence involves a struggle over the "nature" of motherhood itself. Motherhood and patriarchy are actively reconstructed through feminist discourses and practices, state institutions, and the individual women who leave their abusive husbands. The women I interviewed expressed their agency through elaborating their roles as mothers and stressing the private character of motherhood. The hegemonic (and counterhegemonic) is thus woven through and between lived social identities (Williams 1977).

One issue facing domestic violence researchers is how to consider the agency of an abused woman in relation to her partner and to society. Most sociologists and psychologists have conducted their research according to either "family systems" or "social control" theories. Family systems approaches take individual families as their units of analysis. The individual life experiences of men and women predict whether they will be abusers or victims. The internal dynamics among individuals in the family will then either inhibit or promote domestic violence (Gelles 1987; Straus and Gelles 1990; Giles-Sims 1983). A woman's behavior within a relationship is seen as having an impact on whether violence is used against her.

Social control approaches focus on social systems of dominance and subordination based on gender. Rape, domestic violence, and sexual harassment are fields in which women's actions and choices are circumscribed by male violence (e.g., Dobash and Dobash 1979; Hanmer and Maynard 1987). This perspective argues that the sexism in society is the cause for domestic violence. Men use violence as one way to control women (Hanmer and Maynard 1987; Kelly 1988). Marriage institutionalizes the domination of wives by husbands through the structure of husband and wife roles (Dobash and Dobash 1979). Women's economic dependence enables husbands to be abusive because of the costs involved in establishing an independent household (Edwards 1987).

In both of these approaches, women's agency is rendered problematic. Family systems approaches view women as agents who can precipitate the violence used against them. In social control approaches, women's agency is undertheorized against patriarchy and the state. The more complex and subtle relationships between action and resources, representations and practices, and hegemony and resistance are backgrounded in these traditions. By contrast, Linda Gordon, a historian, studied social workers' interventions in domestic violence cases in Boston (1988). Gordon uses the word "gender" to "describe a power system in which women are subordinated through relations that are contradictory, ambiguous, and conflictual—a subordination maintained against resistance, in which women have by no means always defined themselves as other, in which women face and take choices and action despite constriction"(1990: 852). Abused women in Boston shrewdly represented themselves and their children to social service agencies to receive assistance (Gordon 1988), drawing upon middle-class sympathy. Gordon's formulations of gender and patriarchy leave open the possibility of addressing resistance and transformations within particular patriarchies. "Patriarchy," according to Gordon, must be used to describe a system larger than the family, a system where some individual women do have a measure of power (1990).

Johanna

I met Johanna at a friend's apartment in Reykjavík.[1] When I told her about my project on Icelandic domestic violence, she expressed interest in being interviewed about her experience as an abused wife. Johanna does not conform to the Icelandic and American media stereotypes of battered women, which include passivity, helplessness, introversion, and a lack of interpersonal skills (Jónsdóttir 1991; Samtök um kvennaathvarf 1991b; Einarsdóttir 1991; Loeske 1992). She is strong, powerful, and, some might think, intimidating. She told me the following story as we sat in her kitchen over coffee.

> The day before our daughter's birth my husband had completed a five-day drinking binge. That evening he had a hangover. While I was washing the dinner dishes, he held a shotgun, the kind used in war. He called for me. I said, "Wait, I have to finish cleaning up."
>
> Then he got angry. He said, "Come here, I am going to kill you."
>
> I heard and saw him putting bullets in the gun. Of course I was scared and I went to him. He set the gun at my heart and pulled the trigger. Nothing happened. He said, "Damn it, the safety is on."
>
> He took it off, pulled the trigger again, and nothing happened. Then he became angry, took the gun, threw it out the open window, and then all the bullets fired. I fainted, then he woke me up saying, "My love, my love, I'm not going to kill you."
>
> This occurred at 8:00. My daughter was born at 12:30.

Her clear voice remained steady though indignant as she discussed how she coped in a marriage of over a decade characterized by physical abuse directed against her and her six children. A son and a daughter, now grown, sat with us throughout the interview, helping to recall events and to translate. Johanna periodically stopped to answer a telephone call or to refill our coffee cups.

Johanna met her husband in the mid-1960s, while she was living with another man. She and her future husband worked in the same factory. Physical abuse began early in their relationship; he threatened to hit her at a country dance because she refused to sleep with him. Johanna hit back, knocking him to the ground. After parting with her infant child's father, she felt pressure from her parents to find another boyfriend. They thought her status as an unattached mother reflected badly upon the family. She then began living with and eventually married the man from the factory.

Her husband was extremely jealous and prohibited her from speaking to other men. If any man, including a friend of his, visited their home, Johanna was accused of having affairs with him. His jealousy extended to her girlfriends and he allowed them little time to socialize. Throughout their marriage he threatened to kill her and to slash her face and breasts. If Johanna refused sex, he said he would "kill one child to make room for another."

She tried to enlist her parent's support for a divorce, telling them simply that it was an unhappy marriage. They offered to take custody of her children. Fearing that her parents were trying to take the children away from her, Johanna abandoned her plans to separate. She was committed to keeping her children, even if it meant remaining in an abusive marriage. Throughout the marriage the distance between Johanna and her parents increased, with their contact limited to sporadic telephone calls.

Johanna received voluntary child support payments from her first child's father, often the only income the family had. Her husband worked irregularly in construction, and Johanna was a housewife. Because her husband spent all of their disposable income on alcohol, she requested financial assistance from a city official. This assistance often took the form of personal loans, because she was unaware of any social welfare programs available to her.

Johanna's departure was precipitated by a hallucination. One weekend evening she and her husband planned to go to a public dance. He left first and Johanna stayed behind to tuck the children into bed. As she prepared to leave, she heard a voice saying, "Your time has come." She immediately called a girlfriend to pick up her and the children. The mayor lent her transportation money to her parents' house. Her parents helped her secure temporary housing. She independently supported herself and her children with wages from a service-sector job. When her husband tried to move into her house, she called the police to remove him. The children have no ties with their father and do not use his name. Johanna has been involved in helping others through her involvement with women's groups. Johanna and her children have recently been assisting Alma, a Filipina woman recently separated from Johanna's ex-husband.

Since Johanna's divorce in the late 1970s Icelandic public awareness of domestic violence and institutional responses to it have increased dramatically. In the summer of 1991 I spoke with six other women who left their abusive husbands after the establishment of the Women's Shelter in Reykjavík (Kvennaathvarf). Most shelter women return to their abusive husbands within a few days. The women I spoke with were atypical; all established independent households with their children after their stay at the Women's Shelter. Inspired by the battered women's movement in nearby countries, a group of feminist activists met to establish the Women's Shelter in 1982. Since opening its doors in December of that year the Women's Shelter reports having provided refuge for over 1,000 women and 800 children (*Samtök um kvennaathvarf* 1991a). The shelter is a place where women who have experienced domestic violence can meet, support one another, share stories. Abused women no longer confront male domination as isolated individuals, but can draw upon a network of support and the resources provided by the organization.

The Women's Shelter draws upon international discourses to explain domestic violence to the Icelandic public. *Ofbeldi gegn eiginkonum*, a Shelter publication, was translated from a book by a Danish psychologist, Else Christensen. The Women's Shelter participates in conferences with other Nordic women's shelters, where some of their staff members have worked. Videos of American made-for-TV movies concerning domestic violence and sexual abuse are often screened in the shelter's living room. The shelter thus engages the international feminist community and draws upon its resources in its fight against domestic violence.

Nationalism, Gender, and Purity

The occurrence of domestic violence is at odds with the romantic image of Iceland as a classless, nonsexist, antimilitaristic, crimefree society. Nationalist discourses stress the uniqueness and purity of things Icelandic, including the language (Pálsson 1989b), the countryside (Brydon 1992), and traditions (Jónsson 1989, 1990).

The middle and upper classes define and represent that which is pure in state discourses. For example, the speech that marks the middle classes is the standard; the nonstandard forms of the lower class are "diagnosed" as "diseased" (Pálsson 1989b). A state commission closely protects the Icelandic lexicon from outside influences, providing the public with "pure" Icelandic words, derived from Old Norse, to use instead of Danish, English, or other foreign-derived terms. Some work places and schools fine people for using foreign words. In terms of language, both foreigners and Icelandic lower classes are marginalized as non-Icelandic. Gísli Pálsson and E. Paul Durrenberger (1992) argue that the individualistic and egalitarian national discourse prevents people from understanding that these differences are products of social class differences.

Lower-class linguistic patterns, according to the dominant ideology, represent unclear thoughts. Pálsson and Durrenberger (1992) explain that in national discourse the cultivation of language is the same as the cultivation of thought. By extension, lower-class people cannot think rationally or communicate properly; hence they are more likely to communicate through violence. Notions of purity also figure in dominant ideas about violence against women. There is a tendency to view domestic violence, and other forms of violence, as an issue which is not truly Icelandic. Abusive men are thus constructed as the inarticulate working class who cannot control themselves, drunk or sober.

In addition to increased public awareness of rape and domestic violence, Iceland has been experiencing an increase in violent crime and crimes against property since World War II (van den Hoonaard 1991). The murder rate has tripled in the past two decades (*Dagblaðið-Vísir* 1991). Mobbing, the attack by a large group of young men on a single person or a small group, is the most recent form of physical violence, one which is increasingly frequent. W. van den Hoonaard suggests: "The public explains crime in terms of individualistic causes and attributes, while downplaying the social aspects of crime. . . . we see a series of self-presentations to the larger, outside world where the myth of a crimeless Iceland sustains and fosters the uniqueness of that society in a world fraught with crime" (1991: 109).

The weekend paper *Pressan* (1991) ran a front-page headline stating that four out of seven women in the Women's Shelter were from Asia, the "mail order" brides of "drunken old men" (*brennivínskarlar*). The occurrence of domestic violence in middle- and upper-class families was not mentioned in this article; nor was the fact that the high proportion of foreign women in the shelter at a single time was an anomaly. One woman was from Africa, not Asia, and the other three were friends who left their abusive husbands at about the same time.

Some of these men had Icelandic partners before marrying foreign women, including Johanna's former husband.

One of the first Icelandic newspaper articles concerning domestic violence as a social problem was titled "It Doesn't Happen Here?" (*Gerist þetta ekki hér?*), revealing the author's cognizance of her audience's perception that violence originates from abroad (Ingadóttir 1981). An upper-class woman I interviewed was preparing to leave the country shortly after leaving the Women's Shelter. She believed that her husband's abuse indicated a more general problem, saying, "I don't trust myself to raise my kids in Iceland, not with the way society is here now." Given Emily Martin's (1987) suggestion that dominant gender ideologies are more penetrable by the marginalized lower classes, this woman's perception of domestic violence as a fundamentally Icelandic issue is unexpected.

Inga Dóra Björnsdóttir (1989) discusses the problems that women involved with foreign soldiers faced during World War II. Three hundred Icelanders left the country after marrying their soldier boyfriends, and many more were romantically involved with military men. Concerned with how the actions of these women would affect the nation's moral character, the surgeon general declared these dating relationships "a dangerous disease or a plague" (Björnsdóttir 1989: 102). Women's moral duty was to bear Icelandic children, endowing them with Icelandic language and culture. The Ministry of Health established an active propaganda campaign and two residential institutions for women caught fraternizing with soldiers. Women, the incarnations of Fjallkonan (literally, the Mountain Woman), the icon of Icelandic independence, were constructed to be the guardians of Icelandic purity and national culture.

Fifty years later Icelanders with one foreign parent may not be considered truly Icelandic, especially if that parent is not of northern European heritage. The fact of a child's "mixed" parentage is often fodder for schoolyard taunts and adult scorn. Though marriages to foreigners are becoming more common and accepted, one woman's family disowned her when she married an American serviceman from the Keflavík NATO base. Her family thought that it was "horrible that an Icelandic girl would marry an American soldier." At this time, they were unaware of the gross physical violence he used against her.

The Mountain Woman image is that of a nurturing mother, the guardian of national identity, morality, and culture. Proper motherhood implies proper (Icelandic) paternity of one's children. The public acceptance and support of single mothers reflects this ideology. Natal families, a fluid procreative family structure, and social welfare programs accommodate children and encourage motherhood.[2] Iceland's birth rate is among the highest in Europe (Chadwick 1989). Women receive considerable state support on the basis of their motherhood. This support has increased in the 1970s and 1980s as a result of the women's movement (Kissman 1989). All women with infants receive a "mother's wage." In 1991 the minimum was 20,000 kronur a month (about $500). Fathers may have to pay child support, starting at 5,000 (about $100) kronur a month. The state invests more money in child-rearing than fathers are required to. Children are promoted as the nation's "future." It is the public's collective responsibility to ensure that the Icelandic cultural legacy lives on.

Björnsdóttir (1992) has proposed that the Icelandic women's political party (the Women's Alliance, Kvennalistinn) employs the image of Fjallkonan and the maternal essence of womanhood to claim political and social legitimacy. The Women's Alliance is able to muster support through its identification of women as mothers and caretakers who are culturally distinct from men (Kristmundsdóttir 1989; Björnsdóttir 1992). Betsey Chadwick (1989) reports that mothers spoke from a privileged position at Women's Alliance meetings.

There are continuities between these sites of Icelandic feminism, the Women's Alliance and the Women's Shelter. The Women's Shelter draws upon these discourses of the public nature of motherhood as well. In order to obtain a sympathetic hearing from state funding sources, shelter workers stress the importance of the Women's Shelter for mothers' and children's safety. Women receive assistance from the state as mothers, not as individuals who need assistance and protection.

The shelter's written materials (e.g., *Samtök um kvennaathvarf* 1991a) stress the importance of mothers and of family dynamics in disseminating information about the "cycle of violence." The cycle of violence theory proposes that children from abusive families not only suffer emotionally when they witness (or experience) domestic violence, but will repeat the behavior of their same-sex parent when establishing families of their own. This explanation for the occurrence of domestic violence tells women that they have the power to end domestic violence by leaving their abusers and sparing their children from the lives they have led, emphasizing women's responsibility to others.

Whereas women are constructed as mothers in feminist and non-feminist discourses, men's relationship to child-rearing and reproduction is disregarded. Men can be men without being attentive fathers. Their voices will be considered at political meetings without regard to their paternal status. Fathers do have certain rights to visit their children and some degree of financial responsibility toward them. The vast majority of Icelandic children are given a patronym for their second name. Johanna's children must sign their father's name to legal documents, but they use another second name in all other contexts. Johanna's son attempted to change his legal name, but the state prohibited him from doing so. His paternity is thus inscribed onto his legal identity, out of his control. It is possible for an infant to receive her maternal grandfather's name when the father is unknown (or disliked); but once the child reaches adulthood, changes are difficult to obtain.

A man, as decision maker within the patriarchal family, is *húsbóndi* (master of the house). Johanna said that her father never abused her mother. However, she did tell me that her father was *húsbóndi*; she, her siblings, and her mother did not contradict him. Another woman said her father decided everything for the family. Men's decision making in these families was similar to that of abusive husbands and boyfriends; the men had the final word.

Icelandic national and private identity is closely tied to independence (Pálsson and Durrenberger 1992). To be "independent" (*sjálfstæð/ur*) indexes many different things. Depending on the context, it could mean independence from Danish monarchs, American political domination, or the interference of family members and/or self-sufficiency and self-fulfillment. Independence of the nation and self-determination are tightly bound. Independence may, however, mean different things to men and women. Men position themselves to maintain independence. Women, as mothers who have primary responsibility for the care of their children, simply do not have access to this kind of independence. Financial dependence on men, or the state, and roles as mothers preclude most women from engaging in this search for self-fulfillment, at least until their children reach adolescence. Independence is an upper-class masculinist ideal, from which most women are excluded during their child-bearing years.

The single mothers Kris Kissman (1991) interviewed preferred to be called *sjálfstæð móðir* (independent mother) as opposed to *einstæð móðir* (single mother), signaling their desire for independence from men and from their parents. This is an interesting reworking of "independence" and, perhaps, a plea for the privacy of their families.

Icelandic feminists' use of a discourse of motherhood illustrates the complex relationship between hegemony and counterhegemony. The counterhegemonic must resonate with something that people are familiar with and must be located in familiar positions, which can be transformed and resisted as they are being engaged. Raymond Williams says: "All or nearly all initiatives and contributions, even when they take on manifestly alternative or oppositional forms, are in practice tied to the hegemonic; that the dominant culture, so to say, at one produces and limits its own forms of counter-culture" (1977: 114). Williams identifies hegemony as "saturation of a process of living" "lived identities and relationships" and "practices and expectations" (1977: 10). A major point of contestation is the meaning of Icelandic motherhood, its importance to the nation, the extent to which it is a public activity, and how it should be monitored. Social forces, such as the state, weave feminist counterhegemonic discourses back into dominant discourse. Icelandic feminists are expanding women's political and social positions through engaging dominant discourses about motherhood and women's role in the propagation of the nation. The Women's Alliance uses and then subverts these discourses, arguing that motherhood's centrality to the nation warrants a more public role for women in constructing the nation and increased representation of women in the state apparatus.

State welfare agencies invest resources in ensuring the health and care of infants. Icelandic public health nurses visit new mothers at home, checking their infants' weight, home life, and fitness. The public quality of mothering is thus constructed by the state as an activity subject to public intervention and control. Mothers are the guardians of Icelandic culture and the propagators of the nation. At the same time, they must be monitored. This intervention is also a reflection of the decreasing autonomy of the patriarchal family from state intervention and control, which may be related to the increasing number of female-headed households in recent years.

In its support of single mothers, the state appears to be taking over the role of male wage-earner in a female-headed household. As Kissman's (1991) observation that Icelandic single mothers prefer to be called "independent mothers" illustrates, some women are constructing a new vision of private motherhood, without male intervention. Mothers are insisting upon the independence enjoyed by their children's fathers, although because of limited employment and educational opportunities they do appreciate state financial support.

Domestic Violence and the State

The Women's Shelter argues that domestic violence is a social problem, which should receive attention from state authorities. Domestic violence may involve the intervention of police, activists, families, child welfare workers, the social services, medical personnel, and mental health professionals.

When engaging the police concerning domestic violence, feminist activists are forced into the position of translating their concern from an issue of male domination and privilege to one of criminality and broken laws. The shelter is in the paradoxical position of having to request an organ of public patriarchy to monitor private patriarchy (thus bringing private patriarchy under the public eye). A police official I spoke with lauded the foundation of the Women's Shelter, stating that the shelter was better equipped to handle domestic violence than the police. Because abusive husbands repeat the abuse, it is preferable to enable women to leave their husbands, rather than arrest the husbands for assault. Also, only a woman's departure can end the cycle of violence.

None of the women I interviewed successfully prosecuted their partners; none went to court. Many, however, contacted the police. The women thought that the police were more willing to intervene after they had separated from their husbands, especially when the abuser was an alcoholic. Johanna called the police to remove her ex-husband from her family's new home on numerous occasions, and they assisted her. During the marriage she tried to enlist their help, but was told that there was nothing they could do. As "individuals," men are granted a degree of autonomy by the state, which extends to the use of physical violence against their female partners.

Two other women interacted with the police, with similar results. Alma, Johanna's ex-husband's second wife, found the police to be helpful. Once when her husband came home drunk and disruptive they arrested him. When I visited Alma at her new home, the police arrived to help keep him away from her. Another woman contacted the police when her former boyfriend kicked her in the face. The officers counseled her to reconcile. Through further interactions with the police concerning his abuse, she noted that the police response improved as the period of separation lengthened. The shelter maintains that the police are more likely to intervene to arrest the man if he appears to be drunk. This pattern is a result of convergence of the responding officers' discretion, not of official police protocol.

Although it handles over 500 domestic disturbance calls annually (Lögreglan í Reykjavík, 1990) the Reykjavík police department has no protocol for domestic violence calls. According to the police official I interviewed, each situation is different and requires its own solution. There are, however, many elements which often crosscut these situations. A possible police response appropriate to nearly all domestic violence calls would be to inform the women about the shelter and offer to escort them there. It is likely that many officers do this on their own. The lack of protocol is not an example of "incompetence" on the part of the police department, but it is an illustration of a nationalist emphasis on the individual at the expense of the social, and the individual case at the expense of larger patterns (see Durrenberger, this volume).

Johanna took personal loans from the mayor to feed and clothe her children and to pay for transportation when she left her husband. Formal help from state-supported social services was unavailable to her when she was married. After her divorce, she received financial assistance from the social welfare office for only three months. Aside from the programs directed toward mothers and children, the social welfare office pays shelter residents' daily fees and can arrange for day care once women establish their own households. Social workers are limited in their ability to help women find housing. Women with small children face difficulty securing housing because homeowners and landlords are often unwilling to rent apartments to single mothers. Johanna was fortunate that her divorce settlement included the family apartment.

Iceland's state-supported religion is the Lutheran Church. Couples must receive counseling from a Lutheran minister before they are granted a divorce, regardless of their religious affiliation. If a minister believes reconciliation to be possible, she or he can prolong the divorce process. One minister told me that, if a pastor suggested that an abused woman remain with her husband, the woman would likely follow this advice. The Women's Shelter refers its clients to a sympathetic minister who does not attempt to reconcile women with abusive husbands. The minister Johanna contacted recommended that the court grant her divorce and helped her apply for financial assistance.

Most of the women contacted Iceland's state-run medical system. Nurses at the hospital helped Johanna move her children to her friends' houses when she was giving birth, another extension of a bureaucratic role that she facilitated. Emergency room doctors did not press the women about the origins of their injuries. Men, as individuals, have the right to privacy, which may facilitate their abuse. A notable exception was the young Icelander married to an abusive American soldier. When she contacted an emergency room physician to document her injuries legally, he berated her for marrying a foreign soldier, telling her that the abuse was her fault. The importance of mothering and bearing Icelandic children is again promoted by state authorities. In this case, the foreign husband was not an "individual" whose privacy was to be respected.

State-supported institutions, such as the Women's Shelter, and state agencies direct their efforts to assist women victims, rather than disciplining men perpetrators. Police allow the shelter to respond to domestic violence. Before it was established, women often called upon the police for assistance. They sometimes offered women sanctuary in a jail cell. The contradiction is striking: women victims are, though willingly, placed in jail, and their abusers remain free. There is a degree of continuity between a state that places soldiers' girlfriends in work schools and one that places abused women in shelters.

The state refuses to direct its attention to the behavior of the abusive husband. It is the women who are under examination, who are thus constructed as "deviant," and who are subjected to institutional power. Many of these abusive men are alcoholics. Although it is problematic to suggest that domestic violence is caused by alcoholism (Gordon 1988), the state officials I spoke with recognized a link between domestic violence and alcoholism. They oppose coercing men into treatment because "[alcoholic men] have to really want to change." The state denies its own power of coercion by denying its ability to intervene in private patriarchy. Abused women can be subject to state authority and their husbands free from it through the construction of public motherhood and private patriarchy. According to police, domestic relations between a husband and wife, sexual or violent (or both), are a "private matter." Motherhood and child-rearing is not a private matter, but a public one that involves the propagation of culture, "race," and nation.

The Women's Shelter is a feminist organization, which fights bitter battles for state financial support. It has saved lives. It is also an institution which operates very similarly to other modern state institutions discussed by Michel Foucault (1979). The monastic setting, an isolation where an individual confronts her soul and conscience, structures the shelter. A woman is encouraged to spend her first three days alone to "recover." Contact with her husband is discouraged, and she is not expected to talk with the staff or other residents for her first three days. Each resident gets assigned a case number and is thus individuated. The assignment of numbers is to protect a woman's identity, but it simultaneously provides her with a new identity, that of "abused wife."

In the shelter, a mother's interactions with her children become public. After much deliberation, the staff members will comment upon and criticize a woman's behavior toward her children if they feel the need to intervene. Motherhood is under surveillance.

The shelter staff is aware of the irony that women are institutionalized while their partners are free. Activists are engaged in making domestic violence a public matter and making abusers the objects of state surveillance. In 1991 staff and residents discussed whether the Women's Shelter's location should be disclosed to the public, in order to construct domestic violence as a more public issue and to mitigate the stigma of having been abused by a partner. However, women are institutionalized while their partners remain free, which makes women the targets of power both while they are in their relationships and as they are involved in leaving them.

Families and Friends

Families are another institution which women contact for support. Johanna received more help from her friends than from her family, and most of the women I talked to first enlisted help from their friends when they decided to separate. This pattern challenges Ann Pinson's (1979) argument that people rely less upon connections between friends than upon kin connections. After telling their friends about the abuse, the Icelandic women then disclosed it to their siblings. Finally, the women told their parents.

The Icelandic women expressed shame at their abuse, trying to hide the violence from their parents and siblings. Many blamed themselves for the abuse. Others, such as Johanna, were afraid that their fitness as mothers would be called into question. However, when they decided to leave, they solicited support from their natal families. During their marriages all of the women experienced a distance from their parents and siblings due to their husbands' jealousy or their own attempts to conceal the abuse. Some of the most brutal instances of abuse occurred when the husband thought that his wife stayed too long with a parent or sibling. Johanna dissolved her connection with her parents after they expressed an interest in taking her children from her. If her parents telephoned during the holidays, she told them her marriage was secure and happy.

None of the Icelandic women told their families about the abuse before deciding to leave their husbands. None returned after their families were aware of the abuse. Many of the women I interviewed said they went to the shelter because their families, for financial reasons or due to lack of housing space, were unable to help them and their children. When women ask for assistance from their families, they are in a similar position as when they request assistance from the state. Like the police, the women's families treat domestic violence as a private matter, without interfering with or confronting their kinswomen's husbands.

Interviews

Motherhood and maternal status figure prominently in the lives of the women that I talked to. These women represented their agency in their marriages in terms of their positions as mothers, protecting their children. Johanna and Alma stated that they stayed with their husbands out of concern for their children's welfare. Johanna married her husband because she felt pressure from her parents to have a partner and stayed married to keep custody of her children. Alma resided in the Women's Shelter twice. Having no family in Iceland to help her, she decided to return to her husband after her first stay, fearing that she could not support her children alone. Only two of the women I interviewed had paying jobs. One of these women was a foreigner, whose husband arranged with her employer for her wages to be paid to him. The other five women, like Johanna, were housewives without secondary education and had few opportunities for high-paying work.

The women described their decision to leave in terms of their children's safety. At the beginning of their marriage, Johanna's husband threatened to throw her crying child out the window. After Johanna warned him she would leave if he continued his threats, his behavior improved for a short time. Concerned about her children's safety, she tried to separate after the attempted shooting, but was unable to receive assistance from police and social welfare offices. Alma left her husband the second time out of concern for her children, after he broke their baby's piggy bank for alcohol money. One woman resolved to leave her boyfriend after he woke their child and attempted to take the infant out of their house. Another decided to divorce after one of her husband's blows caused her baby to fall from her arms.

A young woman left her boyfriend after their first child was born, but returned following his threats to kill her. He berated the children and called them names, although he never physically abused them. When her eldest child began asking "whether dad could move away" she contemplated divorce. She moved into the shelter after her husband punched her in the face in front of her children, resolving not to expose them to his violence.

Curiously, Johanna did not discuss her final decision to leave in terms of motherhood, but in terms of a supernatural experience, a voice which told her that her time had come. The woman married to the American soldier left him after he kicked her in the face and badly injured her. Unlike the other women I talked to, it was not clear from her narrative where her child was at the time or how she got the child away from her husband.

Johanna and the woman married to the soldier did not go to the shelter after leaving these relationships and did not discuss their final departures in terms of their maternal roles and children's safety.[3] Perhaps the shelter plays a role in redefining a woman's "self-interest" into concern for her children. This is not to suggest that these two women were not concerned about their children's welfare. I talked to them; they were. But the incident preceding their departure was not discussed with the shelter staff and counselors, who may have focused on how the abuse was affecting the children.

Unlike shelter and state discussions of the mother-child relationship, the women I interviewed discussed their relationship with their children as a private matter. Johanna said that she enjoyed her post-divorce life with her children and that they took care of each other. The women said that after their separations and after finding housing they looked forward to spending time alone with their children, as an autonomous unit. One woman took her children out of the country. They were not talking about their roles as mothers in terms of a public responsibility, but in terms of private fulfillment, perhaps tapping into discourses of independence.

Media Representations

Shelter residents have also made their stories public by giving media interviews. Media representations make domestic violence and private patriarchy subjects of public discussion. One of the most interesting aspects of these interviews is the relationship between the interview material and accompanying pictures and photographs. The counterhegemonic nature of the interviews (as an indictment of private patriarchy, state response, or Icelandic society) is often woven back into dominant, hegemonic representations through the use of images.

The magazine *Vikan* (Jónsdóttir 1991) ran an article which contained interviews with three residents of the Women's Shelter. The first page was a photograph of a bruised woman, shirt torn, bra exposed, eyes averted. There were two accompanying photographs of an abused woman who came forth to be named in an interview. Unexpectedly for the viewer, perhaps, she looked straight into the camera.

The graphic pictures which accompany these articles can shape and reinforce certain ideas about domestic violence which contradict what women themselves are saying. The use of photographs of bruised women posits vast difference between abusive families and private patriarchy. One woman interviewed in the *Vikan* article said that the emotional abuse she endured was as bad as physical violence.

Physical violence was represented in a similar manner in another recent magazine article (Guðlaugsson 1991). Throughout the article are pen-and-ink drawings of a woman running from a man who is trying to hit and grab her. An inset labeled "Emotional Abuse" explained that insults, jealousy, and threats are also forms of domestic violence and can be just as damaging. Accompanying this inset was a picture of a man pinning a woman to the ground.

Interviews with incest victims (*Vikufréttir* 1990) and articles about child sexual abuse (*Helgarblað* 1991) have been accompanied by photographs of beautiful, nude adult women. The images in *Helgarblað* were artistic and could have appeared in a soft-porn magazine. Those in *Vikufréttir* were tawdry. Although the victims discussed in these articles were children, the papers showed their bodies as adult and hence as desirable.

Although many women are coming forward for media interviews, I have not seen a discussion in the papers with Icelandic offenders. One magazine article (Guðlaugsson 1991) carried interviews with British offenders in a wife batterers' treatment program. This omission also creates the impression that domestic violence is not an Icelandic problem. Susan Gal (1991) argues that speech and silence are not necessary monosemic signifiers. By remaining silent about their behavior, abusive Icelandic men cannot defend themselves, but neither do they corroborate the women's stories.

By making their stories public, giving voice to a previously muted group, and exposing private patriarchy to public view, regardless of the content or how they embrace the notion of motherhood, abused women's accounts appearing in newspapers are an inversion of the cultural apparatus (Hannerz 1992). Battered women, once silenced even in their own homes, produce publicly available discourses and meanings. However, the forms these meanings take and their possibilities are constrained by editors, illustrators, and the viewing public.

Conclusion

Elizabeth A. Povinelli (1991) reveals that stories are more than a protest against oppression—they work, they invite people to political action. Johanna began her interview by saying that "it was so unbelievable that no one would think it true." One of the purposes of this essay has been to provide another medium through which abused Icelandic women, whose presence is denied by Icelandic dominant ideology and romanticized foreign accounts (e.g., Chapple 1984), could have their stories heard.

At the heart of the discussions and responses to Icelandic domestic violence is the contestation of public/private motherhood and public/private patriarchy in relation to the state, feminist groups, and abused women trying to leave their partners. Women are the targets of domestic violence and of institutional responses to it. The state encourages (but scrutinizes) motherhood, constructing it as a public function, and treats domestic violence as a personal matter, owing to the privacy afforded to Icelandic men as individuals.

Representations of gender are contested as they are constructed (Gordon 1990; Williams 1977). According to Chandra Talpade Mohanty, agency is possible only when alternate representations are imaginable:

>Resistance is encoded in the practices of remembering, and of writing. Agency is thus figured in the minute, day-to-day practices and struggles of third world women. Coherence of politics and of action comes from a sociality which itself perhaps needs to be rethought. The very practice of remembering against the grain of "public" or hegemonic history, of locating the silences and the struggle to assert knowledge which is outside the parameters of the dominant, suggests a rethinking of sociality itself. (1991: 38–39)

Feminist struggles are located within representations and shared memories, as well as within lived experience (Mohanty 1991).

As Theresa De Lauretis (1987) argues, however, representations are practices. The problem with constructing truly antiessentialist discourse on gender is that feminist representations are no less constructions than dominant ideologies; they simply have a different purpose and cannot be constructed as politically or socially "innocent." These representations have very real consequences in terms of the kinds of resources available to women and the kinds of power they are subjected to.

De Lauretis suggests that gender emerges as a representation through lived experience. Gender is constructed through practices and representations, as opposed to a distributive system of meanings divorced from social action and agency. Gendered social positions can have variable meanings, such as motherhood and the husband/wife relationship. "To assert that the social representation of gender affects its subjective construction and that, vice-versa, the subjective representation of gender—or self-representation—affects its social construction, leaves open a possibility of agency and self-determination at the subjective and even individual level of micropolitical and everyday practices . . ." (De Lauretis 1987: 9). Gender is constructed not only through discourses, but through practices as well. These practices are meaningful. Representing one's self as a gendered subject (male or female, mother or father, married or single) draws upon these meaning effects. Abused women's public telling of their stories may generate more support for motherhood as a private function. However, this formulation of motherhood may serve other interests too—for example, lessen state support for unwed mothers or for the shelter. Icelandic motherhood is both being redefined as a public issue and being defined as a private one. Feminists can appropriate the dominant ideology's public motherhood to garner support for projects like the Women's Shelter and votes for the Women's Alliance. The women I interviewed see motherhood as a private affair, free from the interference of men, and are in the process of defining themselves as independent individuals.

Acknowledgments

This article is based upon field research in Reykjavík in the summer of 1991. I would like to thank the staff and residents of the Women's Shelter, Stígamót, and Johanna for their kind assistance in this project. I am also grateful to the following people for their comments on earlier versions of the article: Ana Alonso, Myrdene Anderson, E. Paul Durrenberger, Deborah Kallmann, Sigríður Dúna Kristmundsdóttir, Carlota McAllister, Gísli Pálsson, Mary Whelan, Margery Wolf, and Hallfríður Þórarinsdóttir. The American-Scandinavian Foundation and the University of Iowa's Anthropology Department generously funded this research.

Notes

1. All names of informants in this paper are pseudonyms. In addition, some details have been changed to protect their identities.

2. Kissman (1991) examines how early mothering has very real effects in terms of women's (and hence children's) financial stability. Despite state programs designed to assist mothers, Icelandic women receive the lowest wages of women in all the Scandinavian countries: 64% of men's earnings. Day care is difficult to obtain, especially for women with male partners. One explanation Kissman provides is that when women have children at a young age their careers and education are interrupted.

3. The woman who was married to an American soldier sought refuge at the shelter after leaving a subsequent abusive Icelandic boyfriend.

PART III NATURE AND NATION

DANIEL E. VASEY

8

PREMODERN AND MODERN
CONSTRUCTIONS OF POPULATION REGIMES

The well-rooted image of Iceland's premodern human ecology is
of a population struggling to survive in an inhospitable environment, pursuing European-style farming too near the Arctic and some
highly active volcanoes, always on the margin of survival. It has been
a "thousand years struggle against ice and fire" (Þórarinsson 1956)
and a "millennium of misery" (Tomasson 1977) in a "beautiful night-
mare" of a place (Griffiths 1969). Though the struggle began with
settlement, conditions supposedly declined with a cooling climate
and the fall of the medieval Commonwealth, and the worst centuries
were the seventeenth and eighteenth, when all hope of victory over
nature and tyranny had for the moment died. Argument has been
less over the extent of the misery than over whether the Danes or the
elements were more to blame (Gunnarsson 1984). Insofar as misery
can be romantic, this is a romantic view of history: the Icelanders,
heroic in the days of the Commonwealth, fell into the depths only to
rise once more.

Granted, the anthropology and historiography of Iceland are on a turn away from romanticism, and when I searched for pithy descriptions of misery the choicest were not only fairly old, but were by foreigners or by Icelanders writing in English for a foreign readership; quite possibly, however, my limited command of Icelandic does not allow me to appreciate its pithiness. A terse but representative quote, this one on the years following the 1602 imposition of the trade monopoly: "The people were on the verge of starvation" (Briem 1945: 58). At more length:

> The Danes humiliated and impoverished them. . . . the Icelanders were tenant farmers, living in wretched poverty. . . . The poor people lived in sod houses, the well and sick together, some with smallpox, and others with leprosy. (Jensen 1954: 29)

> The hopeless struggle for a meagre existence deprived them of all spiritual enterprise and activity, and as time passed they fell into a state of dull shiftlessness and general wretchedness. (Nordal and Kristinsson 1975: 46)

> For centuries the people of Iceland lived in the gloom of fear and insecurity. Like the Horsemen of the Apocalypse there rode across the sky, fire, flood, famine and pestilence. And following in their wake was the sinister spectre of the trade monopoly. (Danielsson 1946: 106)

The idea that the struggle was a losing one goes back to Hannes Finnsson (1796), who wrote in the wake of the great 1784–1785 famine, but was not prompted by it alone. Finnsson and some contemporaries put into the record the story that the Danish government seriously considered removing everyone to Jutland, a tale that, despite its having been discredited some years ago, "seems deeply rooted in the consciousness of Icelanders, many of whom still believe it" (Andresson 1984: 88).

Icelanders and foreigners alike have found redeeming value in the enduring misery. Jóhannes Nordal and Valdimar Kristinsson (1975: xii–xiii) quote Arnold Toynbee approvingly, to the effect that, since nations' challenges and hardship produce triumph, "Would the repetition of the same challenge with twice its Icelandic severity have resulted in a repetition of the Scandinavian response with twice its Icelandic brilliance?" The same theme echos in popular image-building. Some of my informants and acquaintances in the summers of 1969 and 1970, or at least the intellectuals among them, linked past battles against a harsh nature with present resourcefulness.

A population that suffered under such conditions must have had high fertility to compensate for the high mortality. There have been some striking claims. K. Hastrup (1990: 174–175) cites contemporary writers that some sixteenth-century women had twenty to thirty births and that ten to fifteen births were the norm in the eighteenth century, in spite of generally late marriage, and that from so many children most couples raised only two or three to adulthood. Such high fertility would be without precedent. The average Hutterite married woman, in arguably the most fertile population on record, averaged nine live births after marrying in her late teens.

R. F. Tomasson (1976, 1977, 1980), after noting from the 1703 census that many persons never married, takes the view that a substantial number of births must have resulted from sexual relations outside marriage. These he judges to have always been tolerated, arguing mainly on the basis of the behavior of wealthy men in the sagas and creative rethinking of early censuses. For this kind of evidence he has been roundly criticized (Gunnarsson 1980). It may be that Tomasson was under the "influence of the romantic tradition in Icelandic historiography . . ." (Gunnarsson 1980: 21). He also did some ethnography, which seems to have been an influence. On two visits to Iceland a few years before Tomasson's, I was repeatedly told that premarital sexual relations are widely approved or knowingly ignored, and a few persons even offered that toleration was an old practice and one more way that Icelanders are different. A common theme was that young people got it out of their systems and remained faithful in subsequent marriages, unlike, it was implied or stated, Europeans and North Americans. One host told me, apropos of nothing, "You know, there's not a virgin on this island over the age of twelve," while his fifteen-year-old daughter served coffee.

This essay examines the demographic substance behind the myth, in particular the idea that premodern Iceland's mortality was exceptionally high. Although that part of the myth and some others prove to be false, I use "myth" to mean a construction of history and self-image together, whether based on demonstrable historical fact or not, and I do not deny all of the myth's substance. Some detail of the past is needed, it being necessary for a time to step outside the modern theme to examine modern mythology.

Premodern Iceland

"Premodern" here refers to all periods before the last half of the nineteenth century, not to just one, because premodern Iceland was not static. But particular attention here is paid to the eighteenth century and early nineteenth centuries, for which vital data are available.

Over the whole premodern era probably the best candidate for a historical constant is a primary reliance on sedentary pastoralism, widely supplemented by marine and freshwater fishing. Accounts of the first settlers note the importance of access to good pasture. While fishing has produced more food energy or value than farming only in the modern era, fish often made up a large share of exports. Between 1625 and 1785 fish varied from as little as 38% to as much as 82% of the value of exports, at prices when sold abroad, and the balance consisted almost entirely of meat, hides, wool, and other farm products (Gunnarsson 1983a: 34).

Farmers dominated politics. In the seventeenth and eighteenth centuries only a handful of officials were wholly on salary. Important Icelanders usually held positions of authority in the church or the state apparatus, but were farmers too.

After the establishment of Norwegian rule ca. 1280 the loose association of chieftains that had controlled medieval Iceland was replaced by royal rule and a state bureaucracy whose structure persisted with few changes into the nineteenth century. Officials included sheriffs (*sýslumenn*) and civil district officers (*hreppstjórar*) and several lesser grades. There was already a church hierarchy, Catholic until ca. 1536, then Lutheran.

Wealth and power were in the same hands and highly concentrated. A few families owned most farms other than those in church hands, which were about 32% of all farms in 1695 (Lárusson 1967: 60). The families that owned most private land were also the usual fief-holders of church and crown lands (Gunnarsson 1983a: 17) and tended to occupy the top positions available to Icelanders in the state and church hierarchies.

Next down the social ladder, apart from a few small land-owning farmers, were tenant farmers. These had probably become more numerous toward the close of the medieval era (McGovern et al. 1988; Durrenberger 1992a: 39) and occupied 96% of farms in 1695, 90% in 1800 (Lárusson 1967). Tenure tended to be insecure. Only 15% of

tenants had contractual life tenancy in 1829 (Jónsson 1988: 105).
Most leases were renewed annually around 1800 (Lárusson 1967).

Main, or tax-assessed, farms (*heimajarðir*), whether owner-
operated or rented, were as a rule ranked above two kinds of dependent households enterprises: dependent farms (*hjáleigur*), and cottages (*kot*) that were not self-sufficient farms. This principle probably
held most of the time, though *hjáleigur* were occasionally more prosperous than many *heimajarðir*, and some *kot* may have kept the name
after becoming independent farms. Local officials controlled the number of cottages. Some of the country's few artisans were cottagers,
some farmers.

Fishing houses were common enough in places, most notably in
Gullbringa county west of modern Reykjavík and on the Snæfellsnes
peninsula. These too were on land controlled by a main farm, and the
farmers exercised some control over their numbers and operation. Inshore fisheries had long been considered the property of farms on the
adjacent shore; where there were no fishing households, the work
was done by persons from the farm household or by seasonal workers hired from other, often distant, farms.

Farmers headed most households. Cottagers, who were mostly
day-laborers or employed in fishing (including a few women in
fishing-related work), headed many others.[1] House-folk (*húsfólk*),
most of them single or widowed, were about 1 of every 100 persons
in the censuses. They were supposedly allowed to form households
even though they lacked the means to start a farm, but were in practice a varied lot. Some were day-laborers or fishers, often with some
livestock, in which case they may have differed from cottagers mostly
in name and relation to the main household. Others were servants in
the main household or paupers on the poor rolls or lived on savings.

Boarders filled most of the remaining occupational roles. Servants were the most numerous. A few artisans boarded. *Lausamenn*
were boarders who paid rent to the householder and worked for a
freely negotiated salary—whether with the same householder or
another—unlike servants, who worked on annual contracts whose
terms were fixed by law. Ordinarily *lausamenn* obtained better pay
than did servants, but there was a means requirement, the equivalent
of ten cows in 1720 (Gunnarsson 1983a: 22–23, 27), a standard that
some farmers could not have met. A statute in effect from 1783 to
1865, a measure previously sought by the farmer leadership but

resisted by the Danish crown, required all persons who were not householders to enter service, thus abolishing the freely bargaining *lausamenn.*

Paupers were fairly numerous, principally, but not only, the elderly and orphans. Most paupers were boarded in households, some supported by the private "alms" of the householder or by parish funds, but by the eighteenth century the civil districts (*hreppar*) bore most of the responsibility, and a large share of taxes went for this purpose.

Fosterage and adoption were very common. The Icelandic terms for the children varied (e.g., *fósturbarn, tökubarn, uppeldis barn*) and no one term consistently denotes one specific relationship with the householders (Gunnlaugsson 1993: 124–125).

The modal household included married householders, children, one or two servants, and possibly a foster child or pauper. The great majority of households were variations on this structure. Because of a high rate of remarriage, householders were often half-parents of one or more sets of children. The law required that one child be sent out into service at age sixteen, and in practice most left before age twenty (Guttormsson 1983: 99–102; Gunnlaugsson 1988: 60), though among the many households headed by elderly persons, whether couples or widowed, one finds quite a few in which grown children remained as servants. In farming districts most households, even among cottagers, included servants, but these were somewhat less general in fishing households. Live-in relatives were fairly common, most often widowed parents or single siblings of one or both householders, while married parents, siblings, and children were less common. Wealthy households tended to include both larger numbers of servants, sometimes a dozen or more, and several foster children and paupers.

There were single-person households, though any estimate of their numbers depends on interpretation of the status of house-folk. Official household counts have placed all house-folk, many of which were single, in separate households, a practice which lowers mean household size, probably misleadingly. There is good reason to doubt that all were really independent. Often they lived in outhouses of the main house of a farm. Some who were alone were described in the censuses as sick and incapable (*veik og vanfær*), while others were in their nineties.

Eighteenth-century Iceland, though subject to European influences, was a society under tight controls. A trade monopoly, granted by the crown in 1602, operated under prices and terms fixed in Copenhagen, with the effect of discouraging innovation in either trade or production (Gunnarsson 1983a). Internal trade was largely by barter, trade over any distance was officially discouraged, and there were no full-time Icelandic merchants. Inland farms obtained fish more by letting out servants to work in the fisheries than by trading.

The Modernization Process

The *ancien régime* of Iceland, already an anachronism in several respects by the late eighteenth century, came under mounting pressure for change in the nineteenth. The old farmer elite exercised for the most part a profoundly conservative influence. Change came slowly, from grass-roots action, a few reformers, and often the intervention of the Danish crown.

Even in the eighteenth century farmers had expressed concern that the development of fishing would draw away labor. District councils along the coast limited inmigration and the building of new cottages, often voicing fears of increased demands for poor relief. There was resistance to technical innovations in fishing that were already in use elsewhere in the North Atlantic. Some courts banned lines with multiple hooks and the use of worms as bait (Gunnarsson 1983a: 69). After the Royal Trade Company tried decked fishing boats in Faxaflói in the period 1776–1787, landed Icelandic interests successfully fought the venture and brought it to an end (Magnússon 1985: 49–50).

Change was piecemeal for most of the nineteenth century. In agriculture tenancy declined slowly, to 83% in 1829 (Jonsson 1988) and 70% in 1900 (Gunnlaugsson and Guttormsson n.d.). Magnús Magnússon (1985: 74) maintains that the only important technical innovation of the century was the adoption of the Scots scythe during the 1860s. However, the number of sheep in 1851 was 1.12 times that in 1820, while sheep and horses were 1.85 and 1.41 as many, respectively (calculated from Kristjánsson and Gunnlaugsson 1990: 31). The extra animals had to be fed, and many yield-raising techniques, such as small-scale drainage and plowing homefields, had long been known, but were underutilized. Good national data series on hay production, which only begin in the 1880s, show a steady rise from the outset.

Fishing grew more impressively. Combined exports of salt fish and dried fish rose 4.5 times from 1816 to 1840 (Magnússon 1985: 67).

Yet resistance to the development of a specialized fishing industry and fishing towns had to be overcome. The increase in production was at first due to greater or more efficient use of the old open rowboats (Magnússon 1985: 85). Decked sailing vessels finally took over late in the century, followed in the next century by motorboats and steam trawlers.

The crown helped promote the growth of internal trade, by extending trading rights first to all Danish subjects, including Icelanders, in 1787, then to foreigners in 1854. At the end of the century commercial centers, ranging from banks and shipping companies in Reykjavík to the ubiquitous rural cooperatives, began their rapid growth, despite an economic depression in the 1880s.

Population, under 50,000 from 1707 to the 1820s, reached 58,558 in 1845, 72,445 in 1880, 85,183 in 1910 (despite unprecedented large-scale emigration in 1880–1900), and 121,474 in 1940 (Hagstofa Íslands 1992: 21). The development of fishing and commerce combined with population growth to spur the movement of people to coastal towns and to Reykjavík. The more modern, highly capitalized forms of fishing were beyond the means of most coastal farmers, so that the modernization of fishing necessitated the growth of specialized fishing villages. In the last decades of the nineteenth century migration simply overwhelmed the efforts of the parliament and local councils to conserve a society dominated by farming households (Magnússon 1985; Gunnlaugsson 1988; Pálsson 1991).

The conservatives did not give up easily. About the middle of the century and for several decades thereafter there was a fusion of liberal ideals of nationhood and extreme social conservatism (Hálfdanarson 1991). There was also determined rear-guard resistance not only to the development of fishing, but also to changes in the terms and conditions of labor (Magnússon 1985; Sigurðardóttir 1985; Magnússon 1989), women's movements and roles (Kristmundsdóttir 1989), and household formation and structure (Gunnlaugsson 1984, 1988).

Sources and Methods

The Iceland Database, source of many of the data in this paper, holds records of births, marriages, and deaths from those parish registers that survive in the collection of the Genealogical Society of Utah, microfilm copies made in 1953 from the original registers in the Icelandic National Archives, along with selected censuses from the same source. D. E. Vasey (1991, n.d.) describes in more detail the database and its applications.

In this essay the "reconstruction sample" refers to the reconstructed reproductive histories of 1,215 couples married between 1770 and 1792, out of 3,680 marriages over that period in the database. The other 2,465 were omitted because of missing years in a register where a couple was living or inability to establish the woman's age or the end of her period at risk of pregnancy.

Instructions on each page of the forms used in the 1801 census were to round all ages upward to the nearest year, while most pastors rounded ages at death downward, but the effect of possible inconsistencies had to be weighed. Two entries in the 1801 census were of fractional ages less than one, a sure sign that instructions were not followed, and two were "nýfædd," but these are rare exceptions next to the 1608 entries of "1." Some pastors indicated they rounded ages at death upward (e.g., "a 3e ar"), raising the question of how many did so without so indicating. However, the distribution of ages at death of two years or less is consistent with rounding down, many ages of young children are in days, months, or years, and reconstruction work has generally found that older ages are rounded down.

Ages at death other than years, months, weeks, or days were numerous enough to pose some problems of estimation. Blank age entries, of which there were only 8 (0.02%) in the 1801 census, were troublesome in the death records. Of the 62,215 deaths in the database (not including 1,916 known stillbirths) for the years 1800–1849, age was blank in 1,817 (2.9%). Descriptive ages at death were common in the death records. There were 1,929 *ungbarn* (young child) (3.1%), 288 *nýfædd* (newborn) (0.5%), 621 *barn* (child) (1.0%), 406 *kona* or *maður* (woman or man) (0.7%), 158 *bóndi* (farmer) (0.3%), 59 *piltur* or *stúlka* (boy or girl) (0.1%), 45 *gamall* or *kerling* (old man or woman) (0.1%), and 23 miscellaneous other descriptions (0.03%). The principle that guided estimation of these ages, where some error was inevitable, was to err on the low side.

In the computation of age-specific mortality rates and life expectancies it was only necessary to place age at death within the age intervals of an abridged life table (table 2). Fractional ages were rounded down. *Ungbarn* and *nýfædd* became 0. Basing estimation on experience with the reconstruction sample, three-quarters of the *barn* ages became 0, and one-quarter became 1–4. *Kona, maður,* and *bóndi* were prorated (using the distribution of deaths at known ages) from 25–29 on, *piltur* and *stúlka* from 1–4 to 15–19, and *gamall* and *kerling* from 50–54 on. Exceptionally, *barn, piltur,* and *stúlka* were always recorded as age 0 if no name of the deceased was given or if both parents' names were given, both practices that, where the death and birth records could be linked, have been found only in records of infant deaths. Lastly, blank ages were prorated over all age intervals on the basis of the known ages at death and those estimated from descriptive ages.

In estimating mean ages at death, blanks were disregarded. Fractional ages were used as is. *Nýfædd* became 0, *ungbarn* 0.2, *barn* 0.5, *kona, maður,* and *bóndi* 35, *piltur* and *stúlka* 16, and *gamall* or *kerling* 60. Anonymous *barn, piltur,* and *stúlka* entries, and those with both parents listed, were again put at 0. The error in these estimated means should tend to be on the low side.

Premodern Population Regimes

Icelanders in the early nineteenth century, once past infancy, had life expectancies that compare favorably with those of contemporary European populations. Several independent computations end in that same finding.

Table 1 lists age-specific mortality rates based upon the "1801" census and 1801–1802 mortality. The census forms bear the date "1. Febr. 1801" and are supposed to represent the population at that

Table 1 Annual Age-Specific Mortality Rates, 1801–1802 (per thousand)

Age Interval	Males	Females	Both Sexes	Age Interval	Males	Females	Both Sexes
0	227.2	235.2	231.2	40–44	19.6	13.1	16.1
1–4	17.0	18.4	17.7	45–49	22.3	7.6	13.4
5–9	8.3	8.2	8.2	50–54	21.7	12.9	16.6
10–14	9.3	6.5	7.9	55–59	22.7	19.7	20.9
15–19	9.1	6.3	7.7	60–64	42.6	28.4	35.1
20–24	8.4	4.4	6.4	65–69	58.5	27.6	39.1
25–29	11.9	6.4	9.2	70–74	63.3	58.6	60.2
30–34	10.6	10.0	10.3	75–79	98.7	108.6	104.9
35–39	10.6	11.0	10.8	80+	226.1	192.3	204.3

Table 2   Abridged Life Table, 1801–1802

Age Interval	Probability of Dying in Interval	No. of Survivors at Start of Interval	Life Expectancy at Start of Interval
0	.2260	100,000	41.25
1–4	.0552	77,400	52.15
5–9	.0402	73,127	51.08
10–14	.0387	70,187	48.12
15–19	.0378	67,471	44.96
20–24	.0324	64,921	41.62
25–29	.0435	62,818	37.93
30–34	.0502	60,085	34.55
35–39	.0526	57,069	31.24
40–44	.0774	54,067	27.84
45–49	.0648	49,882	24.96
50–54	.0797	46,650	21.54
55–59	.0993	42,932	18.16
60–64	.1609	38,669	14.89
65–69	.1781	32,447	12.27
70–74	.2616	26,668	9.38
75–79	.4155	19,692	6.82
80+	1.0000	11,510	4.89

time, but a few pastors wrote in a later effective date and the census lists persons born as late as December 1801. Signature dates are mostly in 1802, some as late as December. It was accordingly decided to use 1801 and 1802 deaths. Only census data from those parishes for which 1801 and 1802 death records are available enter into the computations. Their 1801 census population was 31,834, 67.4% of the national population.

Table 2 is the abridged life table, both sexes combined, based on the age-specific mortality rates from table 1. The method of computing probabilities of dying (Chiang 1984: 137–147) takes into account estimated distributions of deaths within the various age intervals.

Taken together, 1801 and 1802 are probably fairly representative of runs of years falling between major mortality crises in Iceland. The year 1801 was at the end of the particularly good period of the 1790s,

Table 3   Mean Age at Death by Decade, 1800 to 1849

| | | | Mean Age at Death | | |
| | | | | | Both |
Years	N	N < 10	Males	Females	Sexes
1800–1809	8187	3520 inclusive	28.17	35.70	31.92
		< 10 excluded	51.86	58.06	55.22
		< 20 excluded	55.69	61.25	58.69
		< 30 excluded	59.93	63.89	62.15
		< 40 excluded	64.99	68.25	66.86
		(N < 10 / Births = .305)			
1810–1819	7816	2721 inclusive	33.05	41.08	37.11
		< 10 excluded	49.81	55.94	37.11
		< 20 excluded	54.72	59.50	57.36
		< 30 excluded	59.87	63.29	61.81
		< 40 excluded	63.74	67.29	65.76
		(N < 10 / Births = .280)			
1820–1829	13010	6534 inclusive			26.68
		< 10 excluded			52.56
		< 20 excluded			56.49
		< 30 excluded			61.25
		< 40 excluded			65.88
		(N < 10 / Births = .502)			
1830–1839	20583	7575 inclusive			27.61
		< 10 excluded			54.95
		< 20 excluded			57.49
		< 30 excluded			60.74
		< 40 excluded			65.72
		(N < 10 / Births = .368)			
1840–1849	18364	7457 inclusive			29.70
		< 10 excluded			53.94
		< 20 excluded			57.14
		< 30 excluded			60.59
		< 40 excluded			64.28
		(N < 10 / Births = .406)			

Note: Virtually all parish registers have survived from 1819 on, but coverage is less for the decades 1800–1809 and 1810–1819.

while 1802 began a decline. Deaths in 1801 in all reporting parishes numbered 735, following a toll of 736 in 1800. The crude death rate was close to that of the 1790s and 1800, but 1801–1802 just preceded the worst mortality crisis since the 1784–1785 famine. Deaths rose to 940 in 1802 and 1,504 in 1803, the worst year since the 1784–1785 famine, before falling again to 1,182 in 1804 and 981 in 1805.

Mean age at death is an alternative estimate of life expectancy, one that would be unbiased by underreporting evenly spread across all ages. In a steady state population, mean age at death equals life expectancy at birth. It equals life expectancy at age x if deaths before age x are excluded. However, age structures change in real populations, resulting in a biased estimate of mean age at death.

Much of the wide variation in decadal inclusive mean ages at death is presumably due to variation in the birth rate. Birth cohorts varied greatly in size, but tended to be high after 1820, as the population began a steady natural increase. In a growing population with high infant and child mortality, the high birth rate results in an elevated and misleading number of deaths of young children. The 1800–1809 population had disproportionately large numbers of children past infancy, a consequence of a birth boom during the late 1780s and the 1790s, when population recovered from the losses of the 1784–1785 famine. The decade 1810–1819 was a hard one, with several years of elevated mortality, and opportunities to obtain a farm and marry were probably few for persons of the postfamine baby boom then reaching adulthood, but in the next decade this same large cohort would have been marrying in considerable numbers, aided by the dying off or retirement of their parents' generation, who had obtained farms in the wake of the famine.

The increase after 1820 in the ratio of deaths under age 10 to births ($N < 10$/Births in table 3) may also indicate improved reporting of infant and child deaths, since much of the procedure for preparing parish registers was standardized after 1816. Once deaths of persons under ten are excluded, the effect of changing age structure on mean ages at death appears to have been small, despite the aging of birth cohorts of greatly varying size. If we therefore put aside the question of age structure stability, we find that mean ages at death indicate life expectancies from age ten on that are slightly less than those of the 1801–1802 life table (table 4).

How much the remaining discrepancies (A–B) are due to underreporting of deaths in 1801–1802, the effect of population growth, or

Table 4   Estimated Life Expectancies at Selected Ages

At Age	A 1801–1802 Life Table	B 1800–1809 Death Records	A – B
0	41.25	31.92	9.33
10	48.12	45.22	2.90
20	41.62	38.69	2.93
30	34.55	32.15	2.40
40	27.84	26.86	0.98

heightened mortality after 1802 is unknown. Rounding downward of ages at death, if the pastors did this consistently, would account for something less than a half-year of the discrepancy.

By either method of computation, Icelandic life expectancies were not too bad for the time.

Age-specific mortalities and life expectancies of eighteenth-century Iceland are not yet available, but crude death rates were fairly close throughout Finland and Scandinavia from 1735 to 1800, a long enough period that it would tend to smooth the effect of fluctuations in age structure. Crude rates per thousand were 28.2 in Iceland, 28.1 in Sweden, 28.1 in Denmark, 28.7 in Finland, and 26.2 in Norway (Gille 1949–1950: 33).

Several independent estimates are available of first-year mortality in eighteenth-century Iceland, and most are comparable to that in table 1. Loftur Guttormsson (1983: 147) has reconstructed rates per thousand of 218–299 (Möðruvallaklaustur, Eyjafjörður county, 1716–1730), 228–272 (Reykholt, Borgarfjörður county, 1732–1747), and 200–255 (Mosfell, Árnes county, 1754–1774). Gísli Gunnarsson (1983b: 15) has estimated a much higher rate, 370, from 1770 to 1800, but this period includes some mortality crises, such as the 1784–1785 famine, which took an extreme toll of infants (Hálfdanarson 1984; Vasey 1991).

Putting aside possible underreporting, a defensible estimate of first-year mortality is 250 per thousand in most years, possibly 300 in the longer term, when mortality crises are taken into account. Higher

Table 5   Life Expectancies in Early Modern Northern Europe

At Age	Britain[a] (ducal families) 1680–1729	1730–1779	France[b] 1700–1770	Sweden[c] 1751–1800	Iceland Early 19th Century	England[d] 1800–1809	France[d] 1800–1809	Sweden[d] 1800–1809
0	33.3	46.5	28.8	36.1	31.9–41.3	37.3	33.9	36.5
10			40.8	45.7	45.2–48.1			
20	32.7	40.6	34.3	38.6	38.7–41.6			
30			28.5	31.8	32.2–34.6			
40	24.7	26.8	22.9	25.1	26.9–27.8			

[a]Hollingsworth (1965: 358–361). The original estimates are for males and females separately, which have been averaged: $(m + f) / 2$.

[b]Duvillard (orig. 1806), in Bourgeois-Pichat 1965: 494.

[c]Calculated from survivorship tables for males and females (Gille 1949–1950: 36). Male and female life expectancies have been averaged. Livi-Bacci (1992: 109) offers a life expectancy at birth of 37.3 for the same years.

[d]Livi-Bacci (1992: 109).

rates, like those that might result from a possible correction for underreporting of infant deaths, would of course lower life expectancy at birth, but not life expectancy at later ages.

Some comparative first-year mortality rates are 204 per thousand in Sweden 1751–1800 (Gille 1949–1950: 36), 370 in Sweden-Finland 1755–1775 (ibid.: 35), and 250 in France "about 1770" and 207 between 1805 and 1807 (Bourgeois-Pichat 1965: 495). A cohort study of British ducal families, in which the influence of underreporting is probably minimal, found that 200 per thousand children born 1730–1779 died before age five and that the rate had been over 300 in previous centuries (Hollingsworth 1965: 360).

That the Icelanders after their first year of life fared well may surprise anyone familiar with the abundant evidence of widespread poverty and, as has often been pointed out, special disease risks. They were among the last Europeans to suffer leprosy in appreciable numbers. Scurvy was an illness mainly of sailors, Icelanders, and others

living near the Arctic. Chronic and acute respiratory illnesses thrived
in the close quarters of Icelandic houses. But overlooked, to my
knowledge, are the historic advantages of being an Icelander.

Most households would have had access to water free from upstream contamination by human feces. Most farms had their backs to
an uninhabited slope, from which a stream usually flowed. Even
where farms fronted a larger stream, this was typically fast-flowing,
farms upstream were few, and there were alternative water sources
near at hand. In Europe fecally transmitted diseases were major kill-
ers. In Sweden typhoid fever killed 0.25% of the population in "normal" years between 1749 and 1800 (Gille 1949–1950: 48), more than
smallpox, which was endemic in much of the country. Dysentery,
which is fecally transmitted, also took a considerable toll.

Insect-transmitted diseases were probably less of a problem in
Iceland than in Europe. Jón Espólín's annals record two plague epidemics, in 1402–1404 and again in the 1490s; mortality in the first
was said to be as severe as that of the Black Death in Europe (Steffensen 1975: 321–339), although Kristín Bjarnadóttir (1986) has given
some reasons to doubt the epidemic was in fact due to *B. pestis*. In any
event the plague came earlier to Europe, then more frequently and
longer. A plague attack confers immunity for only a few years; the
cycle of transmission between rats and people can soon be repeated.
Major epidemics repeatedly swept Europe after the Black Death and
before the end of the fourteenth century (Livi-Bacci 1992: 46–47).
By the seventeenth century it had become in the main an urban disease, but still lethal. Even as plague slowly abated in Europe, typhus
made its appearance or increased noticeably, but not to my knowledge in Iceland.

Smallpox and measles were common to Iceland and Europe; they
were endemic in most of Europe, epidemic in thinly populated fringe
areas of Europe and in Iceland. European adults who escaped smallpox until adulthood were most unusual—hence some contemporary
wonder that England's Elizabeth I had done so. In Iceland smallpox
epidemics were typically twenty to thirty-five years apart (Steffensen
1975: 275–320, 1977). The effect of age on smallpox mortality is
controversial, but certainly the epidemic nature of the disease in Iceland, for all the horror of its visitations, allowed many to reach adulthood before being exposed.

Childbirth deaths were uncommon in late-eighteenth-century

Iceland. Of the 5,998 births in the reconstruction sample, 24 were followed within thirty days by the mother's death (4.0 per thousand), an extraordinarily low rate in a preindustrial population. Among European royal families between 1600 and 1799, the rate of mortality from puerperal causes was 19.4 per thousand births (Peller 1965: 96).

Population Regulation

Famine mortality was a weaker mechanism of population regulation than the raw numbers lost would suggest. Excess mortality in the great famine of 1784–1785 was about 24% of the population, but about half as great among women aged ten to thirty-nine (Vasey 1991), who were in their prime childbearing years or would be within the next fifteen years.

Epidemics, which tended to fell young persons who lacked immunity from previous epidemics, must have had a more lasting effect on population, but evidence that hunger acted through disease to regulate population is weak (Vasey 1991). For instance, the 1786–1787 smallpox epidemic, which arrived on the heels of the great famine, was exceptionally mild (Vasey 1991).

Nuptiality and fertility, not mortality, were the variables that most effectively responded to changing population pressure (Guttormsson 1983: 110–111; Gunnlaugsson 1988: 28–29). Although the law did not absolutely bar any persons from marrying after 1834, and then only paupers (Björnsson 1971: 74–75), regulations and customs enforced by pastors and civil authorities had long restricted marriage mainly to householders (Gunnlaugsson 1988: 92–107). This alone would have tended to stabilize population in the long term. The historic pattern seems to have been one of fluctuating pressure and marriage opportunity, especially in response to mortality crises. Crude birth rates typically rose after mortality crises, usually following a lag of several years (Tomasson 1977, 1980; Jackson 1982).

Mortality in the 1784–1785 famine was high among female householders past forty, and over the next decade young women tended to fill vacant householder niches. Study of parishes for which church censuses were available before and after the famine, an analysis reported in detail in another essay in preparation, found that decreased age of married householders accounts for about 90% of the increase in reported births.[2]

Icelandic marital fertility was among the highest reported for any past or present population, so that the potential for rapid population growth was always there, but ordinarily late marriage and celibacy sharply curbed births. Women in continuous sexual unions from age 15 to 49 should have averaged 12.24 live births, judging from age-specific marital fertility rates in the reconstruction sample. Loftur Guttormsson's (1983: 134) 1856–1860 age-specific marital fertility rates, which are only given from 20–24 to 40–44, are slightly higher. Among the 1,215 couples in the reconstruction sample, the woman's mean age at birth was 28.87 and the couple's mean number of live births was 4.94. Holding the women's age at first marriage constant, removing the factor of widowhood would have raised the mean number of live births to only 5.97, still less than half the potential number. The 1703 census identifies 41.9% of women 40–49 as *ógift* (literally, unmarried, but supposed to mean those who had never married). The 1801 census identifies 25.7% in the same age interval (Guttormsson 1983: 114); a few of the women this census calls *ógift* have turned out to be elderly widows.

The 1703 census reveals heavy population pressure, a relative contrast to the years that followed the 1784–1785 famine. It counted just over 50,000, a level that would not be reached again until the 1820s. The census followed a long run of hard years in the 1690s and was commissioned in part because of official concern over conditions. Not only was celibacy high, but only 27.8% of women ages 15–49 were currently married, fewer than in any later censuses (Gunnarsson 1980: 7), and probably too few to have maintained population numbers (Hajnal 1965: 137–138) in the absence of large numbers of illegitimate births.

Modern Population Regimes

Iceland, like Europe, experienced a long demographic transition, but Icelandic fertility was the highest in Europe throughout much of the twentieth century. This does not necessarily mean that the transition began late in Iceland. By one measure, a 10% drop in marital fertility, a lasting fertility decline began between 1890 and 1910 in 53% of a large sample of European populations, or 59% if French populations (well known for early fertility decline) are excluded (Coale and Treadway 1986: 37–39). Icelandic crude birth rates, plotted in five-year averages (Gunnlaugsson 1988: 18), began a steady decline from 1860, albeit from rates slightly above long-term averages. Rates averaged

33.7 per thousand over the whole of the nineteenth century, and 31.0 in the last decade, but fell to 27.8 in the decade 1901–1910 and 26.5 between 1911 and 1920 (after Tomasson 1980: 65). Since the ratio of illegitimate births to all births was declining from a peak around 1780, and nuptiality was increasing (Gunnarsson 1980: 8, 22; Gunnlaugsson 1988: 43), it is very likely that the Icelandic marital fertility decline had reached 10% by 1910, probably earlier.

Crude death rates did not begin a decisive downward turn until after 1870, at which time, owing to previous improvement in much of Europe, Iceland's mortality did compare unfavorably. Particularly striking is the persistence of high infant mortality, which was 366.8 per thousand in 1838–1840, 341.7 in 1841–1850, and 251.9 in 1861–1870 (Tomasson 1980: 67; see also Heiðdal 1988: 66). Not only were these rates higher than any reported in Europe during this period (Mitchell 1975: 39–44), but they are higher than most earlier Icelandic rates, again raising the possibility of greater underreporting before 1820.

The steady rise of population that began about 1820 begs explanation. By 1850 population had risen by a quarter. There were no major mortality crises during the period, a proposed explanation (Magnússon 1985: 36–37), but an unsatisfactory one, since long-term crude death rates were still high. By this time the old system of fertility regulation was showing signs of weakening. Not that restrictions on marriage were as yet gone. Efforts to tighten restrictions, whether by law or by other means, persisted through much of the nineteenth century, and from 1860 to 1880 nuptiality was at a low ebb, as a slack economy provided few opportunities to meet the old requisites for marriage (Gunnlaugsson 1988).

By the mid-century farmers and many among the clergy were registering complaints about poor and "lazy" persons marrying, protests heard on the floor of parliament and widely voiced in letters and journals. It appears from work with the censuses that young married nonhouseholders were on the increase by 1845, but still the exception. The increase is especially evident in the northeastern part of the country, roughly from Suður-Þingey county to Suður-Múli county, and still more in 1845, when both married servants and married children of householders seem to have contributed. Gísli Gunnlaugsson (1988: 71–72) found only 17 "stem" families out of 289 households in a sample of seven parishes in the 1801 census, but they were three out of 17 in Skútustaðir, Suður-Þingey county.

Gísli Gunnarsson (1980) has charted the progress of illegitimacy from 1770 to 1800 and 1827 to 1978. Data for the eighteenth century were only from the Skalhólt bishopric, but data from the Hólar bishopric from 1791 to 1796 are comparable (1980: 22). The illegitimacy ratio (that is, the percentage of all births that were illegitimate) was 9.6 between 1770 and 1800 and 14.5 between 1830 and 1870 (1980: 23). Nineteenth-century observers held that the rise in illegitimacy began even before 1802, about 1787, "as the trade became freer," according to the nineteenth-century observer Arnljótur Ólafsson (Gunnarsson 1980: 28). The illegitimate fertility rate (the rate of illegitimate births among unmarried women of fertile age) reached a peak between 1866 and 1875 (1980: 32). The illegitimacy ratio continued to rise until the early 1880s, however, because the decline of nuptiality lowered legitimate fertility.

There is a need for longitudinal study of Icelandic illegitimacy. One of the problems in dealing with it is to distinguish births to couples who subsequently married from other types. In the reconstruction sample no less than 42.4% of the women gave birth before marriage or within eight months afterward, but only 8.3% had apparently been pregnant more than a year before marriage, 2.3% more than two years before. These births were nearly 8% of all births to these women, close to Gunnarsson's (1980: 23) estimate of the illegitimacy ratio (9.6%) for roughly the same period, but, since a majority were after marriage, it is unlikely that all were registered as illegitimate.

The great increase in the illegitimacy ratio after 1930, which for several decades was distinctly higher than in the rest of Europe for the first time on record (Gunnarsson 1980: 23), was due to the number of couples having one or more births before marrying and to a slow decline in marital fertility. For example, in 1961–1964 the illegitimacy ratio in Akranes was 25.8%, close to the national figure, but only 9.7% of live births were to parents who were not married, engaged, or cohabiting and likely to be married later (Björnsson 1971). In the remainder, the parents were cohabiting or the baptism was on the day of their marriage. Further study of a household sample found that cohabitation nearly always followed engagement. The practice of marrying on the day of the baptism of a child, usually the first, had largely developed since World War II. Some informants in 1969 and 1970 presented this pattern of reproduction and marriage to me as traditional.

Conclusion

The old myth of Iceland's historical demography and human ecology is in many respects understandable without deconstruction. It has a basis in fact. There was struggle and, though the Icelandic misery was less lethal than many have claimed, it was real. No one should dispute the hardships imposed by the sub-Arctic climate and shifting crust and the cold, damp houses, nor that premodern Iceland was impoverished in cash and disposable goods in comparison with much of Europe. The nationalist tradition of Icelandic historiography that fostered the image of past and contemporary misery dates from the middle and late nineteenth century (Pálsson and Durrenberger 1989), when intellectuals were constructing romantic myths of one sort or another throughout Europe (Hobsbawm 1983a, 1983b), but coincidentally also the one time that Icelandic mortality was demonstrably high in comparison with that of Western and Northern Europe. The findings of this essay do not really challenge the image of a triumph over daunting odds, since the unexceptional mortality of premodern Icelanders could be taken as a token of their success.

The findings do challenge much of the construction of otherness that comes from the romantic tradition (Pálsson and Durrenberger 1989). Iceland's demographic regimes, from the time of the 1703 census to the present day, are unmistakably European. To the degree that they are distinctive—and they are—it is within European parameters. When fertility was high in Europe and marriage came late or, for some, never, Icelandic fertility was particularly high, marriage particularly late, and the number of unmarried persons particularly high. In these respects the best parallel to eighteenth-century or early-nineteenth-century Iceland is rural Ireland in the late nineteenth century (Walsh 1970), except that Iceland lacked the religious celibates found in Ireland.

Other peasantries bore their own crosses, and there are tradeoffs in any comparison. If the Icelanders had a less favorable natural environment than, say, peasants of Tokugawa Japan, and if Iceland's system of rents was not always equitable, the Japanese had to contend with sharecropping arrangements that could take as much as 70% of their crop and were as a matter of policy designed to provide only the bare minimum subsistence (Hane 1982: 5–110). If it were necessary to name a historic European peasantry with the worst burden imposed by combined nature and inhumanity, it would perhaps be that

of Russia (Blum 1961), where life expectancy at birth was still only
27.7 in 1880 (Livi-Bacci 1992: 109).

Acknowledgments

This research has been supported by National Science Foundation Grants
BNS-8820264 and OPP-9222995 and has been made possible by the exchange of machine-readable data with the Genealogical Society of Utah.
The author thanks editors Gísli Pálsson and Paul Durrenberger and other
participants at the Iowa conference for their useful comments. Responsibility for error or misinterpretation is the author's alone, and opinions
expressed are not necessarily those of any of the above-mentioned organizations or persons.

Notes

1. Under cottagers are included the heads of *tómthús* and *þurrabúð*,
which were usually engaged in fishing, appear to have had a legal status
similar to that of cottages, and were usually attached to a main farm.

2. These parishes are Vatnsfjörður and Kirkjubólsþing, Norður-Ísa-
fjörður county; Árnes in Trékyllisvík, Fell-Tröllatunga, and Prestbakki in
Hrútafjörður, Strandir county; Melar in Melasveit, Borgarfjörður county;
Berunes-Berufjörður, Suður-Múli county; Myrká in Hörgárdalur and
Hrafnagil, Eyjafjörður county; and Háls in Fnjóskadalur, Suður-Þingey
county.

9

EVERY ICELANDER A SPECIAL CASE

An Icelandic emphasis on the notion of the autonomous individual at the expense of conceptualization of the social is especially evident in denials of class as a social phenomenon. This emphasis underlies Icelandic everyday as well as academic treatments of the diverse phenomena of language differences, differential success of fishing skippers, crime, and history. The denial of class is informed by an ideology of egalitarianism and homogeneity. If all are equal, there can be no classes, no social differences, hence no sphere of the social as distinct from the individual.

I first present some ethnographic vignettes to illustrate the pattern and some analytical observations to indicate its pervasiveness. I then suggest that this pattern is salient, readily available as a means of constructing discourses or accounts of everyday life not because it represents social realities but because it was propagated as a conscious ideology in service of the romantic and nationalist independence movement. This ideology was favored because it fit expectations of foreign audiences and served the interests of an Icelandic rural agricultural elite who favored independence as a means of maintaining control of labor against demands of the developing competition of a fishing industry. The system of autonomous farms they defended was a result of Iceland's position on the political and economic periphery of Denmark.

The ideology was based on bucolic images of the rural life sponsored and ratified by the rural elite. From the middle of the nineteeth century, though, the social and economic realities were shifting away from farming and toward fishing as the mainstay of the Icelandic economy, which undercut not only the experiential basis of the ideology but adherence to the laws based on it. With the coming of independence in 1944, public policy was used directly to foster the development of the fishing industry. Iceland's more recent engagement with international communications networks, computers, computer games, and other cultural products; immersion in urban life; and the development of the system of individual transferable quotas to regulate fishing have eroded the cultural, political, rhetorical, economic, and experiential bases for this cultural pattern. In the second section of the essay I discuss this dynamic in more detail. In the third section, I offer ideas about how to conceptualize the process in terms of anthropological theory and indicate some questions that this inquiry poses for Icelandic historiography.

The Phenomenon

An Icelander in a bureaucratic position once lamented that Icelanders could comprehend the idea of rules and regulations, and could understand the need for their orderly application, but that each and every Icelander considered himself or herself a special case. R. F. Tomasson conveys the same observation when he argues (1980: 201) that Icelanders are "predominantly empirical—not ideological or theoretical or philosophical—in their approach to experience." W. van den Hoonaard (1991) argues that Icelandic myths of crimelessness can be maintained by particularizing the phenomena as individual symptomatic traits and explaining them in terms of psychology to trivialize the social context rather than seeing crime as a social phenomenon. Gísli Pálsson (1989b) contends in the same way that individualizing language behavior negates the social dimension of language use. Pálsson and I found in our work on the "skipper effect," the idea that some skippers are more successful at fishing than others because of their personal characteristics (Pálsson and Durrenberger

1990; Pálsson 1993a), that Icelanders tend to think of individual characteristics as unrelated to social ones and consider differences to be personal rather than structural.

What Jonathan Wylie (1987) argues of the Faroese and their historiography, which presents local life in fragmented detail, is true of Iceland. Focusing on individuals and leaving the social system perpetually unproblematic and out of focus enhances the sense of continuity (Wylie 1987: 190–191). Because of the same emphasis on individuals rather than social processes, a sociology or an anthropology of the sagas is difficult to imagine. Sigurður Nordal observes, in the same vein, that most of Icelandic history had been "the history of people rather than the history of a people. We have been proficient in genealogy, but less so in politics" (1924: 165).

After studying Icelandic at the University of Iceland and hearing often of the distinctions between "good" Icelandic and disparaged "street" Icelandic, my wife, Dorothy, and I worked on a farm for several summers in the 1980s (Durrenberger 1993). I soon learned that the three tractors had names: "Cab-Tractor" because it had a cab; "Shovel Tractor" because it had a front end loader attachment; and "Lilli." I had complex dualistic models in mind as I inquired about the names of tractors.

"The word for tractor is feminine, isn't it?" I asked, giving the properly pure Icelandic word, *dráttarvél* (from words meaning "pull" and "machine"), devoid of any Latin influences.

"Yes."

"But the name of this one is Lilli?"

"Yes."

"And that is masculine?"

"Yes."

"Why does a feminine tractor have a masculine name?" I asked, waiting for the missing piece of the structuralist puzzle to fall into place to make a model of crystalline and lucid clarity.

"That is a *tractor*," the farmer said, using the borrowed Latinate word (*traktor*), just about like the English "tractor," degenerate and disparaged by the standards of Icelandic purists. "And that is masculine," he continued, ending the matter.

One day after lunch the farmer was looking over some advertising for pickup trucks. He used the word *pikkupp*, "pickup," and I asked if there were an *Icelandic* word for it. He told me that the "real" Icelandic word is *pallbíll*, "platform car," but that everyone called them pickups. There is an Icelandic word for everything, but that does not guarantee that people will use it.

In more academic settings, there have been drawn-out debates about whether to use the Latinate form *ethnografia* in preference to the purely Icelandic form *þjóðlýsing* (the combined words mean "nation" and "description"). The object of the use of the Latinate form was to avoid all of the nationalist connotations of forms that start with *þjóð,* "nation," such as "national bank," "national spirit," "national debt," "national costume," and "nationalist," all of which suggest a nation, national, or nationalist ideology, as the Icelandic word for "folk studies, folklore, and ethnography" surely does. The difference here is between modern international anthropology and folk studies in service of nationalist ideologies. This difference was not easily acknowledged by the Icelandic academic community.

For a long time, until Icelanders were impressed with the inhumanity of the practice as depicted in the film *Roots,* even the personal names of any persons claiming Icelandic nationality had to be Icelandic, though the list of approved names did include some borrowed from the Bible. Foreign persons, like concepts and things, had to be domesticated through their names.

Iceland accommodates new technology, ideas, disciplines, and people, but the language must remain pure and uniquely Icelandic, inviolable. This seems odd to speakers of English, who are accustomed to a vocabulary largely borrowed from the Norman French of William the Conqueror and filled out over the centuries with words and personal names from virtually every language. While English has several registers, the everyday or crude (Germanic), the polite (Norman French), and the technical (Latin, Greek), Icelandic has but one, the Icelandic.

The possibility of manufacturing new Icelandic words for new things and ideas to maintain a "pure" Icelandic is facilitated by the fact that most Icelanders are familiar with several other languages and read, write, speak, or understand them to various degrees. All are taught Danish and English in school. Many learn classroom French and/or German as well. Many have traveled widely in Scandinavia, Europe, and the English-speaking world. Paradoxically, it is the potential for foreign languages to take the burden of detailed discussion for cosmopolitan Icelanders that makes possible the parochialism of language purity. Instead of having distinct registers within the same language, Icelanders use different languages. Surely when one listens to Icelandic around the University of Iceland one hears many foreign words—English or Danish or Latin—in everyday conversation just as one hears the depreciated borrowings from Latin, Danish, and English in the countryside.

The idea of language and cultural purity centered on rural farms was developed and advanced by a local elite in developing an independence ideology to foster their own interests. They could not keep out new ideas and things, but they could try to tame them, bend them into the form of the romantic purity of the sacred countryside by naming the new things in Icelandic instead of creating a new register for technical terms, to Icelandicize all imports and purify them. Should the technology or ideas bring in new words, the language would lose its purity, its use as a marker of distinctiveness. Some even argue that, since language is associated with thought, to pollute the language is to risk pollution of the thought process (Pálsson 1989b), an argument also heard in Greece (Herzfeld 1987).

In our account of the individual over the social in Icelandic conceptualizations of language and skippers Pálsson and I (1992) pointed out the primacy of the axiom of equality in Icelandic culture and ideology. There can be no class-based dialects of Icelandic because the ideology dictates that there are no classes. Icelanders tend to deny the existence of inequality and sociolectic differences, but admit that there are nonstandard varieties of Icelandic. They conclude, as for crime, that those who use nonstandard or "impure" versions of the language are somehow psychologically deficient. Language purists even favor disease metaphors to describe such deficiencies. What makes the idea of departures from language purity being psychological and individual particularly appealing to Icelanders is that the notion of class remains implicit and hidden (Pálsson 1989b).

Because of the conceptual value bestowed upon equality among Icelanders, accounts of differences have to be formulated *implicitly* and in euphemistic language so as to disguise or hide the underlying claim of difference. Explicit accounts are neither acceptable nor convincing. Since the ideology of equality makes class differences a contradiction, and the class differences are undeniable, a euphemistic theory of inequality has developed and the concept of language purity serves this ideological interest. Above all, the phenomenon of class remains disguised and hidden, unavailable for conceptualization, thought, or critique. In everyday life, language then becomes a marker for class difference and use of "street" Icelandic develops as resistance to the ideology (Scott 1991).

Icelandic folk models of skippers, important figures in an economy largely based on fishing and the export of fish products, share common assumptions with concepts of language. Conceptually, individual characteristics are unrelated to social ones and individual differences are held to be personal rather than structural. This mode of thought denies the importance of differential access to resources. Many Icelanders tend to reject the conclusion that differential fishing success is related to the size of boats and effort more than to characteristics of skippers (Pálsson and Durrenberger 1982, 1983, 1992; Durrenberger and Pálsson 1983), on the grounds that it is simply contrary to their experience. As with language, traditionalists see the skipper effect to be an individual characteristic unrelated to social or economic variables. As with language, this allows the comfortable and consistent ideology that inequality is minimal, that opportunities are equal, and that existing differences in terms of resources are due to personal rather than structural differences. The concept of skipper effect promotes an understanding of differential benefits without appeal to concepts of class differences or differential access to resources. While Icelanders deny social and economic inequalities, they project inequality onto personality just as they do onto language use.

Because the nationalist and independence ideology conflated medieval and modern history to democratize elite status to maintain the doctrine of egalitarianism and superiority at the same time, every Icelander can see himself or herself as an aristocrat, a chieftain, a descendant of a Norwegian king. All one needs to make the fantasy real is the goods to prove the prestige. All one needs for the goods is either income or credit. For either, one needs a job, perhaps two. As long as one can maintain sufficient income, the concept of class does not become problematic. As long as one can consume at the same levels as others, one remains within the range of prestige display that defines egalitarian consumer relations, and one does not see class differences in everyday life. This reinforces the ideology of classlessness. This consciousness begins to break up when people become aware that some can become wealthy not by working but by holding quotas through no effort of their own.

Iceland is a hypermodern state. The income that supports the standard of living and incessant consumption of imported goods depends largely on fishing. Both the consumer economy and the fishing industry have developed since Iceland became independent. The fishing economy contributed to a continual inflation. Since it was the center of the economy, the exchange rate of Icelandic currency was manipulated to keep fish competitive on the international market, always revising upward the prices of the locally available imported goods that defined fashion so central to maintaining a sense of worth and prestige consistent with the images perpetuated by the independence romanticism.

The politicians who owe their positions to local support fight to maintain that support by sponsoring programs to help local communities, especially in the form of government guaranteed loans for trawlers to provide the basis of fishing economies along the coast. Political maneuver maintains the economic system by distributing costs of local failure throughout by government guarantees which are backed with either taxes or foreign loans. Until recently, this process contributed to the process of inflation and to the inflationary mentality of spending for immediate consumption. One had to spend money before it lost its value or got taxed away. This was the economic grounding for consumption informed by cultural values of a generalized aristocracy, the democratization of elite status promoted by independence romanticism. Government programs of health insurance and retirement insulate individuals against the necessity for long-term financial planning. Together these fuel the consumer capitalism that maintains those who are not involved in the fisheries.

Process

With a trade monopoly that restricted imports, Denmark withdrew Iceland from the emerging seventeenth-century Dutch-English fish trade to keep its rich fishery under its own control (Chase-Dunn 1989). Iceland developed as a periphery to Denmark, sharing a classical pattern of political and economic forms common throughout other peripheral areas (Chirot 1986). In response to Danish policy, an Icelandic farming elite developed a system of self-contained farms and opposed the development of fishing, which would threaten the secure and enforced supply of cheap labor. This set fishing interests against farming interests, in a process common in peripheral economies (Chase-Dunn 1989: 122–123). With independence, this faction finally lost to the fisheries sector (Magnússon 1985).

The trade monopoly organized Iceland as a tributary state for mercantile purposes and created the Icelandic class of farmers with their own entrenched interests and power to defend them versus fisheries. The Danish trade monopoly created the autonomous Icelandic farm as the primary social, economic, and political unit in the interests of the Danish tributary system. When the tributary system outlived its usefulness and became a hindrance to organizing for capitalism, the Icelandic elite engineered backwardness to serve its interests. But this elite owed its existence to Danish policy that created it and defined its interests.

This resistance to development can be read as local, as the consequence of Icelandic conditions and Icelandic mentalities, only if we ignore history and context. If we place Iceland in its historical and geopolitical context, we see that this "backwardness" was not a local dynamic, and certainly not culturally determined, but part of a larger Danish and international system, part of an embracing world political and economic system.

As Denmark was incorporated into a wider sphere, its absolute monarchy was replaced by a nation-state which redefined relations among its component parts, not only the various possessions, but the individual and the state, and provided a context for Icelandic independence. Though farmers strove to perpetuate their hold over the economy, they failed, and industrial fishing became the backbone of the national economy (Magnússon 1985).

The "independence struggle" started in the mid-nineteenth century, a period of the invention of tradition to serve emerging state elites across Europe (Hobsbawm 1983b). E. J. Hobsbawm (1983a) argues that in a period of a few years traditions were invented and instituted to instill nationalistic values by repetition and reference to continuity with the past. These traditions symbolize group membership, legitimate institutions and authority, and inculcate value systems by reference to views of history appropriated for the tasks. Icelandic nationalism and independence were part of the general restructuring of the European state system, though it was shaped by local conditions. Icelandic nationalist ideology presents the movement as a great awakening that needs no explanation beyond the genealogy of the individual intellectual geniuses who shaped it and their biographies. They sounded the trumpets and down fell the walls that had impeded economic and intellectual development (Hálfdanarson n.d.).

In the service of the independence movement the elite developed distinctive images of what Iceland was and what it was to be Icelandic: historians and legalists developed arguments of law; folklorists collected, purified, and published an Icelandic tradition; and linguists showed Icelandic to be the original language of the northern peoples. These concepts of nation and self responded to the prevailing political and intellectual culture in the colonial metropole of Denmark and the nationalist inventions of other European states. These images described an ideal life-way of an elite. If Greece was the southern foundation for constructions of European identity that caught the Greeks up in new myths created by foreigners (Herzfeld 1987), Iceland was the northern terminus of a similar process. It could be said of Iceland, as Michael Herzfeld said of Greece, "If this region is ancestral to 'us' [Europeans], it is removed from us through mythic time; if merely exotic, then its distance is one of cultural space. In either case, it is 'not us,' even though we claim it as 'our own'" (1987: 7). Its paradoxical status is a consequence of the Eurocentric ideology rather than anything about the region itself.

Motivated by its own nationalistic urges and romantic leanings, the Scandinavian audience was certainly willing to listen to the Icelandic elite's claims and ratify them. Danes thought Icelandic culture embodied that which was most noble in the common Norse experience and looked to Iceland for inspiration (Wylie 1987: 177). The nineteenth-century Danish scholar Rasmus Rask saw Icelandic as the key to Scandinavian languages and advocated its purity (Gjerset 1924: 371–372).

Icelandic leaders could argue effectively, in accordance with the romantic "folkish" ideology of the metropolis, that Iceland's future should match the glories of its past (Wylie 1987: 179). Images of a heroic past were welded to the landscape of contemporary farming in a rhetoric in which Icelanders could imagine a community stretching unbroken from the glorious days of the medieval past to the present. Icelandic students in Denmark began to import ideas of nationalism and romanticism. The Icelandic elite followed the Danes in identifying with a romantic image of a glorious Icelandic past.

As the Danes began to modernize and develop, they set the conditions for Icelandic independence. Finally it was conditions beyond Danish control, occupation by Germany in World War II and the occupation of Iceland by British and then American troops, that pushed Iceland into independence. Given independence and population growth along with new sources of outside capital provided by international events, the new government focused its efforts on the development of industrial fishing and infrastructure to support it.

The first independent government of Iceland of 1944 declared that fishing would be the backbone of a policy of development and set about schemes to improve facilities ashore and develop local fishing capacity (Durrenberger and Pálsson 1989a). This policy defined a "national economy" and the rules for collective action as well as a system of state education to inculcate the values of Icelandicness. Thus the working class identified themselves with national political movements, parties, and operated within the confines of the nation to ratify the elite's vision of Iceland. The state, nation, and society merged, a process Hobsbawm (1983b) suggests was general throughout Europe.

In Iceland members of a farming elite attempted to reserve to themselves the power of the emerging state to retain labor for their farms (Magnússon 1985). The ideology they developed to accompany these legal moves was one of the individual, the holiness and purity of the countryside, and the moral primacy of the farm and farmers. The units at stake, the significant individuals, were not dependents or working people, but the farmers. Independence was to serve their interests.

This ideology was perpetuated in academic writings, schools, and law, and, as in Greece, foreign scholars, anthropologists, and local folklorists created a bureaucratic folklorism with its dual hierarchy of the intellectual as superior to the rural people and the Icelandic (Greek) rural people as the most superior of all "exotics" (Herzfeld 1987). Such constructs could not withstand the sheer contradictions of practice as most Icelanders abandoned the countryside in favor of fishing villages or the burgeoning city of Reykjavík and wage work or salaried positions. Its axiomatic content remained salient as Icelanders generalized and democratized the concept of elite—now everyone was elite—and began to inform and motivate competitive consumerism. This in turn led to a new cultural context with equally strong but less disguised foreign influences and weakened the ideology of the farmer elite in recent years.

The main ideological task of the independence movement was to develop a paradigm to unite the people of the country, a paradigm that would prove that the nationalistic power struggle would change something for the ordinary people. Part of the general process of creating tractable electorates in Europe was reference to the traditionalism of peasants as the ideal model of political behavior (Hobsbawm 1983b). Icelanders made similar reference to rural folk, but elevated everyone in a process of the democratization of aristocratic standing. Folklore was part of the ideology of the independence movement. The collection of folklore since the mid-nineteenth century was an offshoot of German and Danish romanticism and nationalism; like Greece, Iceland was forced into the role of the proto-European (or Ur Europa) and at the same time humiliated vassal (Herzfeld 1987: 19). Just as the native Greek was defined as pure and the imported Turkish as impure, so Icelandic was pure and Danish impure. As the Greeks adopted the Turks as "enemy" (Herzfeld 1987: 29), so Iceland did the Danes. Just as the Turks brought on the fall of Greece, so foreigners were made responsible for the fall of Iceland from the grace of the Commonwealth through either Christianity or royal meddling. The past and the countryside were emphasized as pure. Working people of the city of Reykjavík were trash. Some of the lore of the folk was culture and some was not and only that which the scholars certified as cultural was elevated to the status of folklore to characterize the Icelanders. The folklore movement displaced discussions of competition of power among Icelanders in the here and now to other times (Jónsson 1989: 448–449) and, as in Greece, reduced diversity to uniformity in service of the state (Herzfeld 1987).

If there were the materials for a popular nationalism in folklore, they were displaced by the elite's control of the press and all communication media in favor of an official nationalism that stressed language purity and ancient history and purified folklore of its depravity to elevate it to a more suitable cultural level, just as in Greece. As in Greece, the language had to be purified to serve as a structure of thought, to be transparent, to be abstract and reflect logic itself (Herzfeld 1987: 52). If the society of the isolated farm gave way to the experience of the cooperative association or trade union, the fish-processing factory or trawler crew, these did not become the basis of a popular nationalism; rather the elite defined Iceland as a nation as beheld through its Danish romantic lenses and defined in terms of a farming society and heroic individualistic saga history.

Distinct views of history accompanied the independence movement. The centuries between the end of the medieval period and the modern were forgotten in favor of an ideology of continuity. The farmers could not hold out against history. As the population grew and the economy turned more toward fishing and coastal towns and villages, the farmers lost their economic place and "sought recourse in history, celebrating the traditions and rituals of the past as they could expect nothing of the future" (Hálfdanarson n.d.: 21). They called for preservation of the past and tried to maintain control of the parliament while reinforcing their own symbolic hegemony. The main goal of the nationalist ideology the elite promulgated was to conserve the old Icelandic order. The glory of the sagas was held up as a model for modern Icelanders and certain celebrations were revived to emphasize the connection. The independence movement folklorists and scholars did not see Icelandic culture and language as a living thing of everyday people, but as a thing of books and tradition, as a set of structures, to borrow Herzfeld's (1987) term.

Their goal was to define valid reference points for judging cultural and linguistic practices as either correctly Icelandic and elite or wrong and rubbish to be discarded. Some culture, like some linguistic usage, is good and some is bad. The old and rural is Icelandic and good; the urban, village, fishing, and working class is deplorable and un-Icelandic. The good Icelandic practices and stories have been collected and standardized for mass media presentation to the modern audience. The literature of folklore is a set of manuals for proper observance of properly Icelandic celebrations, a model of how Icelanders are to be (Jónsson 1989).

In Iceland and throughout the nationalizing countries of Europe the institution of the school replaced the church as the arena for the perpetuation of such consciously constructed ideologies and invented traditions. Various local elites struggled to formulate locally relevant ideologies and give them the force of tradition by asserting their antiquity and propriety as well as their legality (Hobsbawm 1983a, b; Herzfeld 1987). These ideologies became encoded as law and in school curricula as history, literature, and citizenship. Together these forces created new settings and motivations (Lave 1988) and moved ideological concepts in a short time from the realm of the manufactured to the realm of the axiomatic, implicit, and cultural, validated in schools, media, and ritual enactments if not always in everyday life. Because the economy did not remain stable, there was a gap between the everyday and the official, the gap that James Scott (1985, 1991) argues is often bridged by acts of everyday resistance.

The program of development in Iceland had consequences familiar to the rest of Europe—people concentrated in Reykjavík and fishing villages and the economic program as well as the ideology argued for the individual over the collectivity, for class against rank, for *Gesellschaft* against *Gemeinschaft*—and weakened the authority of the earlier social order but did not replace it.

Most Icelanders live in the urban complex of Reykjavík and neighboring municipalities. Most of the balance live in fishing villages along the coast. Only very few live in the countryside of the folklorists' fables. Most Icelanders consider Reykjavík to be Iceland proper and consider the countryside to be a distinct burden because of the cost of subsidies to keep farms in operation. People of the fishing villages are proud of providing most of Iceland's exports and consider themselves, rightly, the backbone of the economy. They consider people of the countryside backward and the word "country-person" (*sveitamaður*) is used to label people considered clumsy or ignorant (Einarsson 1990a). Consumption became exaggerated and competitive among the generalized aristocracy as individuals, conceiving of themselves as one among many, attempted to distinguish themselves from each other by consuming as much as and more than others. The competitive consumerism fits well with the developing consumer capitalism and inflationary economy, but as Icelanders bought videocassette recorders to view foreign movies, computers for their work, and computer games for their children's amusement, all with a vast infrastructure of instruction and strategy in English, romantic nationalism became irrelevant to everyday practice.

An international scheme of reference, a wider imagined community, is more relevant as Iceland is inundated by video games and videocassettes as well as media and cinema programing from abroad. When the family, couple, or teenage group sees a film at the cinema or in the living room on television it is more likely by far to be in English than in Icelandic. The actors one identifies with are most likely American or Continental. The television may feature an international ballroom dancing contest in which the Japanese take the tango prize or an international soccer match which the Brazilians win. One can imagine dancing the tango with the perfection of a Japanese partner or winning a soccer game with Pele. Young boys imagine themselves playing basketball in the United States' National Basketball Association's playoffs with the Chicago Bulls or one of their opponents, and much of their everyday conversation concerns such subjects. One's imagined community is global rather than island-wide. Just as the laws that strove to guarantee labor to the landowning elite became irrelevant, so has their ideology, which for some time has been incorporated as individualism in Icelandic culture.

As those who are not of the elite have studied in Iceland and abroad, they have developed a critique of the elite ideology. As city people reassess the costs of supporting the countryside, their attitudes toward farmers and farming are changing and the picture of the holy countryside is beginning to change to one of the demanding farmer.

While until the nineteenth century there had been little beyond the agricultural economy controlled by the Icelandic elite and Danish colonial order, a reality that supported the ideological centrality of the rural elite, even ideological struggle did not halt the decline of the agricultural economy during the nineteenth century. Independence and the fishery developed together. Early in the twentieth century the fishing industry began to develop with the use of motorboats. The new order was based on industrial fishing and it was increasingly unlikely that ordinary people could ever own land in Iceland. Some went west to Canada and America; many went to the coast to participate in the growing fishing industry and as "the rules of the old order turned into oppression [they] were simply not heeded" (Hálfdanarson n.d.: 23). When Icelanders left for Canada and the United States and threatened the labor supply, and bad weather and sheep diseases threatened large landowners from another direction, the elite began to invest in fisheries themselves and local fishing capital began to accumulate (Durrenberger and Pálsson 1989a). As the economy shifted, the asserted homogeneity of Icelandic society disappeared.

As Anne Brydon (1990, this volume) points out, historically, political mobilization, national self-determination, capital investment, wage labor, and the hope of a prosperous future all developed together to link fishing, the sea, prosperity, national, and individual independence into a single gestalt in terms of which Icelanders now understand their recent past and present. These images of Icelandicness are replacing the previous more bucolic ones based on livestock farming (Pálsson and Helgason, this volume). The schools are the arenas for the propagation of romantic-nationalist visions of the past and present, so much of the debate about appropriate curricula is in terms of whether to orient studies toward a nationalist ideology based on the past or an understanding of the current affairs of Iceland in an international world.

As fishing became the basis of the newly independent republic's economy and entered its expansive phase, skippers were conceived through the lenses of independence romanticism as individualistic, heroic persons struggling against the sea. Because of the emphasis on individuals rather than social processes, fostered by independence ideology, it was impossible to conceive of the social basis of skipper-hood as opposed to the individual achievements which became cele-brated as the dimensions of the skipper effect (Pálsson and Durren-berger 1990).

Expansive fishing brought fishing technology beyond the biologi-cal capacity of prey species to support it, and in 1983 the government instituted a system of individual transferable quotas for boats. These have seriously undermined the individualist ideology of the skipper effect and created a new form of wealth which differentiates quota-holders from non-quota-holders through no consequence of their own efforts or characteristics, further undermining concepts of equal-ity and individualism (Pálsson 1991).

In spite of the fact that today Iceland depends on its fishing econ-omy, the cultural traces of this process are still visible. The "real" Ice-land and Icelandic, one is told, is found in the countryside on the farms. City parents still consider it valuable to familiarize their chil-dren with "properly" rural Icelandic values and outlooks by summers spent working on farms.

Anthropological Theory

Allan Hanson (1989) argues that the Maori have combined and re-combined elements from their tradition and others to invent usages and beliefs appropriate to their political agendas, whose practice has made them authentic. Anthropology provided one source for this on-going process. Participants would not conceive themselves as inven-tive, but outsiders can see how different views of Maori culture serve political agendas, and "their status as inventions becomes obvious" (Hanson 1989: 899). So in Iceland: the notions of equality, indepen-dence, and purity have been invented and imported by scholars to serve the interests of a political elite as it strove for independence from Denmark (Pálsson 1989b). In the process such concepts have developed their own authenticity and provided a legacy with which Icelanders must come to terms as they construct themselves as indi-viduals and as a nation in the modern world.

Though Iceland's small homogeneous island population lends it-self to the myth of uniqueness propagated by its nationalist rhetoric, to claim that Iceland is exceptional would be an extension of the

same ideology. Iceland's economy and political rhetoric alike are examples of general patterns that can be observed clearly in other parts
of the world whether in Greece (Herzfeld 1987) or among the Maori
(Hanson 1989) or in Europe (Hobsbawm 1983a, b). The history of individualism in Europe has been discussed from several perspectives
(Dumont 1986; Lukes 1973) and we could rightly see Iceland as one
example of a much wider cultural and historical pattern. Iceland was
also but one instance of a wider pattern of nationalism (Mann 1992;
Smith 1986, 1991; Harris 1990; Hobsbawm and Ranger 1983).

Insofar as we can only comprehend the particular in terms of the
general, we must comprehend the unique instance in terms of general concepts and universal processes rather than historical events
asserted to be specific to the example. In the mid-1980s Sherry Ortner (1984) characterized an emerging approach of practice-oriented
anthropology that explains relationships between human action and
larger systems in terms of evaluative schemes and a holistic understanding of institutions as interrelated and seamless rather than diverse, that develops histories in terms of how action reproduces
systems and changes them at the same time. She discussed the intellectual background to this approach from Pierre Bourdieu to Michel
Foucault; from Karl Marx to Jürgen Habermas.

Jean Lave (1988) develops such an analytical framework which
shifts the boundaries of activity beyond the individual mind or psychology of an economic actor who maximizes according to the theoretical axioms of economics, to motivated persons engaged with the
world as it is given by historical processes with all of its contradictions
and trying to resolve their own dilemmas and in the process of action
shaping their assumptions about reality and modifying the reality itself in a dialectical process. She argues that cognition is not a property
of individuals, but is seamlessly stretched across mind, body, activity,
and setting (1988: 18, 171). People develop analyses of realities in
terms of systems of meaning and types of argument—cultures—they
have learned, act on those analyses and, in the process, change the
realities and their cultures in a never ending cycle. People are agents,
acting in terms of cultures in historically given contexts, changing
both contexts and cultures through their actions, but not always in
ways they anticipate (Pálsson 1992, 1993a).

Such a theoretical stance moves us beyond the problems of static
structures (Herzfeld 1987) and allows us to see the individual, the social, and the configurations of everyday life in terms of which people

live and construct their concepts in action. We can see that being raised in the environment of a fishing village, a rural farm, and an urban complex would create different mentalities. Moving from one life space to another would achieve the same result. In this sense, as Magnús Magnússon (1985) points out, we can trace the patterns statistically as we see the proportions of each age category who are rural dependents increase throughout the nineteenth century along with the rise in unlawful residencies, the growth of fishing villages, immigration to the United States and Canada, and the growth of Reykjavík and the neighboring metropolitan areas. Each individual contribution to the statistics is a person deciding to abandon the countryside for Canada or a fishing village, deciding to risk disobedience to the law and disapproval of others, deciding to be part of the disparaged rabble, if the confrontation of such alternatives can be styled decision. The sheer balance shifts away from the countryside, thus creating the schism between the ideal and the experienced reality. Perhaps it was that distance, represented with such verisimilitude in the writings of Halldór Laxness, that made his work controversial in Iceland at an early period and more acceptable as foreigners awarded him a prize that Icelanders could also respect and as it came to represent the experience of more people in Iceland.

It is clear that not everyone loved the country life. An elderly farm woman discussing her childhood recounted her first experience of farming when she left her home in the West Fjords to join a group for hay making and how she hated the farming life. She vowed she would never live in the countryside and married a herring fisher. She was pointing out the irony that she had ended up on a farm for most of her life in spite of her early wishes to the contrary (Durrenberger 1993). If everyone loved the farming life, there would never have been a movement west to the United States and Canada; Reykjavík would not be so populous, nor fishing so important.

Ethnography can fill in the details of everyday life that shape conceptual systems and define the systems in terms of which people act and think and contrast these with ideological productions, but it cannot recapture the past. Icelandic historians and historiographers of Iceland face that challenge, and it is not at all unproblematic because they, like anthropologists and all other people, are caught up in systems that define their work and thought (Hayles 1990; Herzfeld 1987). As long as Icelandic history remains in the self-referencing institutional context of ideological production, it is difficult to see how it can transcend reproduction of past themes. Romantic scholars serving independence held up the idea that Icelanders were and had been the most egalitarian of people, that all were equal and together and could be proud of a splendid past and a pure language which made them all good Icelanders: "Most of the scholarship in Iceland which has to do with Icelandic culture has been in this paradigm, and has always been more Icelandic than scholarly" (Jónsson 1989: 448–449). Like rock bands, historians have to face the dilemma of whether to write in Icelandic for a traditional audience and contribute to its comfortable debates or, like the Sugarcubes, to risk ostracism in Iceland by embracing the international and writing in English. The international scholarly community cannot sift through all of the nationalist and romantic production to try to detect the divergent historiography that might contribute to new interpretations, but will rely on historians of Iceland to join the discourse at the international level, in the global ecumene (Hannerz 1993).

Some argue (Hayles 1990) that there are but two social levels in the contemporary world—the family and the international network. This may appear true to those who live in an international nation such as the United States constructed of many sovereign local polities; or to Latin Americans or Chinese who live in many independent states but are unified by language, literature, business connections, and culture. In such contexts, the nation or polity may not form a significant level of social and cultural interaction or level of sociocultural integration, as Julian Steward styles it (1951). It is not the same for people who live in lands such as Iceland whose languages and institutional patterns impose on them the level of the nation that embeds and defines their practice, whether it be academic, cultural, or business.

Of course people routinely transcend these limits as Pálsson and I discuss (1989), but it is neither easy nor automatic (Hannerz 1993). It is acquiescent to accept the myth of classlessness and be puzzled by the diversity labeled as *bóndi*, "farmer," in Icelandic. It is surely incorrect to use the term "peasant," as any examination of the large anthropological literature on that topic would immediately suggest (e.g., Wolf 1966). But, as in the United States, the term covers a wide range of practices, patterns, and situations from the dire poverty of sharecropping to rental arrangements to land ownership to gentleman-planter elite status. Members of different classes are called by a single term that disguises the class relationship. Being alert to class differences shows that categories can change their position in a system as quantitative changes become qualitative, as when dependency changes from being an age category to a class category, thus creating a new life space for decision making, action, and thought (Magnússon 1985).

It is not my intention to critique Icelandic historiography except to point to its ideological uses in the past. From the point of view of anthropology, there is room for a viable collaboration if historians and historiographers take up the issue of developing the details of everyday life and social dynamics of the past to show the variety of practice, thought, and resistance. But this requires a shift in view from nationalist paradigms and a shift of context from familiar Icelandic ones bound with the institutional practices and ideologies of the past to international ones. Fortunately, there is evidence that such a shift is now underway as some Icelandic historians seek education off the island, write for international audiences, examine historical problems in a comparative perspective that moves them beyond Iceland (though the anthropological concept of social and cultural forms seems alien to historians as they search for closeness of time or space to legitimate comparison), or even discuss non-Icelandic materials and problems.

Conclusion

The cultural pattern of conceptualizing the autonomous individual at the expense of the social is a consequence of an ideology developed by a farming elite to perpetuate its advantaged position in a political economy that evolved as a dimension of Iceland's peripheral status and Danish policy. The invention of the traditions, academic justifications, literature, and practices around the ideology parallel processes in the rest of Europe and elsewhere in emerging states. In part, the process was forced on Iceland by foreign definitions and expectations; in part it was fostered by a local Icelandic elite. As fishing became economically dominant by the middle of the twentieth century, the realities of everyday practice diverged increasingly from ideological definitions.

Awash with foreign cultural and technological products from entertainment to navigational systems, from hardware to software, Iceland has become embedded in an international culture and practice that is increasingly international rather than tied to rural areas or even to the nation as Icelanders travel and live abroad and communicate in other languages. The challenge to anthropology is to comprehend this process as it affects individuals as well as systems, to see not only the evolution of patterns and political economies and international networks of cause and effect but also everyday practice and how each affects the other to construct the statistical patterns that tell the story of social, economic, and cultural evolution (Hannerz 1993). Part of this story is the form that Icelandic representations of Iceland have taken, but that is only part of the story. The other part is experiential, in the lives of the people, the choices they faced, and the decisions they made, a story that is revealed today by ethnography but obscured by ideological representations. By attending to it perhaps we anthropologists can go beyond what Pálsson (1995) has called neo-Orientalism to the post-Orientalism of living discourse.

Acknowledgments

I thank Gísli Pálsson, Guðmundur Hálfdanarson, Shaun Hughes, Myrdene Anderson, and the participants in the 1993 workshop on the Anthropology of Modern Iceland in Iowa City for their comments on previous versions of the essay.

10

LITERACY IDENTITY AND LITERACY PRACTICE

We examine the tradition of literacy in Iceland and the role this concept has continued to play over the centuries in society, culture, and national identity. Two aspects of literacy act on and influence each other, literacy practices and literacy identity. In Iceland literacy practices have been altering in step with other social changes, whereas the Icelandic literacy identity is just now in the beginning phase of breaking away from the traditional model dating back to the Middle Ages. The new literacy practices—schooled literacy, electronic media literacy, and internationally influenced business literacy—are beginning to change the ways in which Icelanders define their specific literacy identity, an important element of their national identity.

Literacy has been studied cross-culturally, but greatly varying presuppositions about its definition as well as different opinions regarding its appearance in various contexts such as school, home, and the wider community have produced correspondingly variable results. It is now more commonly agreed that no absolute criteria can be applied to a definition of the concept of literacy because its meaning is culturally, historically, and socially variable.

Within the last decade the issue of literacy has taken on new importance among educators and anthropologists. Unfortunately, the debate that has emerged often tends to recycle old assumptions and values. The notion that literacy is a matter of learning a standard script still informs most literacy programs and manifests its logic in the renewed emphasis on technical reading and writing skills. Almost without exception, traditional approaches to understanding literacy have been deeply ingrained in a positivistic method of inquiry. Within programs designed to advance literacy, substance and historical context have been ignored in favor of technical mastery (teaching reading "skills"). The underlying cultural and social notion of literacy—what it means to "be literate" in various cultural or community groups—has not been taken into account. The exclusion of social, political, and cultural dimensions from the study of literacy has contributed to the view of readers as "objects," and reading and writing as purely "mechanical skills" to be acquired and honed.

The new field of research with which our study is aligned has been referred to as a sociocognitive approach to language development and literacy (Garnica and King 1979; Heath 1982, 1983, 1986a, 1986b, 1987; Cochran-Smith 1984; Cole 1985; Cook-Gumperz 1986; de Castell, Luke, and Egan 1986; Schieffelin and Ochs 1986; Schieffelin and Gilmore 1986). This unified model of human development assumes that language, cognitive skills, and social knowledge are interrelated and interdependent. Thus understanding participants' values, attitudes, norms, beliefs, and assumptions concerning the meaning or importance of a literacy event is crucial for understanding the event itself. Particular orientations toward literacy (cultural models) need to be investigated as culture-specific. The initiation of Icelandic children into particular literacy orientations needs to be studied in terms of the larger situational and cultural contexts, especially in relation to the literacy of parents and other adult mentors in the community. This sociocognitive approach dictates that we also consider sociohistorical dynamics, as shared literacy identities and literacy practices which developed throughout Iceland's history continue to act as emblems of national identity today.

Cultural models are the taken-for-granted worlds, the "frames" by which and in which individuals interpret what goes on around them (Quinn and Holland 1987). They are culturally constructed and learned in social interactions and, when externally presented, may act as mediating devices which function to organize knowledge and action (Vygotsky 1978; Holland and Quinn 1987; Holland and Valsiner 1988a, 1988b). A child may come to learn how to read and write, but also comes to learn the cultural model which organizes these skills. We investigate the change from past to current literacy practices in Iceland, which are just now beginning to result in modifications of the cultural model and consequently of what we call literacy identity.

Our analysis draws from two primary areas: Icelanders' interpretations of literacy and literacy events that they consider significant; and the function of the literate community in the lives of Icelanders, both past, as captured in literature, records, and historical sources, and present, as determined through observations, conversations, and taped interviews. We are concerned both with collective representations and with material changes in Icelandic society.

The sociocognitive approach emphasizes the idea of active involvement with the defining of one's "world and mentality": children and adults learning to read are not just passive objects but active participants, bringing information and beliefs about literacy with them into the process. Traditionally, learning to read has been seen as a cognitive problem—something children had to solve on their own, inside their own heads. Only recently has reading been treated as a social phenomenon, which often occurs in groups (Cochran-Smith 1984) and which is intrinsically embedded in the culture of its users (Heath 1983; Street 1984).

Originally, the fieldwork focused on observing specific literacy events (Heath 1983) in both the classroom and the homes of young children developing literacy skills and conceptualizations. In the process, however, the focus of inquiry began to shift to the more abstract issue influencing the specific literacy events in the schools and in the communities—the issue of what it means to an Icelander, to "be literate." The answers given in interviews and the results of observations in the schools and homes seemed to be divided into two realms—literacy identity and literacy practices. This came to be our new focus of study.

Representative rural and urban communities were examined ethnographically for local variations, although the overall community on which this study focused was the nation of Iceland as a whole. One of us (Sizemore) participated in the life of two different communities, first in the city of Reykjavík and then in the northeastern Icelandic countryside, a community we call Blindgötudalur (Cul-de-sac Valley). Sizemore conducted interviews and observations in the communities and in a variety of schools at the class levels for six-, seven-, and eight-year-olds—the ages of initial academic exposure to literacy and literacy events in the school environment.

In Reykjavík, this observation period primarily involved only classroom participation and observation of the students, whereas in the countryside interaction was more extensive both in the classroom and outside of it due to the schools being boarding institutions (*heimavistarskólar*). Students, teachers, and anthropologists all lived there during the school weeks. During nonschool periods Sizemore worked and lived with a three-generation Icelandic family on a sheep farm in the valley.

One of the questions posed in this study concerns the societal changes and their possible effects on the continuity of literacy as a constituent factor in Icelandic national identity. Other questions are: What social and/or cultural factors seem to affect values associated with literacy? With Iceland's purported attainment of virtually 100% literacy, are there shared values and knowledge concerning literacy that override other contextual differences? Is the meaning of literacy in Iceland changing along with other social changes?

The guiding orientation for this study is the idea that society provides an interactional and institutional framework for literacy and that culture provides an interpretive framework. We believe that Icelanders actively participate in socially structured events and distill, reconstruct, and internalize the cultural models pertaining to literacy in everyday social interactions. Both the historical and current contexts of these models continue to constitute a significant factor in the concept of Icelandic national identity. We found this literary identity to be a symbolically conserving force for Icelandic culture and nationality.

Literacy in Transition

The telling and reading of the sagas, the conducting of evening sessions of reading, singing, and handiwork in the home (*kvöldvaka*), and the general practice of home-based reading instruction all acted to reproduce important aspects of a long-standing way of life in Iceland's history. Until World War II these practices were essentially unchanged. There was a slow transition from home to school learning, including beginning school at a late age; a continuing centering of economic activities on agriculture; maintenance of traditional kinship associations; and maintenance of the self-sufficiency of separate, isolated farmsteads. These continuities allowed the culturally constructed literacy identity to survive beyond the changing literacy practices. When asked why they thought Iceland had attained and maintained such a high literacy rate, most Icelanders credited their past as the foremost reason.

> I think the tradition is from far behind. I think it's probably from the interest of reading and the sagas. . . . (parent)

> We are few, I think, that is one point. I would just throw out, also, with this great value, this history, yes, great tradition, it was so precious to be able to learn. Around 1900, there were maybe three or four books in a home and they were a treasure. (parent)

> I don't know, perhaps it was because it was the only thing people had, the only amusement. They had some stories to read. It's a very old tradition also. (teacher)

The quite restricted repertoire of reading materials and literacy practices served to maintain the continuity of the literacy identity that had developed. The *kvöldvaka* acted as a means of continuity between the Saga Age and the present. It appears, however, that the older model of literate Icelanders, at least for the younger generation which has grown up with television and extensive international contact, is now being modified, placing less emphasis on these continuities or legacies of literacy.

We have proposed that the construction of a tradition of literacy has had, and continues to have, an influential effect on Icelanders' perceptions of their country's history, its educational apparatus, and their sense of distinctive national identity. This literacy identity has been inextricably intertwined both with the country's history and with the history of literacy practices. Icelanders have persisted in seeing the purposes, workings, and achievements of their literate world in the light of a historical understanding of past experience which may not always bear a resemblance to past, current, or future realities.

Economic conditions and social arrangements have changed in Iceland, particularly during the last half-century. Literacy practices and literacy events also continue to change accordingly. Literacy in Iceland is currently experiencing an abrupt, condensed transition, thereby distinguishing more distinctly than before two aspects—literacy identity and literacy practices. The "goodness-of-fit" between the cultural construct of literacy identity and the practices, and between those and the current societal context, is just now starting to be examined by some Icelandic educationalists.

Icelandic society and culture are changing from a way of life developed on scattered, isolated, and self-sufficient agricultural farmsteads toward one facing modernization, international markets, and trade opportunities and increasingly concentrated in urban environs. One factor cited for maintaining Iceland's feeling of continuity with the past and contributing to its success in achieving political independence is its language. The Icelandic language has a reputation for conservatism among Scandinavian languages, which, because of its close association with the indigenous literature, seems to have encouraged the retention of Icelandic cultural identity.

A major transition began in the 1940s as a result of World War II, due to British and then U.S. military forces occupying the country. After World War II Iceland began moving rapidly from an agricultural to an urban society, as most of the country's population participated in an urban migration to Reykjavík and other towns. Independence, radio, transistors, television, foreign soldiers, and tourists arrived in succession—the forerunners of videocassette players, satellite dishes, computers, cellular phones, and the latest fad or fashion from Paris or London.

Independence from Denmark in 1944 also had an effect on the nation's education system. The change of lifestyle in the twentieth century has resulted in the virtual abandonment of home-based education carried out on the farmsteads. The tasks of teaching children to read and write and of transmitting the cultural values of the nation have now been thrust upon the schools and other public institutions. The need for an improved relationship between the school and the home has recently been supported with the argument that schools are, to an increasingly large extent, taking over a part of the education and guidance which has always before rested with the family.

Major social changes have been occurring more rapidly in these last fifty years than ever before. Middle-aged and older Icelanders are very aware of the changes in almost all aspects of their lives. It is not "long-ago, distant old ways" that are remembered and compared with the current practice, but ways that have changed since the childhoods of most middle-aged adults in Iceland. The headmaster at Blindgötudalur described the changes in the valley that the two middle-aged women who worked at the school, Anna and Sóla, in their mid-forties and mid-fifties, had seen:

> They have lived through all the changes that have come to Iceland. When young, up to four years old, Sóla lived in a *torfbær* [old-style turf house]. She saw the ways and tools change from the old ways of haying, with a hand-held scythe, to tractors and other machinery. They, and even those younger in their thirties, remember the first car coming when they were children. Sóla has seen radio, television, cars and tractors, new types of housing and household appliances, and telephones as they are now all come into the valley. It was 1985 when individual home telephone lines came to Blindgötudalur. The changes have come a little later to the countryside. It's always been difficult to travel and to transport goods. (teacher)

The education system of Iceland has undergone tremendous change, due primarily to the demographic shift in the country. Educators argue that schools, more than families, are the main force of sociocultural transmission today. The acquisition and development of literacy in young children through the schools differs from the techniques and materials used in home-based instruction. The contexts in which literacy is being acquired are quite different from those of the past. There are acknowledged problems with the centralized educational system trying to keep up with the other changes occurring so rapidly in Icelandic society and trying to meet "equally" the different needs of urban and rural school areas. Educational changes have occurred in the rural areas, though not to the same degree as in the urban Reykjavík area.

Economic changes that people have experienced as different types of employment, inflation, unemployment fluctuations, and world market participation have altered Iceland from a rural, agriculture-based country to one that is urban and service-based. This is a major shift away from both the previous everyday reality of lifestyles and work patterns and the cultural model of Icelandicness where the *bu* (farmstead) acted as the focal point of Icelanders' concept of themselves and their country. This recent rural-to-urban transformation is noteworthy because it lies behind perceived gaps between the old and the young, the rural and the urban, the folk and the modern, as discussed in everyday talk between Icelanders. The shift from a general subsistence founded on self-sustaining, barter-based agriculture to a largely cash economy has forced a certain degree of dispersion of kin, each in pursuit of wages and specialized training. It has also changed literacy practices. Icelanders' literacy identity is now changing, as the old one becomes increasingly archaic relative to the current literacy needs and practices.

The image of a child's teeter-totter provides a useful analogy. The grandparental generation at one end represents the older literacy identity, while the young children at the other end occupy the seat of new and different literacy practices centered around schooling and media. The parental generation straddles the teeter-totter at the fulcrum with one foot reaching back toward their parents and Icelandic heritage, the other stretching toward their children and the future. The teeter-totter has been tilted toward the older identity for a long time. In the last fifty years this position has changed and new literacy practices have grown in number and strength so that the teeter-totter is counterbalanced today. The young, by participating in new, primarily schooled literacy practices and, at some point, by developing a new literacy identity, will soon unbalance the teeter-totter toward their end.

Being literate is still important in Iceland, though not in the same way as it has been up to the last half-century. Literacy, with a focus on the Icelandic language, domestic and international communication through oral and written means, and the cultural transmission of ideas over time and space, has been integral in maintaining continuity with the past. One question, however, is whether or not a new literacy identity will continue to function as such an integral part in Icelandicness as the culture changes. Many Icelanders are beginning to ponder this question. When asked if they thought Iceland would have difficulty maintaining a high literacy rate in the future, quite a few Icelanders thought that new aspects of literacy could lead to problems.

> Yes, I think so still. I think people read as much now as earlier. But I think it will change, because now they have all those videos and other forms of entertainment. (parent)

> Probably children or young people are reading less than before when they only had the radio. (parent)

> I think now, with both mothers and fathers working long hours, they don't have time to talk to their children, to help them to read.

I think that will lead to problems—it's not here yet, but I think in the future it will be. (teacher)

If you come back after twenty to twenty-five years, in Reykjavík, the children of Iceland will possibly be able to read Icelandic, but not to write it. Now, with the television and radio, what the children read and hear is wrong. Many children now, they don't know how to write the words. They can read them, but if they have to write them, they don't know. It's sad to see that. When my older children come home from school with their yearbooks, where all the children write something, it's so horrible to read this. Some of the words are so badly written, you can't know what it's supposed to be. I'm afraid we're losing our language. (parent)

Yes, [we will have problems,] I think so, when we move into that new technology. I think the book has lost its power to some extent, it's declining. If you just look at the books that children read, now many of the books are based on pictures, not the story. If you give the children a book to read in school, most of them start to flip through to see if there are any pictures. If there are no pictures, they don't like it and take the book back. (teacher)

Many aspects of literacy in Iceland are in the process of changing: a shift in the primary sites where children learn literacy conceptualizations and skills from family/child to both teacher/child and audiovisual media/child (television, video, cinema); emphasis away from group oral comprehension toward individual silent comprehension of text; and emphasis away from speed of reading toward understanding of text. One feature which apparently has not changed, for either the general public or educators, is the universal expectation that all Icelanders, barring some debilitating mental or physical handicap, will be literate, though this will mean different things to different people.

The Icelandic Literacy Identity

The Icelandic literacy identity is a unique cultural self-image. One of us (Sizemore) has described this image based on definitions and concepts of literacy obtained through interviews with parents, teachers, ministry researchers, and university professors in education. Their comments reflect the image of literacy identity that is still held by most Icelanders. The parental and grandparental generations generally expressed the traditional view of literacy; however, they also voiced concerns about the youngest generation, their children and grandchildren, and the fear that the Icelandic language and traditions are being eroded by the incursion of outside influences. In spite of this concern, this culturally constructed literacy identity has not really changed for the vast majority, who still hold to the image of traditional, Saga Age Icelandicness.

> It's very important here to read. It's very important to know the word, to use it, to love it. It's a part of living, it's life. It's changing, I know that. For a long time we lived with the sagas, Snorri and all that. It's very special, because it's always been like that, or at least for a very long time. I think it's very much a question about that, why people learn to read, what people around you want you to do. It's not a question of brains or skills in that way. But the social expectations, you're supposed to read. And you have to read to be accepted in a way. And I think it's very difficult for people who have some kind of problem, perhaps more here than in some other countries. (parent)

> Well, I was thinking, when people are talking, Icelandic people, and they say about a man who would read just the most necessary things, they would say he is "hardly literate." If people say that, they talk about it as some handicap. People think it's very bad. The standard for being literate is very high in Iceland. (teacher)

> It's not normal to not be able to read. You look down on the people who can't read. You have to know how to read just to be a man. I'd go crazy if I didn't read. (parent)

The Icelandic literacy identity is strongly based on the sagas and Golden Age of literature. The continuity of this image of literate Icelanders, speaking and reading the same Old Norse language as in the past, has been preserved and maintained with great effort. It has involved language committees and other means by which to protect the "purity" of Icelandicness. At the same time, this cultural image that all Icelanders are literate, saga-reading individuals has been taken for granted by both outsiders and Icelanders themselves until just the past few years. Being literate has been an essential part of being Icelandic, an essential part of the self-image. This literacy identity was originally based on actual literacy practices, but it has not evolved over time in step with those practices and the cultural contexts in which they occur. The literacy identity expressed by many Icelanders today is a myth that no longer corresponds to actual literacy fact.

Inside/Outside Aspects of Icelandic Literacy Identity

The inside/outside dichotomy of "we"/"they" is strongly articulated in Iceland. Icelanders readily suggest that their history has been one of difficult struggles against the sea, volcanoes, earthquakes, the weather, the topography, and isolation. They describe the "we," bound together by survival against natural forces on the island, as opposed to the "they" of outside social forces of colonial rule by first Norway and then Denmark and the cod wars with Great Britain over fishing rights. The image of David and Goliath, the small but successful warrior resisting the foreign giant, comes to mind.

Their literacy identity, associated closely with their language, was one means by which Icelanders distinguished themselves from others. With the advent of a national independence movement, language, literature, and literacy became emphasized for their uniqueness and, Icelanders argued, for their high quality.

Today this image is maintained by a wealth of "first" or "highest per capita in the world" national statistics. The preponderance of these statistically significant claims, bearing in mind Iceland's population of 260,000, is a source of humor among foreigners who spend any time there and among some, if not most, Icelanders. Someone in the Statistical Bureau is kept very busy calculating Iceland's position relative to other countries in a wide assortment of "highest per capita" concerns—number of chess players, number of chess grandmasters, number of swimming pools, number of unwed mothers and their children, number of household computers, televisions, and videotape recorders, number of bookstores and books sold annually, and so on ad infinitum. These claims to fame are important to Icelanders as they continue to maintain their "unique" position relative to the outside world. The strong assertion of being "a literate nation" for centuries is still one of the primary features emphasized in dealings with outsiders:

> "We publish more books [per capita] than other people, we buy more books than others, and, in all likelihood, we read more books than other people do." So wrote Baldvin Tryggvason (1970), the president of the largest publishing house in Iceland. Many Icelanders, and perhaps most Icelandic intellectuals, believe assertions

like this one. Indeed, the alleged addiction of Icelanders to reading
books and the proportionately large number of bookstores are
among the few items of information about Iceland that have
reached the outside world. (Tomasson 1980: 116)

Literacy identity acts to bridge this cognized boundary between
inside and outside. This cultural image, in addition to the literacy
practices closely associated with it, mediates the self-image of Iceland
vis-à-vis others. It is used by Icelanders both to set themselves off
as a separate entity with their own language and literate traditions
and to establish a connecting link with other "literate peoples" in the
world. The sagas and the skaldic and eddaic poetry, along with the
other types of literature, written and oral, were used to strengthen
Icelandic literacy identity both inside and outside the island.

Inside, these devices served to describe common ancestors, specific areas within the country, and famous and infamous activities associated with well-known individuals. Thus they acted as a unifying
force, extolling the merit and character of Icelanders as they engaged
both natural forces and other peoples. A general characteristic of Icelanders emphasized by the literature is their "wit and wisdom," displayed primarily through their use of words, poems, and "fast talking" in a variety of situations. All Icelanders came to see themselves
in the same light as those few who were described in these works of
literature. In the process, these literary devices acquired a metonymic
function. The sagas in particular bring to mind a whole complex of
feelings and thoughts about Icelandic society. Dorothy Holland and
Jaan Valsiner "suggest that this characteristic organization of cultural
models through metonyms may come about because mediating devices . . . are also the primary means by which cultural models are
learned from others, and it is they that come to be the pieces that
stand for the whole" (1988b: 260). Icelanders' constructed images of
the literacy practices of *kvöldvaka*, verse-making, and story-telling were
the specific mediating devices. This enabled all Icelanders, both literate
and nonliterate, to enjoy the benefits of literacy through these orally
and communally based literacy practices. The practices and the model
supported each other in a closed system of continuity with very little
change for centuries. Just as the sagas came to stand for the whole of
Icelandic life, so, too, the traveling skalds (poets) in the outside world
stood for the whole of a generally literate Icelandic population.

The literacy identity continues to mediate for Icelanders in their interactions with others. It creates an individual and social image that they have continued to promote successfully, even though the literacy practices which were associated with this image have all but died out. Today Icelanders still perceive being literate to be a necessary prerequisite for being Icelandic. However, with different media and contexts, different kinds of literacy have become relevant.

Literacy has functioned as a means by which Icelanders have established and maintained a separate identity. They have used this identity in their international relations. The long-standing importance of their literacy identity, based on a foundation of their earliest historical writings such as *Landnámabók* and *Íslendingabók* in addition to the traditional sagas, has made it difficult for Icelanders to relinquish or modify their current views. It is only within the last fifty years that this culturally constructed image has proven to be archaic and no longer valid in relation to the actual literacy practices that are evident in the more frequent use of other media in society today.

Cracks in the Image of Literacy

The literacy identity laypeople and academicians have relied upon most often in response to questions about literacy in Iceland is strongly based both on the country's cultural traditions—the *kvöldvaka*, the sagas, literacy as a prerequisite for catechism rites and marriage, home-based education—and on its national and educational history. One of the few "facts" generally known outside of Iceland about its citizens is the reported very high literacy rate of 99+%. This reported rate is itself an interesting aspect of the discrepancy between literacy identity and literacy practice. We had come across this figure several times in English-language publications about Iceland before our first trip to the country. Once there, however, no one, including teachers, school administrators, university professors, and ministry education specialists, could tell us how this rate was calculated or by whom. Each asked us where we had seen such a figure; most seemed generally accepting of it, but none had any specific knowledge of its calculation. A few seemed somewhat embarrassed when we asked how such a rate could have been calculated, given that no reading tests had been administered or compiled for the past fifteen years. One professor commented:

I have never seen these figures. It must be the Ministry of Education, but I don't know how they would get these figures. I think
these figures are not reliable, because there's no research that I
know of; but we know, of course, the rate is very high. We're very
lucky. This is probably a social thing because the nation is really a
whole, it's a small nation. If we have some illiterate people, well,
lots of people would know about it.

I'm terribly afraid some of these figures have something to do
with advertisement, like the greenhouses and growing bananas in
Iceland.

When asked about the published literacy rate, another profes-
sor/administrator commented:

How in the world did this figure about 99% come about? I heard it
first in the States. It could be right, I don't know. Reading is emphasized in schools, but actually there's no visual sign of what people
can do now. Since 1977, no official testing has been done. Also, it
has been as long as I know back, a kind of unwritten, maybe it's
written, rule that you have to be able to read when you are confirmed. Now this has changed. Now not all children have confirma-
tion. So actually we lose our knowledge there that we had before.

Thus, this actual rate was never verified, though most people accepted the idea of Iceland's literacy rate being "very high." Does this
concept of a "very high" rate correspond to current literacy practices
or to the traditional literacy identity? Is this figure of 99+% literacy
(also stated as "essentially 100%") a mythical statistic? One cannot
verify the calculation. Educators are now beginning to conduct more
research into the actual practices of literacy. One professor lamented,
however: "We're saying we need to think about reading and writing,
but it seems to be that there's more need to put money in building a
bridge or a road. We're spending lots of money on researching the
salmon in the rivers, but it's difficult to get research money for literacy." Another professor and administrator in education concurred:
"They have very little money in education. If you're doing research
on fish it's quite all right, but not on people. There's not much money
for that."

Although no reading tests had been administered in Icelandic
schools since 1977, there was talk of the need to reestablish a new and
different type of measurement of reading based on an individual's

reading comprehension instead of reading speed as checked by a stopwatch. A change in the educators' model of literacy proposes a new emphasis on individual comprehension as opposed to the more traditional rote skills of reading aloud and gaining comprehension through group discussion. Three professors were associated with the International Association for Educational Achievement International Literacy Study in 1991, in which Iceland was one of thirty-one participating nations. It was conducted in the spring with 2,000 students in each country, a very large percentage of the total number of nine- and fourteen-year-old students in Iceland. The researchers hoped to be able to measure the literacy rate in Iceland and compare it with the other countries participating in the survey.

This survey constituted a new form of literacy measurement with emphasis on comprehension; when the analysis is completed, it will be the first official measurement of literacy in Iceland since the educational reforms begun in the mid-1970s. The students were tested in three categories of reading ability: their ability to understand stories, educational material, and maps and graphs. One press report in *News from Iceland* (August 1992) ran the headline: "Icelandic Children Losing Out: Second Worst among the Nordic Countries." The short article states:

> Icelandic children were ranked tenth in a survey on 9- and 14-year-old children's reading ability. . . . Although Dr. Sigridur Valgeirsdottir, head of the Icelandic survey team, said there was no reason to be unhappy about tenth place, one could guess the results did some damage to Icelandic pride. Icelanders have long boasted of their saga heritage and literacy, and like to think of themselves as being a "nation of book lovers." Among the Nordic countries, only the Danish 9-year-olds scored worse than their Icelandic peers. The 14-year-olds, however, managed to restore a bit of the nation's honour by scoring highest in the category of understanding educational material, and taking third place in the category of comprehending stories. Their scores, however, were the lowest in the Nordic countries when it came to reading maps and graphs. Dr. Valgeirsdottir says they hope the survey will help educators to understand how children learn to read, and to discover which factors affect children's reading abilities. (August 1992, 6)

As one examines the monolithic image of Icelandic literacy identity in detail, more cracks are evident. Icelandic educators who are starting to notice the cracks are watching and measuring them closely, trying to contain the damage. If one compares this literacy identity to the windshield of an automobile, an appropriate analogy can be drawn. The majority of roads in Iceland are gravel; flying stones that crack windshields are a constant hazard. These cracks may range anywhere from a small bull's eye to a major cleavage. The cracks will eventually expand and destroy the windshield if not contained. One must diagnose the problem and its severity and decide on a solution; calculate how to pay for it; and, finally, evaluate whether or not the crack has been permanently contained. At some point, one must decide if the windshield is so weakened that it must be replaced completely. Depending on the specific context, such as the extenuating circumstance of frequent travel on gravel roads, the treatment process may need to be ongoing. Iceland is now at the point of information-gathering, trying to see how extensive the cracks are and speculating about what changes might be in order.

"Saga" versus "Functional" Literacy—Emic Perceptions

Although we maintain that the majority of Icelanders continue to mediate the world through their traditional literacy identity, some are aware of the changing nature of literacy practice and reflect this awareness in their definitions of literacy. One of the traditional definitions is: "If you can read the letters . . . smoothly, fast. If you can read without having to spell the words" (parent). This definition is hardly surprising in light of the type of "reading" (speed) test in use for so many years. Nevertheless, some Icelanders, primarily in the field of education, are becoming less comfortable with this definition and more aware of a functional aspect of literacy. A professor said:

> A literate is someone who can read and understand and use reading for getting knowledge, and you can share your knowledge. If this is true, then I'm terribly afraid that we are not as literate as we think we are.
>
> I've been thinking, is there a need to be worried? What worries me is that there's not very much discussion going on about literacy; and if we believe that we are so good, nothing to worry about, that is dangerous.
>
> . . . I think completely illiterate people are very few in Iceland. But if we're talking about "functionally illiterate," especially if we're talking about writing too, this could be something to be worried about.

A research administrator and professor commented:

I think this, what do you call it in English, "functional literacy"—we really know nothing about that, you see, because the requirement of reading in a society today is so greatly different from what it was thirty or forty years ago. Now you have to be able to comprehend something that's presented maybe in tables, graphs; and then you have to comprehend scientific articles and all sorts of things. Before, you were really only required to be able to read stories, to read the Bible. We didn't even have such things as farm journals. So it's quite different and how young people are doing now on this comprehension on what they're supposed to read in high school. That's really a question we're still finding.

Clearly, what was once literacy in the eyes of most Icelanders is no longer adequate. Another professor states it more strongly:

I think there is actually a gap between the demands of literacy. For example, we changed our whole tax system last year and millions was spent on advertising, information being sent out to the public about the changes and many people are still phoning the office to ask "what is this?" I think in some way they're using concepts, they're using sometimes a strange kind of language, a tax kind of language. They think they've done a very good job, but I'm not very sure. I don't know if we are illiterate people or if they are illiterate.

I see there's a huge gap between these two things—between the "nation" and what is expected, or what is supposed to be. This is something I'm just starting to think about. Maybe this functional literacy is a part of this gap between these two things, which means that the schools have to follow.

We're using old methods of teaching reading, yes, quite good methods, not bad because they're old. For example, phonics—we are putting heavy loads on the system and the method itself and the parts, the tiny parts of reading, the skills of reading, but not understanding.

I'm criticizing the school system because we're teaching reading, reading skills, from maybe six to nine or ten, depends on the kids. But afterward, it's absolutely nothing. I'm trying to explain the reading, the teaching of reading as a much, much wider thing than just the teaching of skills. I'm saying that you have to teach reading from ten up, up to the university level, you see.

Although many Icelanders would not distinguish functional literacy from traditional literacy to such a degree as our informants do, they are aware of discrepancies between identity and practice—further cracks in the image. Some have recently expressed consternation that often in today's homes many of the books on the bookshelves, especially beautiful, leather-bound sets of the sagas, are there only for display as material possessions. This has been described as a kind of "required" interior decorating scheme for Icelandic homes. Evidently, many young couples purchase or receive as wedding or housewarming gifts these household decorating items. As one scholar rather sadly put it: "Sagas by the metre are what count" (Griffiths 1969: 164). One parent verified this with the example of her brother: "I know some people just have the sagas for looking at. My brother bought all the books and he has never opened them. I think I'm the only one who has opened them at his home."

R. F. Tomasson (1980), in his questionnaires, found that a vast number of Icelanders had not read and did not "know" the sagas and their characters. This flies in the face of the image touted by academicians and government public relations brochures.

But it is a question to what extent Icelandic culture in its institutional manifestations—the university, museums, theaters, schools— represents the "real" Iceland as it is perceived both by the Icelandic public generally and by foreigners. There is a certain artificiality about the official culture with its emphasis on a vanished past, which is often rather romantic (OECD 1987: 7).

The *kvöldvaka* was the traditional time of reading the sagas in the old days. As a modern equivalent, parents in both Reykjavík and Blindgötudalur commonly reported that they normally read to their younger children at bedtime, though not the sagas. Although this practice was claimed for the home in which one of us lived for over three months with a three- and a six-year-old, it took place only a few times during that entire period. Again, one wonders if the actual practice fits the promoted image.

Iceland has another strong literacy claim regarding the large number of daily and weekly newspapers and their correspondingly large readership. Most of the papers are based in the Reykjavík area; because of Blindgötudalur's rural location, newspapers are delivered at most only two or three times a week with the mail. The mail might also include other reading materials such as government brochures, magazines, or agricultural journals for the parents. The headmaster of the school in Blindgötudalur commented:

> I think, well, in towns like Reykjavík, see, there are not many homes that don't buy newspapers. But there are quite a few homes in Blindgötudalur that don't buy newspapers. In other places in Iceland this would be very unusual.
>
> I think people around here read very much around Christmas [the traditional book-giving period]. At other times, I don't think they read much. Some do, but the average person doesn't read very much. The [school] library is open, twenty-four hours a day, open to everyone who wants, but it's not used much. (teacher)

It was ironic to hear Icelanders in the city say that they thought people out on the farms read less, while the farmers and their wives said they thought that the people in the city read less, due to the stress of a more hurried lifestyle. It seems that Icelanders are becoming aware of a decline in reading, but that each group thinks it is the other who is reading less. Everyone seemed agreed upon the point, however, that what reading they did do was primarily concentrated within the dark winter months, particularly during the Christmas holidays when most people receive books as gifts. This tradition of Christmas book-giving might also be in danger of decline if the heavy pre-Christmas onslaught of advertising by the publishing houses is indicative of a perceived need to convince Icelanders to continue buying books instead of toys, videos, or other new items of interest to both children and adults. Several parents commented on the decrease in number of books their children were now receiving at Christmas in comparison to their memories of gift books received during their childhood. A parent and teacher said:

> We were given books for presents. I think a lot more maybe when we were younger than the kids are now. I had a lot more books when I was younger than my sons get for Christmas. That was the favorite gift. People used to count books for Christmas. When we were growing up, we asked our friends after Christmas, "Did you get this book for Christmas? I got it too, and I got this book and this book and so on."
>
> Also, kids now get picture books, cartoons, comic books—just look at the pictures and forget the texts. And, of course, it's limited text. When I was young, I always got books with text at Christmas.

I don't know, I think "He-Man" [a plastic toy] is the worst thing
Iceland has ever got. We have tons of plastic from the States, which,
for some of them at least, we would like to send right back. And
then there is a lot more television, a lot more television, than when
we were growing up.

Presently, Icelandic popular culture is being heavily influenced
by other cultures, American and British in particular, primarily
through television and video, raising the possibility, some fear, that
the younger generation may reject a large part of traditional culture
entirely. This is deemed possible because Icelanders are beginning to
recognize that new literacy practices are being transmitted through
the schools and the media, replacing those traditional home practices
that were the basis for the monolithic literacy identity. A parent commented: "[It is] changing because of all the television, videos. The
language and reading are as important still today, [to] this [older] generation now; but the younger generation, I don't know. They speak
English, they listen to English."

New Literacies

The transition in Iceland to a "schooled society" has led to a new conceptualization of literacy and a growing realization that the practices
associated with it differ in their consequences from the traditional
ones that made up the cultural model of literacy identity. Another
new literacy which will have important consequences in Iceland involves electronic media.

Iceland's electronic media still have elements of the printed word
(Icelandic subtitles) contained in the majority of transmissions. As in
the past, the two modes of communication, oral and written, are still
very much intertwined. Some of the concepts of literacy gleaned
from my interviews stressed the positive and, in some people's minds,
contradictory connection between reading and television. On the
whole, parents voiced more positive associations between television
and literacy acquisition by young Icelandic children than did professional educators.

I don't know, the children watch television and video, but they have
to read the text, so they want to be able to read the text. If we had
Icelandic talk for everything, it wouldn't matter so much for them
to be able to read. (teacher)

I'm certain if you asked the children "Can you read?" well, if they can read the subtitles on television, they would say, well, "I can read." That's a main goal. And to be able to read all that, they have to be able to read about 160–180 syllables a minute. It comes so fast. You have to be a good reader to keep up. Not all of the parents, the older people, can read all the text because of the speed. It is necessary to maintain this speed or else you get no sense out of what you're watching. (teacher)

I don't know, I think it doesn't help. But perhaps television helps with their beginning to learn to read. (parent)

I think I can agree with reading subtexts being helpful, but on the other hand, I don't really like television. It makes them too passive, inactive. (parent)

I don't think it will have so much influence because we have this law that everything on television has to have the subtexts in Icelandic. The kids have to read the text, they try that. (teacher)

Kids brag about being able to read the subtexts on the television. But it still scares me, I think, as the nation becomes "televised," "videoized," and so on. I don't feel as safe with all the television as we may have been. Some kids have unlimited access to video and television. At the age they are beginning to learn to read, they will watch anything if they are not stopped. They will watch anything, they are just watching the world—it comes from out there. It comes steadily, and you don't have to put any effort into it. I think we should watch our step. (teacher)

So, maybe in the States they should start buying films with different languages so they can test this with young children who are starting to read. Because in the States they watch television very much, it starts early in the morning and goes on all the day. (parent)

Television and video-movies are recent phenomena in Iceland, but ones with which most of the younger generation of Icelanders (mid-twenties and younger) are closely associated. American television shows could be first seen in the 1960s in areas near the NATO base, though laws were quickly passed to stop the infiltration of this new outside influence. The Icelandic government established television Channel One and gradually increased both its broadcast range and duration. In 1989–1990, with the emergence of a new private, paid channel, Channel Two, the government channel increased its hours of operation to include Thursday nights, which had, from the start, been reserved for "nontelevision family time." A majority of homes throughout Iceland, though concentrated in the southwest urban area, bought the "key" for viewing the private Channel Two. In Blindgötudalur, however, television was quite late in its arrival. Channel One was first available to most homes in the early 1980s, and it is still not possible to receive Channel Two.

By law all foreign-language television programs, videocassettes, and movies have to be subtitled in Icelandic. Thus, one hears the foreign language, although some Icelanders turn off the audio, while reading the translation of the dialogue. Unfortunately, the translations, done quickly to keep up with the onslaught of incoming material, are quite simplified, limited to two lines at a time, regardless of the length of the actual dialogue. Many young Icelanders also use the television shows to teach themselves English years before they study it in school. Again, the printed Icelandic text they read can help them to understand and associate the meanings of the foreign words they are hearing.

Although some believe the subtexts aid reading, an association between television viewing and a drop in the average number of books read by children ages twelve to fifteen in Iceland has been reported, from 7.2 books in 1979 to 2.7 books in 1988 (Broddason 1990).

The concept of hearing and seeing the words at the same time is reminiscent of parents and children sharing the reading of a bedtime story, looking at the pictures and text on the pages as the story is read aloud and heard by the child. This idea, a technological adaptation of the generally accepted aid to literacy of bedtime story reading, might change the practice of television viewing both among the public and in the schools. Nevertheless, there are reservations about "television literacy":

> Maybe it helps, but the text is different because you are using just a limited number of letters that will fit on two lines. That means it's very short. I'm thinking about the effect on cohesion, for example. Another thing is that the speed of this is a fixed speed, and we need flexible reading habits. Which means that it can affect the speed of reading but you can't go further—you stay put at "TV speed." I think every text helps, but just in a limited way.

But I think also, to be very nasty, that this idea of the television text is probably an excuse because the parents are watching television and the kids are sitting with them and they know it's probably not good, that it's better for the kids to read. It's really just an excuse. (professor)

In today's Iceland a new definition of being literate, used often by both children and their parents, much more than by educators, is the ability to read subtitles on television. One of its determining factors is the ability to match the speed at which the subtitles are scrolled across the television screen. At this point, television literacy appears to be accepted by most Icelanders as at least a new addition to, and possibly a replacement for, the earlier criterion of being literate—the ability to read the sagas and the Bible.

Many literacy programs emphasize the individual, and one change in literacy practice in Iceland is a shift from a communal to an individual context of reading and comprehension. This shift from the *kvöldvaka* communal reading and discussion of printed materials to the silent individual reading of newspapers, textbooks, and television/video subtexts diminishes the everyday opportunities for development of children's reading skills. One possible consequence in current literacy practices is less complete comprehension of the material due to being able neither to hear the ideas of others nor to test one's perceptions against them concerning the same material. The "scaffolding" effect would exist neither for younger or less experienced readers to climb up to higher rungs of understanding, vocabulary, and reading skills nor for readers of less skill to be equally connected with others in the social context of hearing and discussing basic understandings of social behavior as gleaned from the communal readings. The shift from communal to individual silent reading may mean that some individuals, as opposed to the practice in the past, would be excluded from Icelandic literacy identity and literacy practices.

The only example of this kind of communal literate activity that I observed in the schools was the short story-reading by teachers in several of the schools for the six- and seven-year-olds. There was usually no discussion, just reading of the story to the children. One teacher, however, seemed quite aware of possible lack of knowledge of vocabulary terms by the children and would stop to give a familiar example. This situation exemplifies yet another shift in literacy practice from the home to the school in the process of literacy acquisition and development by children.

In different areas in Iceland (e.g., the countryside, the city, and the fishing villages), and even in individual homes within the same areas, there appears to be a growing variance of literacy practices. We believe that this will have an effect on the cultural identity of Iceland in the future. New social and cultural distinctions and divisions are beginning to be seen which might act to decrease the traditional homogeneity. Based on our participation in and observation of current culture and society, both urban and rural, we believe there will be a diminution of literacy as measured by school literacy tests. This lowering of the national literacy rate will be intimately associated with the transition from the old literacy identity to another based less on the saga tradition and more on current established literacy practices associated primarily with school and media. Thus, rather than continuing to act as a unifying or leveling force, literacy in Iceland has the strong potential of changing to a divisive factor, thereby adding fuel to the fire of other developing social distinctions.

Both literacy identity practices and literacy can act as mediating devices in a culture's interactions with others. By viewing literacy in a culture-specific context, as the sociocognitive perspective allows, we can examine the role of literacy both diachronically and synchronically. This is essential in order to document continuity and change in either or both literacy identities and literacy practices. We believe that literacy, the ideologically/culturally constructed literacy identity, and the concrete social literacy practices have acted as enabling and conserving factors in Icelandic society and culture. Icelandic literacy identity has functioned as a conservative factor rather than as a modernizing force. Literacy was not only used for functional reasons associated with economic, political, and religious needs but was also a powerful force helping to preserve the existing social, economic, political and mental world of Icelanders. We believe that the reliance solely on this older, now outdated, literacy identity to mediate the world will not survive long into the future.

MAGNÚS EINARSSON

11

THE WANDERING SEMIOTICIANS:
TOURISM AND THE IMAGE OF MODERN ICELAND

> *A person in the 20th century can exist honestly only as a foreigner.*
> —*Julia Kristeva*

It is nearly a commonplace in pragmatism that action precedes knowledge. The child must move about to gain experience and a sense of self. This is precisely what happens when people travel. The traveler, characterized by his or her social nature and historical era, tries to incorporate all new experience into a cultural scheme of "the order of things." Traveling is a useful epistemological metaphor for the kind of experience where the remote and the strange become more familiar; the routine pattern of everyday life is altered into a state of liminality in which people reflect on self and Otherness. The practice of anthropology bears close resemblance to this process because the act of understanding the Other, although the boundaries are constantly shifting, also involves self-discovery and the construction of ethnic and self identities.

I am mainly concerned with the ethnicity of the Icelanders and their identity as a modern nation. Modern tourism in Iceland provides Icelanders with a national image through what Roland Barthes called the "rhetoric of the image." Travelers' accounts of Iceland, abundant from the nineteenth century, have played a role in the identity formation among Icelanders, and at times Icelanders responded in defense to construct a separate and more praiseworthy identity. This interaction between different frames of meaning is a dynamic relationship comparable to the one that develops between the observer and the observed. This process is still at work through mass tourism, though the character has changed and the scale has expanded due to industrialization and modernity. Icelandic identity is now interwoven with an ideology of nationalism. Emphasizing the cult of the nation-state and the "glorious past," nationalism is a constructed phenomenon of an imagined community (Anderson 1991 [1983]) that seeks recognition and adherence by means of invented traditions (Hobsbawm 1983a), mythmaking, monuments, relics, and historical memory to create a continuity between the past and the present. The present controls and organizes the past to fit its needs (Lowenthal 1990). Through the display of official and historical buildings, museums, and monuments which represent a sense of roots and project the future, Reykjavík, the capital city, has served as the main site to confirm and defend the nationalistic ideology in the twentieth century. As the tourists gaze at these staged constructions, Icelanders respond. As more Icelanders have responded to the tourist industry and toured in Iceland as well as in southern Europe and the United States, they have shared the tourist perspective in other lands.

Not long ago, tourism was not so evident in the mind of the average Icelander, but now it has become a part of their lives and plays a major role concerning foreign currency earnings. Every sector of the economy is in one way or another geared toward tourism. Recently, local communities have been representing themselves as special tourist attractions with their renovated old houses and other district specialities. Icelanders have become preoccupied with their own image. But, at the same time, they are ambivalent toward tourism and tourists in relation to the natural environment. The romantic nationalist ideology represents the environment, like the language and people, as pure. Foreigners by definition pollute. Icelanders debate whether tourists can grasp the "real" Iceland.

Icelanders now have the opportunity to produce and stage their identity with the help of modern industry, something that was impossible in the past. The whole society is marked by this change; even Christmas, which is highly bound up with nationalism and tourism, bears the characteristics of modernity. Tourism has to be contextualized within modern consumer culture imagery and cultural productions: the realm of aesthetic pleasures, desires, dreams, images, and style. The glossy brochures of the tourist industry create and reify such a realm of image and meaning. Nationalism has become such a sign which Icelanders create at home and to which they respond abroad.

The tourist gaze is visual in two main forms: the romantic and the collective (Urry 1990a). The romantic is looking for the authentic, but the collective does not mind looking at artificial sights or spaces of "staged authenticity" or inauthenticity, because that is the nature of the modern experience. These forms influence the way Icelanders present themselves to render an authentic and romantic appearance of their identity. But tourists visiting Iceland are heterogeneous, seeking different levels of meaning regarding their own national identities and how they are related to Icelandic history, if at all. Some tourists seek meaning in relation to environmental issues, as Iceland has become projected an image of purity.

Historical Perspective and Theory

Until the nineteenth century traveling was only available to a narrow elite and was a mark of status. The late-nineteenth-century development of the railway permitted mass travel for the first time and industrialization and democratization have shaped the modern social structure, which lies at the foundation of mass tourism.

Dean MacCannell, writing about the tourist as the best model of modern people, believes that "the progress of modernity depends on its sense of instability and inauthenticity" and that "for moderns, reality and authenticity are thought to be elsewhere" (1976: 3). But how has all this come about? The answer is to be found in history. The roots of anthropology lie within the historical process of exploration and witnessing the unfamiliar, which is still molding the anthropological perspective. The search for an "Absolute Other" is a theme that runs through the literature and history of Western civilization and is represented in the literature of Odysseus, Gulliver, and Jules Verne as well as Western ethnography. MacCannell states that this theme reaches a final peak in modernity: "What begins as the proper activity of a hero (Alexander the Great) develops into the goal of a socially organized group (the Crusaders), into the mark of status of an entire social class (the Grand Tour of the British 'gentleman'), eventually becoming universal experience (the tourist)" (1976: 5).

The nature of the travel experience is relevant to tourism and the anthropological imagination. Tourism and anthropology may have somewhere "deep down" a common root, but there has always been a discontinuity. In the course of history, relativism developed as an organized perspective in the background of the Renaissance, the age of exploration, and the Enlightenment. The main challenge and problem in anthropology has been the redefinition of the myths of "relativism" and "objectivism" concerning the relationship between self and Other. Bernard McGrane (1989) takes a critical look at what anthropology is and what it cannot be. Self and Other construct each other, and McGrane's study is a critique of the positivist impulse to objectify the Other, which is part of "that egocentric tendency of our Western mind to identify itself as separate from what it perceives as external to it" (1989: 5). Similarly, James L. Peacock (1986) emphasizes the need in anthropology to realize that Other-knowledge and self-knowledge enhance each other rather than merely compete. He believes that "insight into the Self is best obtained through relation to another person" and that an "insight into one's own culture is best obtained through relation to another culture" (1986: 87). The similarity of the anthropological and tourist experiences is curiosity about cultural variations. Thus the problem is to define the differences in the relationship between anthropology and Other, and the relationship between the tourist and Other.

The history of the travel experience and travel writing illuminates how anthropology developed as a perspective. The early civilizations in the Middle East, Asia, and the Mediterranean have left written records of their traveling. Herodotus, among the first pioneers in travel writing, wrote about the nature of travel in psychological terms and about the strange manners and customs in foreign countries. On his trips, Herodotus "reports having heard many stories about strange things, like dogheaded men, one-eyed men, headless men with eyes in their chest and goat-footed men" (Cassen 1974: 111). These kinds of expressions are well known from the history of travelers' accounts, which emphasized or redefined the boundaries of the knowable. Two medieval Icelandic sagas, *Grænlendinga saga* and *Eiríks saga rauða*, describe natives of America as barbarian (*skrælingjar*) and running around on one foot (Karlsson 1989: 70). The construction of Otherness among Icelanders can also be seen in Snorri Sturluson's *Heimskringla* on the history of Norwegian kings. *The First Grammatical Treatise* (*Fyrsta málfræðiritgerð Ormsbókar Snorra Eddu*) provided a basis for constructing a linguistic identity for Icelanders and *Hauksbók*, a version of *Landnámabók*, the medieval *Book of Settlements*, provides a chapter on the "nature of different peoples" (cited in Páls- son and Durrenberger 1989: xii).

European expansion was facilitated by new cartograpic and sail- ing technologies from the Renaissance, when "travel documents multiplied through the newly invented printing press" (Graburn and Jafari 1991: 2). Two centuries later the belief in reason was perva- sive in the Enlightenment. James Clifford (1986: 2, 23) points out that ethnography's traditional vocation of cultural criticism has its roots in the writings of this period, such as the *Essays* of Montaigne and Montesquieu's *Persian Letters* and *The Spirit of the Laws*. The writ- ings of the Renaissance figure François Rabelais fit into this category of "pre-anthropologists." Mary B. Campbell (1988: 166) believes that travel literature may be involved in the development of the modern novel and geography as well as ethnography. Travel accounts are of- ten similar, showing a conflict between "mythic expectation and mundane fact" which has become "one of the generic foci of travel writing" (1988: 116).

This evidence suggests differences between anthropologists and tourists. It is possible to indicate a spectrum with the anthropologist at one end, the tourist at the opposite end, and the traveler/explorer somewhere in between. The spectrum could represent a conflict be- tween "fact" and "myth," and the nature of the relationship between self and Other. The anthropologist is trained to be aware of these questions that pose epistemological problems. Tourists make a dis- tinction between their own "subjectivity" and the "objectivity" of the phenomenon they experience. The greatest gap between anthropol- ogy and tourism becomes evident when the tourist only has access to what has been staged by the tourist industry, as when an Icelander enters Disney World in Florida.

It is illuminating to look at the Renaissance literature as "the re- hearsal of cultures" (see Mullaney 1983). Europeans were facing new dimensions of humanity as they came into contact with other people in distant places. Some of these people were brought back to Europe to be gazed at. Steven Mullaney says that a "rehearsal" of a strange culture is to be looked at as a "self-consuming review of unfamiliar things" (1983: 48–49). The ritualistic incorporation of "Otherness" is the core of Mullaney's discussion.

Ceremonies, rituals, and spectacles are staged events, and very often they are manifestations of power and identity. The staging of history and the performance of the past produce sources of legitimacy for modernity. Such staged events represent authority and community and are vital parts of the modern scene of national celebrations, parades, city planning, and tourist attractions. Thus the celebration of the Fishers' day (Sjómannadagurinn) in Iceland, the celebration of Independence day (Þjóðhátíðardagurinn, June 17), and the setting of parliament (Alþingissetning) in modern Iceland are all ceremonies of identification mainly staged for Icelanders by Icelanders.

Travelers' Accounts of Iceland

Due to increased foreign fishing in Icelandic waters, many foreigners visited Iceland during the fifteenth and sixteenth centuries. The German Dithmar Blefken and the English Andrew Boorde describe Icelanders as "superstitious and uncivilized beasts" (Pálsson and Durrenberger 1989: x). Blefken never visited the country himself and his account was based on seafarers' tales. Blefken talks about the Icelanders becoming 200 years old and parents "giving" their daughters to German merchants in exchange for other goods (see Tomasson 1980: 102–103). The descriptions of these early travelers and writers are manifestations of their own cultural identities, constructed through the dichotomy between their familiar European cultural centers and the unfamiliar strangeness at the periphery of the world.

At times, Icelanders have not been satisfied with the image of Iceland that foreign voices presented. Icelandic scholars responded by presenting "more correct" images with which fellow Icelanders could proudly identify. Those who wrote in Icelandic clearly did not address an audience of foreigners, to whom the language was inaccessible. *Íslendingabók* (Book of Icelanders) and *Landnámabók* (Book of Settlement), from the Commonwealth period, both try to maintain ideas about the virtuous ancestry of Icelanders. Arngrímur Jónsson's *Crymogæa* (Iceland), written in 1609, is a refutation of the idea that Icelanders were "barbarians." In this century, Sigurður Nordal's *Íslensk Menning* (Icelandic Culture), written in 1942, and Guðmundur Finnbogason's *Íslendingar* (The Icelanders), written in 1971, portray what Icelanders want to look like to themselves in the images of romantic nationalism (see Pálsson and Durrenberger 1989: xiv–xv).[1]

Gradually, the image of Iceland changed as the economic and intellectual turmoil changed in Europe, and more scholars became interested in Iceland. The first scientist to visit and write an account of the country was the Danish Niels Horrebow, who spent two years in Iceland (1749–1751) to study topics as diverse as volcanic activity, child-rearing, diseases, diet, housing, and the literary bent of the Icelanders. The purpose of Horrebow's mission was to correct former accounts of Iceland (Tomasson 1980: 23–24). This was due to the influence of the Enlightenment movement in Denmark with an interest in reforming the Icelandic economy in the eighteenth century. The nineteenth century saw a growing tendency toward "positive" remarks that Icelanders were "pure-hearted" and "wonderful" people (Tomasson 1980: 26–27). In 1814–1815 the Scotsman Ebenezer Henderson traveled in Iceland and described his journey as a dangerous and mysterious mission with a feeling of excitement and discovery. The English William Morris visited the country in 1871 and 1873, when he noticed in a rather romantic vision the "egalitarian spirit among Icelanders, which made himself an egalitarian in his politics" (Tomasson 1980: 21–22). Morris envisioned a model for an ideal beauty through the image of Iceland in relation to the sagas, some of which he translated in collaboration with Eiríkur Magnússon. The Icelandic sagas became the model for the future of his Utopia (Solomon 1979: 82). Richard F. Burton, who traveled to Iceland in 1872, says that travelers were impressed by everything they saw, "scenes of thrilling horror, of majestic grandeur, and of heavenly beauty," a condition he called "Iceland on the Brain" (Tomasson 1980: 26).[2]

Iceland provided a scene for romantic fulfillment and the intellectual curiosity that characterized the spirit of nineteenth-century Europe. Thus Iceland was incorporated into European discourses, in the form of naturalism, romanticism, evolutionism, realism, and positivism, which all contributed to a new view of people and nature. In fact, the Icelandic intellectuals studying in Copenhagen, under the influence of this intellectual turmoil, brought back these ideas, which became the foundation for an ideology of independence and national pride that they presented in the form of articles, poetry, and speeches.

Ideas of superiority of the Icelanders are evident from the early twentieth century. In 1916 James Bryce talks about the uniqueness of Icelanders: "nowhere else, except in Greece, was so much produced that attained . . . so high a level of excellence" (Tomasson 1980: ix). The British medievalist W. P. Ker and the American geographer and geographical determinist Ellsworth Huntington wrote, in the early twentieth century, about the "magnificent qualities of the Icelanders relating it to a selective migration from Norway and a thousand years of severe natural-selection" (Tomasson 1980: 121). And in his preface to Vilhjálmur Stefánsson's (1939) book *Iceland: The First American Republic*, Theodore Roosevelt emphasizes the harshness of living in Iceland through the ages and that it is a country for "hardy men and women." He believes that Icelanders are sea wanderers by tradition and that poetry and the saga tradition are deeply embedded in the Icelandic character, which believes in democracy and equality (Roosevelt 1939: v–vii).

Recently, there have been many articles and handbooks on Iceland by foreign authors and Icelanders still feel the urge to correct some of these accounts if they do not fit the "recipe of the image." Certain key themes are always mentioned, such as geology, survival in a harsh country, the sagas, literature, language, literacy, superstition, modernity, technology, and equality (see Levathes 1987). It seems as if people of different nationality, touring Iceland, are looking for themes that they can relate to by comparison with their own sense of national identity and ethnicity. The majority of tourists come from Germany, Scandinavian countries, the United States, Britain, and France, and the motivation to tour Iceland is tied to national relevance-structures of meaning. Iceland may signify different things for people of different nationalities, due to former historical relationships with the island. Tourists are comparing Iceland and Icelanders with their own identity and nationality, which renders the journey meaningful. Thus Sigurður Magnússon (1977: 1) believes that, for Scandinavians, Iceland may be the "Isle of the Sagas" and a place where Nordic culture blossomed some centuries ago; for the British, the place of the cod wars; for the French, the setting of Jules Verne's novel about Iceland and shipwrecked French fishers in the last century. For the Americans, Iceland is the home of Leifur Eiríksson, who discovered America before Columbus; and Germans might be looking for the pre-Christian culture of the Teutonic people. These are not the only themes that the tourists are seeking, although they may be typical of an attitude toward Iceland. Besides this relevance-structure of historical relationship, the tourists might be acting in accordance with a relevance-structure of environmental issues and existential pondering.

The Tourist Experience and the Tourist Gaze

The tourist experience is central to the modern experience (Urry 1990b) and becomes important for the identity of Icelanders as they become aware that they are being looked at and how they have gazed at the people among whom they have toured. Tourism is a dynamic social construction.

In tourist studies there has been a tendency to see the tourist experience as either something superficial, as an extension of the alienated world, or as a serious search for authenticity, as an effort to escape from the alienated world. Thus Daniel Boorstin talks about the tourist experience as a "pseudo-event" (Cohen 1979: 179), and John Turner and John Ash (1975: 159) point out that many aspects of culture become the prey of the "tourist kitsch." In the opposite direction, Dean MacCannell (1976) defines the tourist as a kind of a contemporary pilgrim. Erik Cohen (1979) believes that there are different modes of tourism according to their relation to the "center" of the tourist's cosmos. He argues that the tourist does not exist as a clearly defined type because different kinds of people may desire different modes of tourist experiences, depending on their relation to the "center." This "center," although traditionally linked to the sacred journeys of pilgrimages, is for Cohen a measure of ultimate meanings for the individual (1979: 180–181). Thus it is possible to present a spectrum of tourist experience with "mere pleasure" at one end and "quest for meaning" at the other end. The main difference between pilgrimage and modern mass tourism is that pilgrimage is movement inward from the periphery toward the "center," but tourism is a movement outward away from the "cultural center" into the periphery, where the different or novel is anticipated. Furthermore, Cohen suggests that these differences are often combined in the modern world (1979: 182–183).

This may be seen as a metaphor revealing the experience of doing anthropology. The anthropologist is partly like the tourist seeking to get away from his or her "cultural center" into the periphery and partly like the pilgrim seeking a way into "the center" of a form of life. It is useful to look at the tourist experience as a ritual process and a form of play.

Victor Turner (1978) applies the model of Arnold Van Gennep's *Rites of Passage* in his analysis of the pilgrim's rites of passage. Consequently, tourism as a modern ritual has a threefold structure of traveling away from home, the experience of change in the nonordinary place, and the return to home and ordinary work (Graburn 1983: 12). Through tourism, everyday obligations are suspended or inverted into nonserious behavior which is associated with playfulness, recreation, and anticipation of new or different experiences.

The desires for inspiration and recreation are often integrated at tourist attractions or "sacred places," where the sacred and the profane are common features. This becomes evident by "reading" a city, a site, or a natural landscape.

Þingvellir is among the most famous attractions for Icelandic tourists. It is a place where culture and landscape seem almost identical to Icelanders. This place contains simultaneously a sacred and a profane dimension, by indicating a sacred inspiration and a pleasurable recreation. Culture and history are engraved in the landscape that forms Þingvellir and its surroundings. Historical events took place there for centuries, and it served as one of the main assembly places, especially in the Commonwealth period. The spirit of the romantic movement in the nineteenth century is engraved in the landscape of Þingvellir through the poetry of the romantic poet and naturalist Jónas Hallgrímsson. The mountains Ármannsfell and Skjaldbreiður signify the spirit of the romantic movement. A special graveyard is dedicated to the memory of the "national poets" (þjóðskáldin) Jónas Hallgrímsson and Einar Benediktsson. Þingvellir has been a formal national park since 1928.

But Þingvellir also represents a unique area in geological terms, as part of the Atlantic Ridge and the mechanism of plate tectonics. In that sense Þingvellir and Iceland come to signify universal forces in the eyes of the foreign tourists. And still it is a place of recreational activity. In the minds of the Icelanders it is a good place for fishing, camping, eating, drinking, and even tanning: for relaxing and enjoying life (slappa af og njóta lífsins).

For Icelanders, a trip to the Blue Lagoon (Bláa lónið) is mainly a recreational activity, but it is also an adventure to a place of tremendous forces of nature in the form of high-temperature geothermal resources; the geothermal power station, which in fact produces the Blue Lagoon, signifies the technological advancements of modern Iceland. This place represents at least three levels of meaning for the tourists: nature and environment; history and technology; and recreation and existential meaning. These levels underlie the image in

1   The Blue Lagoon. From a visitor's map.

figure 1, where natural forces have been tamed through modern technology, serving people in their quest of health, pleasure, and leisure. Many other attractions or expeditions may serve as metaphors for a special theme or meanings. An expedition into the interior of Kjölur may become a metaphor for entering wilderness, far-away from modernity, and standing in the steps of the outlaw figures of Icelandic folklore.

To foreigners, an expedition to Iceland might serve as a metaphor for traveling to a "nowhere land," because it is betwixt and between the Old World and the New World; it is "nature's wonderland—jewel of the north," according to the tourist brochures, and always a reminder of the formation of the earth itself. In this sense the tourist experience as a ritual process and a form of play becomes more evident.

The tourist industry is built around some elements of the tourist gaze. The tourist industry is part of cultural productions that formulate a sense of style and image, which have become a vital part of everyday life. Places are chosen to be gazed upon because a great deal of anticipation has been created about them through a variety of media such as films, videos, magazines, brochures, records, and TV, which construct the gaze. These practices provide the signs in terms of which the holiday experiences are understood (Urry 1990a). The gaze is directed to features of landscape, available through photographs, postcards, films, or models that are out-of-the-ordinary.

The gaze is constructed through all three modes of the sign—iconic, indexical, and symbolic—and tourism involves the collection of such signs. The tourists' search is directed at signs of typical Iceland or typical Icelandic behavior: Viking culture, the midnight sun, volcanoes and glaciers, or even a typical small fishing village, which becomes the real and authentic Iceland. The glossy brochures of the tourist industry inform these "wandering semioticians" where these signs are to be found in the country and at what time of the year. The signs become generalized images of Iceland.

In figure 2 the photographic image emphasizes the tranquillity and purity of the landscape, with the special breed of the Icelandic horse grazing freely and unrestrained in the foreground, and in the far distance a mythical landscape opens up a possibility of wilderness. The image supports a romantic vision of "majestic grandeur, and of heavenly beauty."

Attractions and signs emphasize ideas and evoke feelings. Thus the display of signs through the tourist industry resembles the display of signs in the cinema and can be manipulated in the fashion of the Eisensteinian "montage of attractions," by focusing and ordering attention (with stimuli and shock). The study of the sign in the tourist industry is relevant for our understanding of practice, reification, and anthropological theory. V. N. Vološinov's (1973) investigation of the relationship between the sign and ideology indicates that signs do not exist by themselves; they emerge in social interaction and through interaction consciousness becomes filled with signs (1973: 12). Ice-

2 Iceland as nature's wonderland. From a tourist pamphlet.

landic nationalistic sentiments and other sentiments of beauty and glory are expressed through the signs of the tourist industry, and Icelanders identify their nationality through these signs, which also are representative of a cultural identity for the tourists. Icelanders and tourists are constantly negotiating meanings and identities as they interact with each other in practice and in verbal discourse.

The two main forms of the tourist gaze, the romantic and the collective, illuminate the nature of the tourist experience and their expectations. Icelanders have a conflict of interests between the need to increase the income of foreign currencies and the need to preserve their romantic concept of unpolluted natural beauty so dear to the nationalist images. The tourist gaze is related to this dilemma. The romantic form of the tourist gaze (Urry 1990a) revolves around the private and the personal relationship with the object of the gaze. But the collective form of the tourist gaze emphasizes the fact that tourist attractions are designed as public places.

The problem of overcrowding is a major tourism policy issue in Iceland. As tourists have been increasing in numbers over the past two decades, numbering 53,000 in 1970 and 156,000 in 1993, tourism earnings have also been rising. Consequently, Icelanders are getting more interested in extending the tourist season, as they have grown more aware of the possibilities of presenting local features that have normally not been within mainstream tourism. These off-peak holidays are becoming a reality: there is already a sign of tourists coming at the end of each year, to gaze at the strange behavior of Icelanders shooting fireworks into the air on New Year's Eve.

The collective tourist gaze is often looked down upon by those concerned with conserving the environment and maintaining the country's prestige and image of purity. But these tourists are still needed for the growth of the economy. John Urry (1990a: 34) describes them as "post-tourists," people who have no problem with "staged authenticity," because they look at tourism as a game to be played. The lack of authenticity is more of a problem for the romantic tourist gaze, which has been criticized as "middle-age elitism" (1990a: 28), although the notion of romantic nature is fundamentally invented pleasure.

Nationalism and the Tourist Menu

Icelanders are ambivalent toward the presence of tourists and at the same time are ambivalent about their own identities, resembling individuals seeking autonomy and independence from parents. Through the romantic movement in the nineteenth century, Icelanders demanded independence from Denmark, which soon became a foundation for nationalism and a new definition of the nation's identity. Through nationalism and tourism in the twentieth century, Icelanders have established a formal identity, a front stage. The renowned "How-do-you-like-Iceland?" question that Icelanders ask foreigners is perhaps indicative of this ambivalence and the wish for recognition.

Icelanders like to present a romantic image by emphasizing the idea of purity in all spheres of the country—environmental, historic, linguistic, cultural, and culinary (unpolluted waters and food). Thus the marketing of tranquillity (see figure 2), for example, by the Icelandic Farm Holidays (Ferðaþjónusta bænda), which is a rather recent innovation in the tourist industry. Consequently, the collective tourists' reputation is low because they are believed to be too "vulgar" to understand the essence of being Icelandic, the purity of culture, language, and landscape so dear to the image. This finds expression among Icelanders when they describe the typical tourists and make fun of them by uttering the word *túrhestar* (tourhorses): they are just a bunch of wanderers who hardly know what they are doing, their experience must be fake, and they will never understand the real us!

But at the same time Icelanders enjoy the role of the host. They need to show the guests who they really are. They need witnesses to confirm their identity. Gunnar Karlsson (1985) believes that this kind of ambivalence is inherent in the nature of Icelandic nationalism, expressing itself in the "progressive nationalism" of Jón Sigurðsson and the "romantic nationalism" of the contributors to the nationalistic journal *Fjölnir*.

At the same time that Icelanders want to present traditional values and the culture of preindustrial Iceland, they put it away into indoor or outdoor museums, into the realm of nostalgic memory of bravery and glory, so that new technological advancements may take place in the space of the everyday. Icelanders are preoccupied in presenting both the past and the present.

A sightseeing tour around the Reykjavík area illustrates the past and the present and their relationship. In the same sightseeing tour, tourists may observe old buildings from the eighteenth and nineteenth century and the newest restaurant building, Perlan (the Pearl), or a new geothermal power station followed by a modern Blue Lagoon bathing spot. The idea is emphasized that the past projects the present. David Lowenthal's (1990) study of the past illuminates that the past is swallowed up by an ever-expanding present in the form of memory, monuments, and tradition. That is why many governments nationalize their nation's past.

Lowenthal believes that the past, or rather pastness, is enormously important for the identity of the Icelanders and that their future depends on their discourse of their past (1990: 46). Similarly, E. J. Hobsbawm (1983a) argues that traditions are very often recent in origin and sometimes invented to construct an image of rootedness in remotest antiquity. The image of Fjallkonan (the Mountain Woman), a national symbol of purity (see Björnsdóttir 1989, this volume), is a metanarrative to Icelandic culture, creating a sense of har-

3   Connections in time and space. From a tourist brochure.

mony and unity of history. In the decades around independence in 1944, Icelandic nationalism provided a new definition of history and the sagas and a new identity for modern Iceland. The past was defined to serve the needs of the present. Denmark no longer represented Iceland, and Iceland had to represent itself in the international arena. The sagas from the "glorious past" gained importance with links to the present through invented traditions, serving as one foundation of nationalism.

Since the end of World War II Icelanders have been at pains to present an official image of their nation-state as independent on the international scene. The brochures of the tourist industry provide such official images. Figure 3 illustrates a relation between the past and the present. The statue of the first settler of Iceland, Ingólfur Arnarson, and the statue of the discoverer of Vínland, Leifur Eiríksson (presented to Icelanders by U.S. citizens), represent a sense of the "glorious past" of heroic adventures. The airport building Leifsstöð, located on the NATO base which, before the cold war ended, was a site of debates about independence, represents the modern independent character of Iceland, but also emphasizes how much Icelanders value traveling and travelers, due to the fact that the first settlers were travelers.

Icelanders feel the need to define themselves more closely than ever before, because the island is getting more involved in the international scene and moving out of the periphery. They take pride in talking about how well they have adapted to the international scene without having lost their "ancient" identity and traditions. Their emphasis on the nobility of the Icelandic language is a good example.[3]

Icelanders define and stage their identity for themselves through major activities of the year, such as Christmas (*jól*) in the winter and tourism in the summer. Christmas is "high-season" (*há-tíð*), and within its boundaries the fundamental elements of nationalism are nourished. The major publishing of books is just before the Christmas season, and the most popular Christmas gift is a book (*jólabók*). A large portion of these books can be classified under thematic motifs of nationalism in the form of biography, folklore, history, and fiction on Icelandic themes.

The media are loaded with nationalistic themes and images around the Christmas season: for example, the speech given by the prime minister on behalf of the government and the state at the end of the year and the speech of the president on behalf of the nation on New Year's Day. Christmas is a self-consuming review of familiar things, or a period of rehearsal, as Icelanders represent their own identity to themselves through the medium of signs. These signs are later represented through the tourist industry in the tourist season. And even tourism affects the presentation of Christmas. Around Christmas Icelanders talk a lot about Christianity and folklore, which resembles the interest tourists show toward churches and trolls. By looking at the tourists looking at them, Icelanders confirm their identity. Nationalism is present all year round, and Christmas and tourism form a circle with the same economic and nationalistic foundations. The present trend in tourism is the emphasis on regional and local culture. As foreigners have been scrutinizing Iceland more closely in the past decade, Icelanders have become more aware of their local environments. Tourists are looking more at real, living people and their daily social lives and culture. Foreign tourists are now offered visits to farms and milking barns. This development is also reflected in a certain tension between Reykjavík, the cosmopolitan center of Iceland and the center of commerce and official political institutions, and the local communities throughout the country.

Each village is preoccupied in keeping the appearance of the environment clean and neat and in advertising every sector of the community to be gazed at. The most telling sign of this trend is the demand for a special regional tourist guide (*svæðaleiðsögumaður*). The regional tourist guide is trained in focusing on the specialties of each region in geology, history, and culture. A town like Siglufjörður, in the north of Iceland, has been advertising itself as the biggest herring village in the world for some years, where a nostalgic "herring adventure festival" (*síldarævintýri*) is staged in order for Icelanders (not foreigners) to relive golden memories. Another part of this trend is the renovating and reconstruction of old houses which are believed to be endowed with some historical significance; many have been turned into local museums (*byggðasöfn*) to represent the local district.

Icelanders are now also advertising tourism for Icelanders. They are encouraged to get to know the real Iceland by traveling in their own country. Thus an advertisement in the summer of 1993 sent a message directed to Icelanders from the Tourist Bureau of Iceland (Ferðamálaráð Íslands): "Preserve the Icelander within yourself." At the same time that tourists are encouraged to visit Iceland, Icelanders are also encouraged to discover and enjoy their own country. This awareness is associated with closer encounters with the international arena.

Food is another feature that Icelanders like to present to tourists. It is a common statement in anthropology that "food is good for thought" because food is a symbolic display of meanings. When Icelanders began to move into the international scene they became preoccupied with consuming foreignness, of which they wanted to be a part as an independent nation. The consumption of foreign commodities, such as food and clothes, became a sign of social status and an international spirit, thus trying to communicate the message: "We Icelanders are also modern!"

Now, when Icelanders are discovering that the international scene is looking at the island for its renowned fresh fish products and clean air and water, they realize that they are no longer on the periphery. Accordingly, they are confident and proud to offer the tourists some "good and decent traditional Icelandic food" (*almennilegan og góðan hefðbundinn íslenskan mat*) instead of the international fast food.

Hotel managers and other tourist managers are seriously talking about the need to offer something special and "traditional" as representative of the local district or Iceland in general. It has become popular to offer tourist groups milk curds (*íslenskt skyr*) or meat soup (*íslenska kjötsúpu*), both of which Icelanders consider to be unique to Iceland, as dancers perform "traditional" Icelandic folk dances dressed in "traditional" clothes. The tourist industry in general, both local and official, is presently making use of this trend to increase the foreign currency income, by advertising and selling Iceland through the image.

Conclusion

Until the end of the nineteenth century Icelanders did not have a unified voice to represent their ethnic identity. Occasionally, some scholars wrote books or declarations in defense of the identity of Iceland. For travelers coming before the eighteenth century, Iceland represented a strange place with strange people at the periphery of the world. Gradually, the position of Iceland changed in the view of foreign travelers, who came to look at the world through the lenses of the Enlightenment and romanticism. Through the intellectual turmoil in Europe in the nineteenth century Icelanders gained a nationalistic voice. With growing industrialization in the twentieth century, and independence from Denmark, Icelanders have been able to stage their identity through tourism and the tourist industry, with a foundation in a fullblown doctrine of nationalism that has created a continuity between a "glorious past" and an ever changing present. Hence the invention of traditions. The national identity is supported through major practices throughout the year, such as the Christmas season and the tourist season, creating images for Icelanders to nourish and for tourists to gaze at. The images create a sense of style and wholeness, which is a main characteristic of modernity. The images idealize certain features of Iceland and thus resemble the cinema.

But tourism is a ritual process, where identity is constructed through social interaction and communication. The tourists affect Icelanders by the way they gaze at things and Icelanders affect the foreigners by staging their identity, through tourism, which has been rehearsed over the Christmas season when Icelanders apparently travel to the center of their identity. Thus the images that Icelanders create for foreigners affect Icelanders' own perceptions of themselves.

There is a marked change in the presentation of the identity of Iceland. The emphasis has moved to the local level of regions and villages. Icelanders want to introduce the more informal side of their identity, as they now know that they are no longer located on the periphery. They have been moving into the international arena, the center, knowing that foreigners are interested in the "quality of living in Iceland." At the same time, Icelanders take pride in presenting their struggle in the past with harsh nature and today's technological advancements. The tourist gaze is a complex phenomenon, which needs more thorough investigation. Icelanders have mainly been interested in the romantic tourist gaze, because they present their own identity with a romantic image. But modernity is all-persuasive in Iceland today, with the collective tourist gaze as part of the playful potential of postmodernism, to which Iceland has much to offer in the form of staged authenticity. Iceland is no more and no less authentic than other countries of the Western world.

The construction of identity and Otherness is crucial for anthropological theory and the traveling metaphor illustrates that the anthropologist's experience must be one of engagement by simultaneously seeking to move into the periphery and into the center. By looking at tourism in Iceland the anthropologist needs to observe what meanings are being displayed in the interaction between the tourist industry as a set of signs and the tourist as a wandering semiotician. But the main focus is on the hosts, the spectators of their own dramatization, the Icelanders.

Notes

1. Nordal was writing at a critical time in Icelandic history. The island was occupied by British and U.S. armed forces that provided work for the Icelanders. A special relationship developed between some Ice-

landic women and the foreign soldiers. Inga Dóra Björnsdóttir's study (1989) of this relationship shows that the construction of Icelandicness and foreignness (self and Other) revolved around ideas of national purity, pride, and unity. Nordal was also writing at a period when Iceland had put an end to the official colonial relationship to Denmark, due to the outbreak of World War II. Icelanders were preparing a declaration of complete independence from Denmark. Finnbogason was writing at a time when Icelanders were receiving the medieval Icelandic manuscripts from Denmark. The following year Iceland extended its fishing limits to fifty miles.

2. Romantic literature in Europe and the "horror genre" of such novels as *Dracula, Frankenstein,* and *Dr. Jekyll and Mr. Hyde* bear witness to Burton's expression of the travelers' image of Iceland as "scenes of thrilling horror, of majestic grandeur, and of heavenly beauty."

3. Pálsson argues (1989b) that Icelandic ethnolinguistics is characterized by a romantic and nationalistic attitude regarding the uniqueness of Icelandic and its place among other languages. Consequently, purism distorts the social realm of language in everyday use of actual utterances.

CONTRIBUTORS

Inga Dóra Björnsdóttir holds a Ph.D. degree in social anthropology from the University of California, Santa Barbara. An article based on her Ph.D. thesis, "Nationalism, Gender, and the Contemporary Women's Movement in Iceland," is forthcoming in *Nordic Feminist Thought*. Björnsdóttir has also done research and a documentary film (*Love and War*) about Icelandic war brides in the United States. She has taught at the University of Iceland but is currently associated with the Center of Women's Studies at the University of Stockholm, Sweden.

Anne Brydon is assistant professor of anthropology at the University of Western Ontario in London, Canada. She studied music at the same university (B.A., 1980) before turning to anthropology at McMaster (M.A., 1987) and McGill universities (Ph.D., 1992). She has written about Icelandic-Canadian ethnicity and representations of women, Icelandic nationalism, the Icelandic travel writings of Richard

Burton and William Morris, and contemporary Canadian art. Her interests include the culture of nature, the cultural life of things, and the anthropology of space and place. In cooperation with Unnur Dís Skaptadóttir, she is currently studying representations of urban spatiality in Reykjavík.

E. Paul Durrenberger (Ph.D. in anthropology, University of Illinois, Champaign, 1971) is professor of anthropology at the University of Iowa. His publications include *The Dynamics of Medieval Iceland: Political Economy and Literature* (University of Iowa Press, 1992) and *It's All Politics: South Alabama's Fishing Industry* (University of Illinois Press, 1992). He has translated two Icelandic sagas in collaboration with Dorothy Durrenberger, co-edited *The Anthropology of Iceland* (University of Iowa Press, 1989), and edited *Chayanov, Peasants, and Economic Anthropology* (Academic Press, 1984). He has also published a number of articles on economic and cognitive anthropology, peasants, and maritime anthropology.

Magnús Einarsson studied anthropology at the University of Iceland and the University of Wisconsin, Madison, where he completed his M.A. degree in 1992. Presently he is teaching in Iceland and occasionally working as a regional tour guide. His research interests include travel literature, identities, nationalism, and gender.

Níels Einarsson studied anthropology at the universities of Iceland, Uppsala, and Oxford. He has done field research on Icelandic small-scale fishing and has also studied British environmental and animal welfare groups. Currently he is a researcher at the Fisheries Research Institute, University of Iceland.

Julie E. Gurdin is in the linguistic anthropology Ph.D. program at the University of Arizona. She received her master's in anthropology at the University of Iowa in 1992. Her master's thesis, "The Strategies of Survivors: Domestic Violence in Iceland," was based upon fieldwork carried out in the summer of 1991 in Reykjavík. She is continuing to work with issues related to violence against women in Iceland and in the United States.

Agnar Helgason is a graduate student at the University of Cambridge. Earlier, he studied anthropology at the University of Iceland

and Brunel University. His M.A. dissertation (University of Iceland, 1995) deals with the social context of fisheries management in Iceland, focusing on notions of equity and the rhetorics of economics. His interests lie in the fields of economic anthropology and the interface between social and biological anthropology.

Gísli Pálsson (Ph.D. in anthropology, Manchester University, 1982) is professor of anthropology at the University of Iceland and currently Research Fellow at the Swedish Collegium for Advanced Study in the Social Sciences in Uppsala, Sweden. His writings include *Coastal Economies, Cultural Accounts* (Manchester University Press, 1991), *The Textual Life of Savants* (Harwood Academic Publishers, 1995), and a number of articles published in anthropological journals. He is the editor of *Beyond Boundaries: Understanding, Translation and Anthropological Discourse* (Berg Publishers, 1993) and *From Sagas to Society: Comparative Approaches to Early Iceland* (Hisarlik Press, 1992) and co-editor of *The Anthropology of Iceland* (University of Iowa Press, 1989). Major fields of interest include ecological anthropology, fishing economies, and cognition and language.

Beverly A. Sizemore earned her B.A. in psychology at the University of Virginia and her M.A. and Ph.D. in anthropology at the University of North Carolina at Chapel Hill. Her area of specialization is cognitive anthropology and her dissertation focuses on sociocultural aspects of literacy and education in Iceland, where she lived and conducted research for two years. She is a research associate at Horizon Research, Inc., an education evaluation firm involved primarily in the evaluation of government-funded systemic reform initiatives. She has published and presented papers on a broad range of topics, including North Carolina archaeology and cognitive aspects of the use of the *Farmer's Almanac.*

Unnur Dís Skaptadóttir studied anthropology at the University of Iceland, the University of Massachusetts, Amherst (B.A.), and the Graduate School and University Center of the City University of New York (M.A., 1994; Ph.D., 1995). Her doctoral dissertation focuses on women in Icelandic fishing communities. Skaptadóttir is presently teaching anthropology in the Faculty of Social Sciences, the University of Iceland. Her current interests include theories of globalization, ethnicity, feminist perspectives, and the structure and experience of urban life. At present she is doing research on the social production of space in Reykjavík in cooperation with Anne Brydon.

Daniel E. Vasey earned his Ph.D. in anthropology at Southern Illinois University. He is currently professor and chair in the Department of Cross-Cultural Studies, Divine Word College, Iowa. His writings include *An Ecological History of Agriculture, 10,000 B.C.–A.D. 10,000* (Iowa State University Press, 1992) and numerous articles in international journals. He spent several years in Papua New Guinea and has traveled extensively in England and Iceland.

Christopher H. Walker received his B.A. in anthropology from Duke University and his M.A. and Ph.D. in anthropology from the University of North Carolina at Chapel Hill. His concentration is the anthropology of symbol and ritual and his dissertation focuses on the symbolic aspects of worship among Pentecostals on the Caribbean island of Tobago. He worked and traveled extensively in Iceland for a period of fifteen months. His papers and publications include comparative studies of ritual in the American South and the Caribbean. He has also recorded, produced, and edited videotapes of a number of fundamentalist church services for the University of North Carolina. He currently works in the computer software publication industry and continues to write.

REFERENCES

Anderson, Benedict. 1991 [1983]. *Imagined communities: Reflections on the origin and spread of nationalism*. Revised ed. London: Verso.

Andresson, Sigfús Haukur. 1984. Missagnir um fyrirhugaðan flutning Íslendinga. *Saga* 12: 57–91.

Antler, E. 1977. Maritime mode of production, domestic mode of production or labor process: An examination of Newfoundland fishery. Paper presented to North Eastern Anthropological Association, March 24–26, 1977, Fishermen and Mariners Symposium.

Appadurai, Arjun. 1981. The past as a scarce resource. *Man* 16: 201–219.

———. 1990. Disjuncture and difference in the global cultural economy. In *Global culture: Nationalism, globalization and modernity*, ed. M. Featherstone, pp. 295–310. London: Sage.

———. 1991. Global ethnoscapes: Notes and queries for a transnational anthropology. In *Recapturing anthropology*, ed. Richard G. Fox, pp. 191–210. Santa Fe: School of American Research Press.

Árnason, Ragnar. 1990. Aflakvótar og hagkvæmni í fiskveiðum. In *Hag-*

sæld í húfi: Greinar um stjórn fiskveiða, ed. Þorkell Helgason and Örn D. Jónsson, pp. 64–69. Reykjavík: Fisheries Research Institute.

———. 1991. Efficient management of ocean fisheries. *European Economic Review* 35: 408–417.

———. 1993a. The Icelandic individual transferable quota system: A descriptive account. *Marine Resource Economics* 8: 201–218.

———. 1993b. Icelandic fisheries management. In *The use of individual quotas in fisheries management*, pp. 123–144. Paris: OECD.

Arnórsson, Kári. 1980. Kjör Vigdísar lyftistöng fyrir þjóðina. *Morgunblaðið*, June 8.

Ásgeirsson, Ásgeir. 1953–1955. New Year speeches. *Morgunblaðið*, January 3.

———. 1954. Án ábyrgra ríkisstjórna er lýðræðinu hætt við falli. *Morgunblaðið*, January 3.

———. 1959. Fjallkonan hefur ríkulega blessað sín börn og ætlast til nokkurs af þeim. *Morgunblaðið*, January 3.

Babb, F. E. 1986. Producers and reproducers: Andean market women in the economy. In *Women and change in Latin America*, ed. J. Nash and H. Safa, pp. 53–64. South Hadley, Mass.: Bergin and Garvey Publishers.

Barth, Fredrik (ed.). 1969. *Ethnic groups and boundaries*. Boston: Little, Brown.

Bauman, Richard. 1992. Contextualization, tradition, and the dialogue of genres: Icelandic legends of the *kraftaskáld*. In *Rethinking context: Language as an interactive phenomenon*, ed. A. Duranti and C. Goodwin, pp. 125–145. Cambridge: Cambridge University Press.

Beechey, V. 1988. Rethinking the definition of work: Gender and work. In *Feminization of the labour force: Paradoxes and promises*, ed. J. Jenson, E. Hagen, and C. Reddy, pp. 45–61. Oxford: Polity Press.

Benediktsson, Árni. 1993. Forsetaembættið hefur breyst. *Tíminn*, January 21.

Beneria, L., and G. Sen. 1986. Accumulation, reproduction and women's role in economic development: Boserup revisited. In *Women's work: Development and the division of labour by gender*, ed. E. Leacock and H. Safa, pp. 141–157. South Hadley, Mass.: Begin and Garvey Publishers.

Berlin, Isaiah. 1978. *Concepts and categories: Philosophical essays*. London: Hogarth Press.

Bjarnadóttir, Kristín. 1986. Drepsóttir á 15. öld. *Sagnir* 7: 57–64.

Björnsdóttir, Inga Dóra. 1989. Public view and private voices. In *The An-*

thropology of Iceland, ed. E. P. Durrenberger and G. Pálsson, pp. 98–118. Iowa City: University of Iowa Press.

———. 1992. "Nationalism, gender, and the contemporary women's movement in Iceland." Ph.D. thesis, University of California, Santa Barbara.

———. 1994. Þeir áttu sér móður. *Fléttur: Rit Rannsóknastofu i Kvennafræðum* 1: 65–85. Rit Rannsóknastofu Háskóla Íslands.

Björnsson, Björn. 1971. *The Lutheran doctrine of marriage in modern Icelandic society.* Oslo: Universitetsforlaget.

Björnsson, Sveinn. 1945–1952. New Year speeches. *Morgunblaðið,* January 3.

———. 1957. *Endurminningar Sveins Björnssonar,* ed. Sigurður Nordal. Reykjavík: Ísafoldarprentsmiðja.

Bleaney, Michael, and Ian Stewart. 1991. Economics and related disciplines. In *Companion to contemporary economic thought,* ed. David Greenaway, Michael Bleaney, and Ian Stewart, pp. 729–741. London and New York: Routledge.

Bloch, Maurice. 1977. The past and the present in the present. *Man* 12: 278–292.

Bloch, Maurice, and Jonathan Parry. 1988. Introduction: Money and the morality of exchange. In *Money and the morality of exchange,* ed. Maurice Bloch and Jonathan Parry, pp. 1–32. Cambridge: Cambridge University Press.

Blum, J. 1961. *Lord and peasant in Russia, from the ninth to the nineteenth century.* Princeton, N.J.: Princeton University Press.

Boniface, Priscilla, and Peter J. Fowler. 1993. *Heritage and tourism in "the global village."* London: Routledge.

Böröcz, József. 1992. Travel-capitalism: The structure of Europe and the tourist. *Comparative Studies in Society and History* 34: 708–741.

Bourdieu, P., L. Boltanski, R. Castel, and J.-C. Chamboredon. 1965. *Un art moyen: Essai sur les usages sociaux de la photographie.* Paris: Editions de Minuit.

Bourdieu, Pierre, and Loic J. D. Wacquant. 1992. *An invitation to reflexive sociology.* Chicago: University of Chicago Press.

Bourgeois-Pichat, J. 1965. The general development of the population of France since the eighteenth century. In *Population in history,* ed. D. V. Glass and D. E. C. Eversley, pp. 474–506. London: Arnold.

Boyd, Rick O., and Christopher M. Dewees. 1992. Putting theory into practice: Individual transferable quotas in New Zealand's fisheries. *Society and Natural Resources* 5: 179–198.

Bradley, H. 1989. *Men's work, women's work: A sociological history of the sexual division of labour in employment.* Minneapolis: University of Minnesota Press.

Briadotti, R. 1992. Gender and post-gender: The future of an illusion? Unpublished manuscript.

Briem, Helgi. 1945. *Iceland and the Icelanders.* Maplewood, N.J.: McKenna.

Broddason, Th. 1990. Bóklestur og ungmenni. *Bókasafnið* 14 (March): 17–19. Reykjavík: Bókavarðafélag Íslands.

Broddason, Th., and K. Webb. 1975. On the myth of social equality in Iceland. *Acta Sociologica* 18: 49–61.

Bromley, Daniel W. 1990. The ideology of efficiency: Searching for a theory of policy analysis. *Journal of Environmental Economics and Management* 19: 86–107.

Brow, James. 1990. The incorporation of a marginal community within the Sinhalese nation. *Anthropological Quarterly* 63: 7–17.

Brown, Wendy. 1988. *Manhood and politics: A feminist reading in political theory.* Totowa, N.J.: Rowman and Littlefield.

Bruner, Edward M. 1993. Introduction: The ethnographic self and the personal self. In *Anthropology and literature*, ed. Paul Benson, pp. 1–26. Urbana: University of Illinois Press.

Brydon, Anne. 1987. Celebrating ethnicity: The Icelanders of Manitoba. Master's thesis, McMaster University.

———. 1990. Icelandic nationalism and the whaling issue. *North Atlantic Studies* 2(1/2): 185–191.

———. 1992. The eye of the guest: Icelandic nationalist discourse and the whaling issue. Ph.D. dissertation, McGill University.

Buckoke, Andrew. 1993. A bitter jumbo bill. *Guardian*, September 10.

Burling, Robbins. 1964. Cognition and componential analysis: God's truth or hocus pocus. *American Anthropologist* 66: 22–28.

Butterworth, D. S. 1992. Science and sentimentality. *Nature* 357: 532–534.

Cameron, Catherine M., and John B. Gatewood. 1994. The authentic interior: Questing *Gemeinschaft* in post-industrial society. *Human Organization* 53(1): 21–32.

Campbell, Mary B. 1988. *The witness and the other world.* Ithaca: Cornell University Press.

Carrier, James G. 1992. Introduction. In *History and tradition in Melanesian anthropology*, ed. James G. Carrier, pp. 1–37. Berkeley: University of California Press.

Cassen, Lionel. 1974. *Travel in the ancient world*. London: George Allen/ Unwin.

Chadwick, Betsey. 1989. Under one roof: The juncture of natal and procreative families in Iceland. Master's thesis, University of Massachusetts.

Chapple, S. 1984. Reykjavik rocks. *Mother Jones* 9(7): 26–31.

Chase-Dunn, Christopher. 1989. *Global formation: Structures of the world economy*. Cambridge: Basil Blackwell.

Cherfas, Jeremy. 1992. Whalers win the numbers game. *New Scientist* 1829 (July 11): 12–13.

Chiang, Chin Long. 1984. *The life table and its applications*. Malabar, Fla.: Krieger.

Chirot, Daniel. 1986. *Social change in the modern era*. New York: Harcourt Brace Jovanovich.

Clifford, James. 1986. Introduction: Partial truths. In *Writing culture: The poetics and politics of ethnography*, ed. James Clifford and George E. Marcus, pp. 1–26. Berkeley: University of California Press.

Coale, A. J., and R. Treadway. 1986. A summary of the changing distribution of overall fertility, marital fertility, and the proportion married in the provinces of Europe. In *The decline of fertility in Europe*, ed. A. J. Coale and S. C. Watkins, pp. 31–181. Princeton, N.J.: Princeton University Press.

Cochran-Smith, Marilyn. 1984. *The making of a reader*. Norwood, N.J.: Ablex Publishing Corporation.

Cohen, Erik. 1979. A phenomenology of touristic experience. *Sociology: Journal of the British Sociological Association* 13(2) (May): 179–201.

Cole, Michael. 1985. The zone of proximal development: Where culture and cognition create each other. In *Culture, communication, and cognition: Vygotskian perspectives*, ed. James V. Wertsch, pp. 146–161. Cambridge: Cambridge University Press.

Cole, S. 1991. *Women of the Praia: Work and lives in a Portuguese coastal community*. Princeton: Princeton University Press.

Comaroff, John, and Jean Comaroff. 1992. *Ethnography and the historical imagination*. Boulder: Westview Press.

Connelly P., and M. MacDonald. 1986. Women's work: Domestic and wage labor in a Nova Scotia community. In *The politics of diversity: Feminism, marxism and nationalism*, ed. R. Hamilton and M. Barett, pp. 53–80. New York: Routledge, Chapman, and Hall.

Cook-Gumperz, Jenny. 1986. *The social construction of literacy: Studies in interactional sociolinguistics*. Cambridge: Cambridge University Press.

Copes, Parzival. 1986. A critical review of the individual quota as a device in fisheries management. *Land Economics* 62(3): 278–291.

———. 1992. Individual fishing rights: Some implications of transferability. Sixth IIFET Conference, Paris, July 6–9.

Coulter, Philip B. 1989. *Measuring inequality: A methodological handbook.* Boulder: Westview Press.

Dagblaðið-Vísir. 1991. June 5. Manndráp jukust gífurlega á síðasta áratug.

Danielsson, Holmfridur. 1946. The Dark Ages in Iceland. In *Iceland's thousand years,* ed. Skuli Johnsson, pp. 95–110. Winnipeg: Icelandic Canadian Club.

Davis, D. L. 1979. Social structure, sex roles and female associations in a Newfoundland fishing village. Paper presented at a CESCE meeting Banff, Alberta.

de Beauvoir, S. 1961. *The second sex.* New York: Bantam Books.

de Castell, Suzanne, Allan Luke, and Kieran Egan (eds.). 1986. *Literacy, society, and schooling: A reader.* Cambridge: Cambridge University Press.

De Lauretis, Theresa. 1987. *Technologies of gender.* Bloomington: Indiana University Press.

Dewees, C. M. 1989. Assessment of the implementation of individual transferable quotas in New Zealand's inshore fishery. *North American Journal of Fisheries Management* 9: 131–139.

———. 1991. *Industry and government negotiation: Communication and change in New Zealand's individual transferable quota system.* Pamphlet. Department of Wildlife and Fisheries Biology, University of California.

Dilley, Roy. 1992. Contesting markets: A general introduction to market ideology, imagery and discourse. In *Contesting markets: Analyses of ideology, discourse and practice,* ed. Roy Dilley, pp. 1–34. Edinburgh: Edinburgh University Press.

Di Stefano, Christine. 1991. *Configurations of masculinity. A feminist perspective on modern political theory.* Ithaca: Cornell University Press.

Dobash, R., and R. Emerson Dobash. 1979. *Violence against wives: The case against the patriarchy.* New York: Free Press.

Donham, Donald. 1992. Revolution and modernity in Maale: Ethiopia, 1974 to 1987. *Comparative Studies in Society and History* 34(1): 28–57.

Dumont, Louis. 1977. *From Mandeville to Marx: The genesis and triumph of economic ideology.* Chicago and London: University of Chicago Press.

———. 1986. *Essays on individualism: Modern ideology in anthropological perspective.* Chicago: University of Chicago Press.

Durrenberger, E. P. 1992a. *The dynamics of medieval Iceland: Political economy and literature.* Iowa City: University of Iowa Press.

————. 1992b. *It's all politics: South Alabama's seafood industry.* Champaign: University of Illinois Press.

————. 1993. Working Efra Sel: Change on a family farm in Iceland. *The World & I* (July): 256–265.

Durrenberger, E. Paul, and John Morrison. 1979. Comments on Brown's ethnoscience. *American Ethnologist* 6: 408–409.

Durrenberger, E. Paul, and Gísli Pálsson. 1983. Riddles of herring and rhetorics of success. *Journal of Anthropological Research* 39(3): 323–336.

————. 1985. Peasants, entrepreneurs and companies: The evolution of Icelandic fishing. *Ethnos* 1–2: 103–122.

————. 1986. Finding fish: The tactics of Icelandic skippers. *American Ethnologist* 13(2): 213–229.

————. 1989a. Forms of production and fishing expertise. In *The anthropology of Iceland*, ed. E. Paul Durrenberger and Gísli Pálsson, pp. 3–18. Iowa City: University of Iowa Press.

————. 1989b. Icelanders and West Icelanders in the modern age. *The World & I* 4(3) (March): 660–667.

Edwards, Anne. 1987. Male violence in feminist theory: An analysis of changing conceptions of sex/gender violence and male dominance. In *Women, violence and social control*, ed. Jalna Hanmer and Mary Maynard, pp. 13–29. Atlantic Heights, N.J.: Humanities Press International.

Eggertsson, Thráinn. 1992. Analyzing institutional successes and failures: A millennium of common mountain pastures in Iceland. *International Review of Law and Economics* 12: 423–437.

Einarsdóttir, Ólafía. 1984. Staða kvenna á þjóðveldisöld. *Saga* 22: 7–30.

Einarsdóttir, V. 1991. Hvers vegna láta konur berja sig? *Morgunblaðið*, March 8.

Einarsson, Ágúst, and Ragnar Árnason. 1994. Veiðiheimildir á fáar hendur? *Morgunblaðið*, January 27.

Einarsson, Níels. 1990a. From the native's point of view: Some comments on the anthropology of Iceland. *Anthropologiska Studier* 46/47: 69–77.

————. 1990b. Of seals and souls: Changes in the position of seals in the world-view of Icelandic small-scale fishermen. *Maritime Anthropological Studies* 3(2): 35–58.

————. 1993a. All animals are equal but some are cetaceans: Conservation and culture conflict. In *Environmentalism: The view from anthropology*, ed. Kay Milton, pp. 73–84. London: Routledge.

——. 1993b. Environmental arguments and the survival of small-scale fishing in Iceland. In *Green arguments and local subsistence,* ed. Gudrun Dahl, pp. 117–127. Stockholm: Stockholm University.

Eldjárn, Kristján. 1969–1980. New Year speeches. *Morgunblaðið,* January 3.

England, Paula. 1993. The separative self: Androcentric bias in neoclassical assumptions. In *Beyond economic man: Feminist theory and economics,* ed. Marianne Ferber and Julie A. Nelson, pp. 37–53. Chicago and London: University of Chicago Press.

Ergang, Robert R. 1931. *Herder and the foundations of German nationalism.* New York: Columbia University Press.

Ferber, Marianne, and Julie A. Nelson. 1993. Introduction: The social construction of economics and the social construction of gender. In *Beyond economic man: Feminist theory and economics,* ed. Marianne Ferber and Julie A. Nelson, pp. 1–21. Chicago and London: University of Chicago Press.

Fernandez-Kelly, M. P. 1983. *For we are sold, I and my people: Women and industry in Mexico's frontier.* Albany: State University of New York Press.

Finnbogadóttir, Vigdís. 1981–1993. New Year speeches. *Morgunblaðið,* January 3.

——. 1985. *Morgunblaðið,* October 25.

Finnsson, Hannes. 1796. *Um mannfækkun af hallærum á Íslandi.* Reykjavík: Rit þess Konunglega Íslenzka Lærdómslista-Félags.

Flaaten, Ola, and Kenneth Stollery. 1994. The economic effects of biological predation. Theory and application to the case of the northeast Atlantic minke whale's (*Balaenoptera acutorostrata*) consumption of fish. Manuscript.

Foster, Robert J. 1991. Making national cultures in the global ecumene. *Annual Review of Anthropology* 20: 235–260.

Foucault, Michel. 1979. *Discipline and punish.* Tr. Alan Sheridan. New York: Vintage.

——. 1986. Of other spaces. *Diacritics* 16: 22–27.

Freedman, Maurice. 1963. A Chinese phase in social anthropology. *British Journal of Sociology* 14: 1–19.

Freeman, Milton M. R. 1990. A commentary on political issues with regard to contemporary whaling. *North Atlantic Studies* 2(1/2): 106–116.

Friðriksson, Guðjón, and Gunnar Elísson. 1980. *Forsetakjör 1980.* Reykjavík: Örn og Örlygur.

Gal, Susan. 1991. Between speech and silence: The problematics of research on language and gender. In *Gender at the crossroads of knowledge: Feminist anthropology in the postmodern era*, ed. Micaela di Leonardo, pp. 175–203. Berkeley: University of California Press.

Galey, Jean-Claude (ed.). 1990. *Kingship and the kings*. London: Harwood Academic Publishers.

Garner, Robert. 1993. *Animals, politics and morality*. Manchester: Manchester University Press.

Garnica, Olga K., and Martha L. King (eds.). 1979. *Language, children and society: The effect of social factors on children learning to communicate*. Oxford, England: Pergamon Press.

Gatewood, John B. 1993. Ecology, efficiency, equity, and competitiveness. In *Competitiveness and American society*, ed. Steven L. Goldman, pp. 123–155. Bethlehem, Pa.: Lehigh University Press.

Geertz, Clifford. 1973. *The interpretation of cultures*. New York: Basic Books.

Geirsson, Smári. 1993. Í hvalnum fyrir austan. *Sjómannadagsblað Neskaupstaðar* 16: 69–83.

Gelles, Richard. 1987. *Family violence*. Newbury Park, Calif.: Sage Publications.

Giddens, Anthony. 1985. *The nation-state and violence*. Cambridge: Polity Press.

———. 1990. *The consequences of modernity*. London: Polity Press.

Giles-Sims, Jean. 1983. *Wife battering: A systems theory approach*. New York: Guilford Press.

Gille, H. 1949–1950. The demographic history of the northern European countries in the eighteenth century. *Population Studies* 3: 3–65.

Gjerset, Knut. 1924. *History of Iceland*. New York: Macmillan.

Gordon, H. Scott. 1954. The economic theory of a common property resource: The fishery. *Journal of Political Economy* 62: 124–142.

Gordon, Linda. 1988. *Heroes of their own lives*. New York: Penguin.

———. 1990. Book reviews: Response to Scott. *Signs* 15(4): 852–853.

Graburn, Nelson H. H. 1983. The anthropology of tourism. *Annals of Tourism Research* 10(1): 9–33.

Graburn, Nelson H. H., and Jafar Jafari. 1991. Introduction: Tourism in social science. *Annals of Tourism Research* 18(7): 1–11.

Greenwood, Davydd J. 1985. Castilians, Basques, and Andalusians: An historical comparison of nationalism, true ethnicity, and false ethnicity. In *Ethnic Groups and the State*, ed. Paul Brass, pp. 202–227. London: Croom Helm.

Griffiths, J. C. 1969. *Modern Iceland*. New York: Praeger.

Grímsdóttir, Vigdís. 1993. . . . sókn og vaka: eining hörð og hrein. *Ný menntamál* 11: 6–13.

Gröndal, Gylfi. 1991. *Kristján Eldjárn, ævisaga.* Reykjavík: Forlagið.

———. 1992. *Ásgeir Ásgeirsson, ævisaga.* Reykjavík: Forlagið.

Gudeman, Stephen. 1986. *Economics as culture: Models and metaphors of livelihood.* London: Routledge.

———. 1992. Markets, models and morality: The power of practices. In *Contesting markets: Analyses of ideology, discourse and practice,* ed. Roy Dilley, pp. 279–294. Edinburgh: Edinburgh University Press.

Guðlaugsson, S. 1991. Kvennakvalarar. *Nýtt Líf* 14(1): 34–39.

Gunnarsson, Gísli. 1980. *Fertility and nuptiality in Iceland's demographic history.* Lund: Lunds Universitet.

———. 1983a. *Monopoly trade and economic stagnation: Studies in foreign trade of Iceland 1602–1787.* Lund: Lunds Universitet.

———. 1983b. *The sex ratio, the infant mortality, and adjoining societal response in pretransitional Iceland.* Lund: Lunds Universitet.

———. 1984. Voru móðuharðindin af manna völdum? In *Skaftáreldar 1783–1784,* ed. Gísli Ágúst Gunnlaugsson et al., pp. 235–242. Reykjavík: Mál og menning.

Gunnlaugsson, Gísli Ágúst. 1984. Viðbrögð stjórnvalda í Kaupmannahöfn við Skaftáreldum. In *Skaftáreldar 1783–1784,* ed. Gísli Ágûst Gunnlaugsson et al., pp. 187–214. Reykjavík: Mál og menning.

———. 1988. *Family and household in Iceland 1801–1930: Studies in the relationship between demographic and socio-economic development, social legislation and family and household structure.* Uppsala: Uppsala University.

———. 1993. Everyone's been good to me, especially the dogs: Fosterchildren and young paupers in nineteenth-century southern Iceland. *Journal of Social History* (Winter): 124–140.

Gunnlaugsson, Gísli Ágúst, and Loftur Guttormsson. n.d. Transitions into old age: Poverty and retirement possibilities in late eighteenth and nineteenth-century Iceland. In *Poor Women and Children in the European Past,* ed. R. Wall and J. Henderson. London: Routledge. In press.

Gupta, Akhil, and James Ferguson. 1992. Beyond culture: Space, identity, and the politics of difference. *Cultural Anthropology* 7(1): 6–23.

Gustavson, A. 1986. Women and men in the coastal district on the Swedish west coast: Ethnologia Europea. *Journal of European Ethnology* 16(2): 149–172.

Guttormsson, Loftur. 1980. Um hvað snúast forsetakosningarnar? *Þjóðviljinn,* June 26.

———. 1983. *Bernska, ungdómur og uppeldi á einveldisöld: Tilraun til félagsle-*

grar og lýðfræðilegrar greiningar. Ritsafn Sagnfræðistofnunar 10. Reykjavík: Sagnfræðistofnun Háskola Íslands.

———. 1989. Læsi. In *Íslensk þjóðmenning VI: munnmenntir og bókmenning,* ed. Frosti F. Jóhannsson, pp. 118–144. Reykjavík: Þjóðsaga.

Hagstofa Íslands. 1992. *Landshagir 1992.* Reykjavík: Hagstofa Íslands.

Hajnal, J. 1965. European marriage patterns in perspective. In *Population in History,* ed. D. V. Glass and D. E. C. Eversley, pp. 101–143. London: Arnold.

Hákonardóttir, Inga Huld. 1992. *Fjarri hlýju hjónasængur.* Reykjavík: Mál og menning.

Hálfdanarson, Guðmundur. 1984. Mannfall í móðuharðindum. In *Skaftáreldar 1783–1784,* ed. Gísli Ágúst Gunnlaugsson et al., pp. 140–162. Reykjavík: Mál og menning.

———. 1991. *Old provinces, modern nations: Political responses to state integration in late nineteenth and early twentieth century Iceland and Brittany.* Ph.D. dissertation, Cornell University, Department of History. Ann Arbor, Mich., University Microfilms.

———. n.d. *Individuals, class and nation: Political culture and cultural politics in nineteenth-century Iceland.* Unpublished paper.

Hane, M. 1982. *Peasants, rebels, and outcasts: The underside of modern Japan.* New York: Pantheon.

Hanmer, J., and M. Maynard. 1987. *Women, violence and social control.* Atlantic Highlands, N.J.: Humanities Press International.

Hanna, Susan S. 1990. The eighteenth century English commons: A model for ocean management. *Ocean and Shoreline Management* 14: 155–172.

Hannerz, Ulf. 1986. Theory in anthropology: Small is beautiful? The problem of complex societies. *Comparative Studies in Society and History* 28(2): 362–367.

———. 1992. *Cultural complexity.* New York: Columbia University Press.

———. 1993. Mediations in the global ecumene. In *Beyond boundaries: Understanding, translation and anthropological discourse,* ed. Gísli Pálsson, pp. 41–57. Providence: Berg.

Hanson, Allan. 1989. Making the Maori: Culture invention and its logic. *American Anthropologist* 91(4): 890–902.

Hardin, Garrett. 1968. The tragedy of the commons. *Science* 162: 1243–1248.

Harding, S. 1986. *The science question in feminism.* Milton Keynes: Open University Press.

Harris, Nigel. 1990. *National liberation.* Reno: University of Nevada Press.

Hart, Keith. 1990. The idea of economy: Six modern dissenters. In *Beyond the marketplace: Rethinking economy and society*, ed. Roger Friedland and A. F. Robertson, pp. 137–160. New York: Aldine de Gruyter.

Harvey, David. 1982. *The limits to capital.* Oxford: Basil Blackwell.

Hastrup, K. 1990. *Nature and policy in Iceland 1400–1800.* Oxford: Clarendon.

Hauksson, Erlingur. 1989. Selir og áhrif þeirra á fiskveiðar. *Ægir* 82(6): 290–295.

Havsteen, Jul. 1930. Landhelgi Íslands. *Ægir* 23: 41–43.

Hayles, N. Katherine. 1990. *Chaos bound: Orderly disorder in contemporary literature and science.* Ithaca: Cornell University Press.

Heath, Shirley Brice. 1982. What no bedtime story means: Narrative skills at home and school. *Language in Society* 11(2): 49–76.

———. 1983. *Ways with words: Language, life and work in communities and classrooms.* Cambridge: Cambridge University Press.

———. 1986a. Critical factors in literacy development. In *Literacy, society, and schooling: A reader*, ed. Suzanne de Castell et al., pp. 209–232. Cambridge: Cambridge University Press.

———. 1986b. The functions and uses of literacy. In *Literacy, society, and schooling: A reader*, ed. Suzanne de Castell et al., pp. 15–26. Cambridge: Cambridge University Press.

———. 1987. Foreword. In *The labyrinths of literacy: Reflections on literacy past and present*, ed. Harvey J. Graff, pp. vii–ix. New York: Falmer Press.

Heiðdal, Dagný. 1988. Þeir sem guðirnir elska deyja ungir. *Sagnir* 9: 65–71.

Helgadóttir, Sigrún, Ævar Pedersen, and Stefán Bergman. 1985. *Selir og hringormar: Greinargerð í tilefni af verðlaunaveitingum Hringormanefndar.* Pamphlet. Reykjavík: Landvernd.

Helgarblað. 1991. Kynferðislegt ofbeldi: Gæti verið hver sem er. August 3.

Herder J. G. 1968. *Reflections on the philosophy of the history of mankind.* Abridged and with an introduction by Frank Manuel. Chicago and London: University of Chicago Press.

Herzfeld, Michael. 1987. *Anthropology through the looking-glass: Critical ethnography in the margins of Europe.* Cambridge: Cambridge University Press.

Hirdman, Y. 1990. Genussystemet *Democrati och makt i Sverige.* 44: 73–116. Stockholm: Statens offentlige utredningar.

Hobsbawm, E. J. 1983a. Inventing traditions. In *The invention of tradition,* ed. Eric Hobsbawm and Terence Ranger, pp. 1–14. Cambridge: Cambridge University Press.

———. 1983b. Mass-producing traditions: Europe, 1870–1914. In *The invention of tradition*, ed. Eric Hobsbawm and Terence Ranger, pp. 263–306. Cambridge: Cambridge University Press.

Hobsbawm, Eric, and Terence Ranger (eds.). 1983. *The invention of tradition*. Cambridge: Cambridge University Press.

Hoel, Alf Håkon. 1985. *The International Whaling Commission 1972–1981: New members, new concepts*. Polhogda: Fridtjof Nansens Institutt.

Holdgate, Martin. 1993. Using wildlife sustainably. *People and the planet* 2(3): 26–27.

Holland, Dorothy, and Naomi Quinn (ed.). 1987. *Cultural models in language and thought*. New York: Cambridge University Press.

Holland, Dorothy, and Jaan Valsiner. 1988a. Cognition, symbols, and Vygotsky's developmental psychology. *Ethos*: 247–271.

———. 1988b. Cultural models and Vygotsky's mediational devices. Unpublished manuscript, University of North Carolina at Chapel Hill.

Hollingsworth, T. H. 1965. A demographic study of the British ducal families. In *Population in History*, ed. D. V. Glass and D. E. C. Eversley, pp. 354–378. London: Arnold.

Holt, Sidney. 1985. Let's all go whaling. *Ecologist* 15(3): 113–124.

Iceland Review Publications. 1992. Icelandic children losing out: Second worst among the Nordic countries. *News from Iceland* (August): 6.

Ingadóttir, Álfheiður. 1981. Gerist þetta ekki hér? *Þjóðviljinn*, November 29.

Ingold, Tim. 1992. Culture and the perception of the environment. In *Bush base, forest farm: Culture, environment and development*, ed. Elisabeth Croll and David Parkin, pp. 39–56. London: Routledge.

———. 1993. The art of translation in a continuous world. In *Beyond boundaries: Understanding, translation and anthropological discourse*, ed. Gísli Pálsson, pp. 210–230. Providence: Berg.

INWR Digest (International Network for Whaling Research). 1993. April.

Jackson, E. L. 1982. The Laki eruption of 1783: Impacts on population and settlement in Iceland. *Geography* 67(1): 42–50.

Jakobsdóttir, Laufey. 1980. Lesendabréf. *Vísir*, January 15.

Jasper, James M., and Dorothy Nelkin. 1992. *The animal rights crusade: The growth of a moral protest*. New York: Free Press.

Jensen, A. E. 1954. *Iceland: Old-new republic*. New York: Exposition.

Jónasdóttir, A. 1985. Kyn, völd og pólitík. Paper presented at a conference on Icelandic women's studies, University of Iceland, Reykjavík.

Jónsdóttir, Valgerður. 1991. Rótin að öðrum ofbeldisverkum. *Vikan* 53(10): 18–24.

Jónsson, Finnur. 1945. *Þjóðhættir og ævisögur frá 19. öld.* Akureyri: Bókaútgáfa P. H. Jónssonar.

Jónsson, Guðmundur. 1988. Sambúð landsdrottna og leiguliða: Yfirvöld skrifa um leiguábúð 1829–35 (English summary, pp. 104–105). *Saga* 26: 63–106.

Jónsson, Hjálmar. 1942. Þjóðfundarsöngur 1851. *Ljóðmæli.* Reykjavík: Bókaútgáfa Menningarsjóðs.

Jónsson, Hjörleifur Rafn. 1989. Haltu hátíð. *Skírnir* 163: 446–458.

———. 1990. Trolls, chiefs and children: Changing perspectives on an Icelandic Christmas myth. *Nord Nytt* 41: 55–63.

Kalland, Arne. 1993. Management by totemization: Whale symbolism and the anti-whaling campaign. *Arctic* 46(2): 124–133.

Kapferer, Bruce. 1988. *Legends of people, myths of state.* Washington, D.C.: Smithsonian Institute Press.

Karlsson, Gunnar. 1985. Spjall um rómantík og þjóðernisstefnu. *Tímarit máls og menningar* 46(4): 449–457.

———. 1986. Kenningar um fornt kvenfrelsi á Íslandi. *Saga* 24: 45–77.

———. 1989. *Samband við miðaldir.* Reykjavík: Mál og menning.

Keesing, Roger M. 1972. Paradigms lost: The new ethnography and the new linguistics. *Southwestern Journal of Anthropology* 28: 299–332.

———. 1989. Creating the past: Custom and identity in the contemporary Pacific. *Contemporary Pacific* 1(1–2): 19–42.

Keesing, Roger M., and Margaret Jolly. 1992. Epilogue. In *History and Tradition in Melanesian Anthropology*, ed. James G. Carrier, pp. 224–248. Berkeley: University of California Press.

Kelley, John D., and Martha Kaplan. 1990. History, structure, and ritual. *Annual Review of Anthropology* 19: 119–150.

Kelly, Liz. 1988. *Surviving sexual violence.* Minneapolis: University of Minnesota Press.

Kissman, Kris. 1989. Single heads of household in Iceland: Dual roles and well-being. *International Journal of Sociology of the Family* 19: 77–84.

———. 1991. Women's political representation and wage equality in Iceland. *International Social Work* 34: 133–142.

Kristjánsdóttir, B., and F. Björnsdóttir. 1988. Oft verða söfnin til fyrir tilviljun eina. *Hús og híbýli* 53(5) (October/November): 20–23.

Kristjánsson, Aðalgeir, and Gísli Ágúst Gunnlaugsson. 1990. Félags- og hagþróun á Íslandi á fyrri hluta 19. aldar. *Saga* 27: 7–62.

Kristmundsdóttir, Sigríður Dúna. 1989. Outside and different: Icelandic women's movements and their notions of authority and cultural separateness of women. In *The anthropology of Iceland*, ed. E. P. Durrenberger and Gísli Pálsson, pp. 80–97. Iowa City: University of Iowa Press.

———. 1990. Doing and becoming: Women's movements and women's personhood in Iceland 1870–1990. Ph.D. dissertation, University of Rochester.

Lamphere, L. 1985. Bringing the family to work: Women's culture on the shop floor. *Feminist Studies* 11(3): 519–554.

Lárusson, Björn. 1967. *The Old Icelandic land registers*. Monographs in Economic History No. 7. Lund: Lund University.

Lave, Jean. 1988. *Cognition in practice: Mind, mathematics and culture in everyday life*. Cambridge: Cambridge University Press.

———. 1991. Situating learning in communities of practice. In *Perspectives on socially shared cognition*, ed. L. B. Resnick, J. M. Levine, and S. D. Teasley, pp. 63–82. Pittsburgh: University of Pittsburgh Learning Research and Development Center.

Leach, Edmund R. 1954. *Political systems of highland Burma: A study of Kachin social structure*. Boston: Beacon Press.

———. 1964. Anthropological aspects of language: Animal categories and verbal abuse. In *New directions in the study of language*, ed. Erik H. Lenneberg, pp. 23–63. Cambridge, Mass.: MIT Press.

Leacock, E., and J. Nash. 1981. Ideologies of sex: Archetypes and stereotypes. In *Myths of male dominance*, pp. 242–263. New York: Monthly Review Press.

Leacock, E., and H. Safa. 1986. *Women's work: Development and the division of labour by gender*. South Hadley, Mass.: Bergin and Garvey Publishers.

Lee, Richard. 1994. The primitive as problematic. *Anthropology Today* 9(6): 1–3.

Lefebvre, Henri. 1991. *The production of space*. Tr. D. Nicholson-Smith. Oxford: Blackwell. Originally published 1974.

LeGrand, Julian. 1990. Equity versus efficiency: The elusive trade-off. *Ethics* 100 (April): 554–568.

———. 1991. *Equity and choice: An essay in economics and applied philosophy*. London: Harper-Collins Academic.

Levathes, Louise E. 1987. Iceland: Life under the glaciers. *National Geographic* 171(2) (February): 184–215.

Lévi-Strauss, Claude. 1955. *Tristes tropiques*. Paris: Plon.

———. 1968. *Structural anthropology*. Middlesex: Penguin Books.

———. 1972. *The savage mind*. Trowbridge: Redwood Press.

Lindquist, Ole, and María Tryggvadóttir. 1990. Whale watching in Iceland: A feasibility study. Manuscript.

Livi-Bacci, M. 1992. *A concise history of world population*. Tr. C. Ipsen. Cambridge: Blackwell.

Lloyd, Genevieve. 1987. Selfhood, war and masculinity. In *Feminist challenges*, ed. C. Pateman and E. Gross, pp. 63–76. Boston: Northeastern University Press.

Loeske, Donileen. 1992. *The battered woman and shelters: The social construction of wife abuse*. Albany: State University of New York Press.

Lögreglan í Reykjavík. 1990. *Ársskýrsla*.

Lowenthal, David. 1990. *The past is a foreign country*. Cambridge: Cambridge University Press.

Lubasz, Heinz. 1992. Adam Smith and the invisible hand—of the market? In *Contesting markets: Analyses of ideology, discourse and practice*, ed. Roy Dilley, pp. 37–56. Edinburgh: Edinburgh University Press.

Lukes, Steven. 1973. *Individualism*. New York: Harper and Row.

MacCannell, Dean. 1976. *The tourist: A new theory of the leisure class*. New York: Schocken Books.

Macdonald, Sharon. 1993. Identity complexes in Western Europe: Social anthropological perspectives. In *Inside European identities*, ed. Sharon Macdonald, pp. 1–26. Oxford: Berg.

Macinko, Seth. 1993. Public or private? United States commercial fisheries management and the public trust doctrine, reciprocal challenges. *Natural Resources Journal* 32: 919–955.

Magnússon, Finnur. 1989. Work and the identity of the poor: Work load, work discipline, and self-respect. In *The anthropology of Iceland*, ed. E. P. Durrenberger and Gísli Palsson, pp. 140–156. Iowa City: University of Iowa Press.

———. 1990. *The hidden class: Culture and class in a maritime setting: Iceland 1882–1942*. Monographs 1. Århus: North Atlantic.

Magnússon, Magnús. 1985. *Iceland in transition: Labour and socio-economic change before 1940*. Lund: Økonomisk-Historiska Föreningen.

Magnússon, Sigurður A. 1977. *Northern sphinx*. Montreal: McGill University Press.

Malkii, Liisa. 1992. *National Geographic*: The rooting of peoples and the territorialization of national identity among scholars and refugees. *Cultural Anthropology* 7(1): 22–44.

Mann, Michael. 1992. The emergence of modern European nationalism.

In *Transition to modernity: Essays on power, wealth and belief,* ed. John A. Hall and I. C. Jarvie, pp. 137–166. Cambridge: Cambridge University Press.

Martin, Emily. 1987. *The woman in the body.* Boston: Beacon Press.

Matthíasson, Þórólfur. 1994. En sivilisert lösning! *Aftenposten,* July 9.

Matthíasson, Þorsteinn. 1980. Hvers vegna Albert? *Morgunblaðið,* June 27.

McCay, Bonnie. n.d. *Public trust and private alienation.* Tucson: University of Arizona Press. In press.

McCay, Bonnie M., and J. M. Acheson (eds.). 1987. *The question of the commons: The culture and ecology of communal resources.* Tucson: University of Arizona Press.

McCay, B. M., and C. F. Creed. 1990. Social structure and debates on fisheries management in the Atlantic surf clam fishery. *Ocean and Shoreline Management* 13: 199–229.

McCloskey, Donald N. 1985. *The rhetoric of economics.* Madison: University of Wisconsin Press.

———. 1993. Some consequences of a conjective economics. In *Beyond economic man: Feminist theory and economics,* ed. Marianne Ferber and Julie A. Nelson, pp. 69–91. Chicago and London: University of Chicago Press.

McDonald, Maryon. 1993. The construction of difference: An anthropological approach to stereotypes. In *Inside European identities,* ed. Sharon Macdonald, pp. 219–236. Oxford: Berg.

McGovern, T. H., G. Bigelow, T. Amorosi, and D. Russell. 1988. Northern Islands, human error, and environmental degradation: Social and ecological change in the medieval North Atlantic. *Human Ecology* 16(3): 225–270.

McGrane, Bernard. 1989. *Beyond anthropology: Society and other.* New York: Columbia University Press.

Meillassoux, C. 1975. *Maidens, meal and money: Capitalism and the domestic community.* Cambridge: Cambridge University Press.

Mintz, Sidney W. 1985. *Sweetness and power: The place of sugar in modern history.* New York: Elisabeth Sifton Books.

Mitchell, B. R. 1975. *European historical statistics 1750–1970.* New York: Columbia University Press.

Mohanty, Chandra Talpade. 1991. Introduction. In *Third World women and the politics of feminism,* ed. Chandra Talpade Mohanty et al., pp. 1–47. Bloomington: University of Indiana Press.

Monbiot, George. 1994. Lost outside the wilderness. *BBC Wildlife* 12(7): 28–31.

Moore, Henrietta. 1988. *Feminism and anthropology*. Minneapolis: University of Minnesota Press.

Morris, Brian. 1992. *Western concepts of the individual*. New York: Berg.

Mullaney, Steven. 1983. Strange things, gross terms, curious customs: The rehearsal of cultures in the Late Renaissance. *Representations* (Summer) 7(3).

Munk-Madsen, E., and M. Husmo. 1989. *Kjønnsmyter med konsekvenser: En analyse af skillet mellom kvinner og menn i industriell fiskeforedling til lands og til vanns*. Kvinnes Sysselsetning i Fiskeridistriktene. Rapport 1, Tromsø: Norges Fiskerihogskole.

Murphy, Robert F., and Julian H. Steward. 1956. Tappers and trappers: Parallel process in acculturation. *Economic Development and Culture Change* 4: 335–355.

Nadel-Klein, J., and D. L. Davis. 1988. *To work and to weep: Women in fishing economies*. Social and Economic Papers No. 18. Institute of Social and Economic Research. St. Johns: Memorial University of Newfoundland.

Nash, J., and M. P. Fernandez-Kelly. 1983. *Women, men and the international division of labor*. Albany: State University of New York Press.

Neher, P. A., Ragnar Arnason, et al. 1989. Foundations of rights based fishing. In *Rights based fishing*, ed. P. A. Neher, Ragnar Arnason, and Nina Mollet, pp. 5–10. Dordrecht: Kluwer Academic Publishers.

Nelson, Julie A. 1993. The study of choice or the study of provisioning? Gender and the definition of economics. In *Beyond economic man: Feminist theory and economics*, ed. Marianne Ferber and Julie A. Nelson, pp. 23–36. Chicago and London: University of Chicago Press.

Nordal, Jóhannes, and Valdimar Kristinsson. 1975. *Iceland 874–1974*. Reykjavík: Central Bank of Iceland.

Nordal, Sigurður. 1924. Átrúnaður Egils Skallagrímssonar. *Skírnir* 48: 145–165.

Noyes, J. K. 1992. *Colonial space: Spatiality in the discourse of German south west Africa 1884–1915*. Chur: Harwood Academic Publishers.

O'Brien, D. P. 1991. Theory and empirical observation. In *Companion to contemporary economic thought*, ed. David Greenaway, Michael Bleaney, and Ian Stewart, pp. 49–67. London and New York: Routledge.

Odner, Knut. 1974. Economic structures in western Norway in the Early Iron Age. *Norwegian Archaeological Review* 7: 104–112.

Okun, Arthur M. 1975. *Equality and efficiency: The big trade-off*. Washington, D.C.: Brookings Institution.

Ólafsson, Oddur. 1993. Þjóðarsáttin 30. júní 1968. *Tíminn*, June 30.

Ólason, Vésteinn. 1989. Bóksögur. In *Íslensk þjóðmenning VI: Munnmenntir og bókmenning*, ed. Frosti F. Jóhannsson, pp. 159–227. Reykjavík: Þjóðsaga.

Olwig, Karen Fog. 1993. *Global culture, island identity: Continuity and change in the Afro-Caribbean community of Nevis*. New York: Harwood Academic Publishers.

Olwig, Kenneth Robert. 1993. Sexual cosmology: Nation and landscape at the conceptual interstices of nature and culture; or, what does landscape really mean? In *Landscape: Politics and perspectives*, ed. Barbara Bender, pp. 307–343. Providence: Berg.

Organization for Economic Co-operation and Development (OECD). 1987. *Education Committee: Review of educational policy in Iceland, examiners' report and questions*. Reykjavík: Menntamálaráduneytið.

Ormerod, Paul. 1994. *The death of economics*. London: Faber and Faber.

Ortner, Sherry B. 1984. Theory in anthropology since the sixties. *Comparative Study of Society and History* 26(1): 126–166.

Óskarsdóttir, Þórkatla. 1982. Idea and nationality in Icelandic poetry 1830–1974. Ph.D. thesis, University of Edinburgh.

Pálsson, Gísli. 1989a. The art of fishing. *Maritime Anthropological Studies* 2: 1–20.

———. 1989b. Language and society: The ethnolinguistics of Icelanders. In *The anthropology of Iceland*, ed. E. Paul Durrenberger and Gísli Pálsson, pp. 121–139. Iowa City: University of Iowa Press.

———. 1991. *Coastal economies, cultural accounts: Human ecology and Icelandic discourse*. Manchester: Manchester University Press.

———. 1992. Introduction: Text, life and saga. In *From sagas to society: Comparative approaches to Early Iceland*, pp. 1–26. Enfield Lock: Hisarlik Press.

———. 1993a. Household words: Attention, agency, and the ethnography of fishing. In *Beyond boundaries: Understanding, translation and anthropological discourse*, pp. 117–139. Providence: Berg.

———. 1993b. Introduction: Beyond boundaries. In *Beyond boundaries: Understanding, translation and anthropological discourse*, pp. 1–40. Providence: Berg.

———. 1994. Enskilment at sea. *Man* 29(4): 901–927.

———. 1995. *The textual life of savants: Ethnography, Iceland, and the linguistic turn*. New York: Harwood Academic Publishers.

Pálsson, Gísli, and E. Paul Durrenberger. 1982. To dream of fish: The causes of Icelandic skippers' fishing success. *Journal of Anthropological Research* 38(2): 227–242.

————. 1983. Icelandic foremen and skippers: The structure and evolution of a folk model. *American Ethnologist* 10(3): 511–528.

————. 1989. Introduction: Toward an anthropology of Iceland. In *The anthropology of Iceland*, ed. E. Paul Durrenberger and Gísli Pálsson, pp. ix–xxiv. Iowa City: University of Iowa Press.

————. 1990. Systems of production and social discourse: The skipper effect revisited. *American Anthropologist* 92(1): 130–141.

————. 1992. Icelandic dialogues: Individual differences in indigenous discourse. *Journal of Anthropological Research* 48(4): 301–316.

Pálsson, Gísli, and Agnar Helgason. 1995. Figuring fish and measuring men: The quota system in the Icelandic cod fishery. *Ocean and Coastal Management* (in press).

Pálsson, Heimir, et al. 1990. *Yrkja*. Reykjavík: Iðunn.

Parker, Andrew, Mary Russo, Doris Sommer, and Patricia Yaeger. 1992. Introduction. In *Nationalisms and sexualities*, ed. Andrew Parker, Mary Russo, Doris Sommer, and Patricia Yaeger, pp. 1–18. New York: Routledge.

Peacock, James L. 1986. *The anthropological lens: Harsh light, soft focus.* Cambridge: Cambridge University Press.

Peller, S. 1965. Births and deaths among Europe's ruling families since 1500. In *Population in history: Essays in historical demography*, ed. D. V. Glass and D. E. C. Eversley, pp. 87–100. London: Edward Arnold.

Pinson, Ann. 1979. Kinship and economy in modern Iceland: A study in social continuity. *Ethnology* 18(2): 183–197.

————. 1985. The institution of friendship and drinking patterns in Iceland. *Anthropological Quarterly* 58(2): 75–82.

Povinelli, Elizabeth A. 1991. Organizing women: Rhetoric, economy, and politics in process among Australian Aborigines. In *Gender at the crossroads of knowledge: Feminist anthropology in the postmodern era*, ed. Micaela di Leonardo, pp. 235–254. Berkeley: University of California Press.

Prakash, Byan. 1990. Writing post-Orientalist histories of the Third World: Perspectives from Indian historiography. *Comparative Studies in Society and History* 32: 383–408.

Pressan. 1991. Fjórar af sjö konum í kvennaathvarfinu eru frá Asíu. June 6.

Quinn, Naomi, and Dorothy Holland. 1987. Culture and cognition. In *Cultural models in language and thought*, ed. Dorothy Holland and Naomi Quinn, pp. 3–40. Cambridge: Cambridge University Press.

Ragnarsson, Ólafur. 1981. *Gunnar Thoroddsen: Ólafur Ragnarsson ræðir við Gunnar Thoroddsen.* Reykjavík: Vaka.

Rappaport, Roy. 1971. *Pigs for the ancestors: Ritual in the ecology of a New Guinea people*. New edition. New Haven: Yale University Press.

Renan, Ernest. 1990. What is a nation? In *Nations and narration*, ed. Homi K. Bhabha, pp. 8–22. London: Routledge. Originally published 1882.

Reykvíkingur 1952. 1(6).

Roosevelt, Theodore. 1939. Preface. In Vilhjálmur Stefánsson, *Iceland: The first American republic*, pp. v–vii. New York: Doubleday, Doran and Company.

Rosaldo, M. Z., and L. Lamphere. 1974. *Woman, culture and society*. Stanford: Stanford University Press.

Rosaldo, Renato. 1993. Ilongot visiting: Social grace and the rhythms of everyday life. In *Creativity/Anthropology*, ed. Smadar Lavie, Kirin Nayaran, and Renato Rosaldo, pp. 253–269. Ithaca: Cornell University Press.

Roseberry, William. 1989. *Anthropologies and histories: Essays in culture, history, and political economy*. Rutgers: Rutgers University Press.

Rothschild, Kurt W. 1993. *Ethics and economic theory: Ideas, models, dilemmas*. Aldershot: Edward Elgar Publishing.

Sacks, K. 1982. *Sisters and wives. The past and future of sexual equality*. Urbana: University of Illinois Press.

Sagoff, Mark. 1988. *The economy of the earth: Philosophy, law and the environment*. Cambridge: Cambridge University Press.

Said, Edward. 1978. *Orientalism*. New York: Vintage Books.

Samtök um kvennaathvarf. 1991a. *Ársskýrsla fyrir árið 1990*. Reykjavík: Samtök um kvennaathvarf.

———. 1991b. *Ofbeldi gegn eiginkonum*. Reykjavík: Samtök um kvennaathvarf.

Schieffelin, Bambi B., and Perry Gilmore (eds.). 1986. *The acquisition of literacy: Ethnographic perspectives*. Volume 21 in the series Advances in Discourse Processes, ed. Roy O. Freedle. Norwood, N.J.: Ablex Publishing.

Schieffelin, Bambi B., and Elinor Ochs (eds.). 1986. *Language socialization across cultures*. New York: Cambridge University Press.

Schneider, David. 1977. Kinship, nationality, and religion in American culture: Toward a definition of kinship. In *Symbolic anthropology: A reader in the study of symbols and meanings*, ed. J. Dolgin, D. Kemnitzer, and D. Schneider, pp. 63–71. New York: Columbia University Press.

Scott, Anthony D. 1989. Conceptual origins of rights based fishing. In *Rights based fishing*, ed. P. A. Neher, Ragnar Arnason, and Nina Mollet, pp. 11–45. Dordrecht: Kluwer Academic Publishers.

Scott, David. 1992. Anthropology and colonial discourse: Aspects of the demonological construction of Sinhala Cultural Pracice. *Cultural Anthropology* 7(3): 301–326.

Scott, J. W. 1988. *Gender and the politics of history*. New York: Columbia University Press.

Scott, James. 1985. *Weapons of the weak*. New Haven: Yale University Press.

———. 1991. *Domination and the arts of resistance*. New Haven: Yale University Press.

Sen, Amartya. 1973. *On economic inequality*. Delhi: Oxford University Press.

———. 1985. The moral standing of the market. In *Ethics and economics*, ed. Ellen F. Paul, Jeffery Paul, and Fred D. Miller, Jr., pp. 1–19. Oxford: Basil Blackwell.

———. 1987. *On ethics and economics*. Oxford: Basil Blackwell.

Service, Elman R. 1955. Indian-European relations in colonial Latin America. *American Anthropologist* 25: 411–423.

Sigurðardóttir, Anna. 1985. *Vinna kvenna á Íslandi í 1100 ár*. Reykjavík: Kvennasögusafn Íslands.

Sigurðardóttir, Steinunn. 1988. *Ein á forsetavakt*. Reykjavík: Iðunn.

Sigurjónsson, Jóhann, and Gísli A. Víkingsson. 1992. Investigation of the ecological role of cetaceans in Icelandic and adjacent waters. Paper presented at the annual meeting of the International Council for the Exploration of the Sea (ICES).

Sinclair, P. R., and L. F. Felt. 1992. Separate worlds: Gender and domestic labour in an isolated fishing region. *Canadian Review of Sociology and Anthropology*, 29(1): 55–71.

Skaptadóttir, Unnur. 1992. Frá saltfiski til færibands: Breytingar á stöðu kvenna í sjávarþorpum með tilliti til heimilis og atvinnuhátta. Paper presented in the conference Social Research on the Fisheries, University of Iceland, Reykjavík.

Skýrsla til sjávarútvegsráðherra. 1994. Manuscript. Reykjavík.

Smith, Anthony D. 1986. *The ethnic origins of nations*. Oxford: Oxford University Press.

———. 1991. *National identity*. Reno: University of Nevada Press.

Smith, Neil. 1984. *Uneven development: Nature, capital, and the production of space*. Oxford: Basil Blackwell.

Solomon, Maynard (ed.). 1979. *Marxism and art: Essays classic and contemporary*. Detroit: Wayne State University Press.

Sorenson, John. 1992. History and identity in the Horn of Africa. *Dialectical Anthropology* 17: 227–252.

Sperber, Dan. 1975. *Rethinking symbolism*. Cambridge: Cambridge University Press.

Spong, Paul. 1992. Why we love to watch whales. *Sonar* 7: 24–25.

Stefánsson, Magnús. 1974. Comments on economic structures in the Early Iron Age. *Norwegian Archaeological Review* 7: 130–138.

Steffensen, Jón. 1975. *Menning og meinsemdir*. Reykjavík: Sögufélag.

———. 1977. Smallpox in Iceland. In *Nordisk Medicinhistorik Årsbok 1977*, pp. 41–56. Stockholm: S. M.

Steward, Julian H. 1951. Levels of sociocultural integration: An operational concept. *Southwestern Journal of Anthropology (Journal of Anthropological Research)* 7: 370–390.

Stjórnarskrá Lýðveldisins Íslands. 1986. Forsætisráðuneytið.

Straus, Murray, and Gelles, Richard (eds.). 1990. *Physical violence in American families: Risk factors and adaptations to violence in 8,145 families*. New Brunswick: Transaction Publishers.

Street, Brian. 1984. *Literacy in theory and practice*. Cambridge Studies in Oral and Literate Culture 9. New York: Cambridge University Press.

Thompson, P. 1985. Women in the fishing: The roots of power between the sexes. *Comparative Studies in Society and History* 27(1): 3–32.

Tomasson, R. F. 1976. Premarital sexual permissiveness and illegitimacy in the Nordic countries. *Comparative Studies in Society and History* 18(2): 252–270.

———. 1977. A millennium of misery: The demography of the Icelanders. *Population Studies* 31: 405–425.

———. 1980. *Iceland: The first new society*. Minneapolis: University of Minnesota Press.

Tonnesen, J. N., and A. O. Johnsen. 1982. *The history of modern whaling*. London: C. Hurst and Company.

Turner, John, and John Ash. 1975. *The golden hordes: International tourism and the pleasure periphery*. London: Constable.

Turner, Victor. 1978. *Image and pilgrimage in Christian culture*. New York: Columbia University Press.

Urry, John. 1990a. The consumption of tourism. In *Sociology: Journal of the British Sociological Association* 24(1): 23–35.

———. 1990b. *The tourist gaze: Leisure and travel in contemporary societies*. London: Sage Publications.

Valdimarsson, Sigurjón. 1990. Ritstjórnargrein. *Sjómannablaðið Víkingur* 1: 5.

van den Hoonaard, W. 1991. A nation's innocence: Myth and reality of crime in Iceland. *Scandinavian-Canadian Studies* 4: 97–114.

Vasey, D. E. 1991. Population, agriculture, and famine: Iceland, 1784–85. *Human Ecology* 19(3): 1–28.

———. n.d. Manual for the Iceland database. Forthcoming mimeo. Reykjavík: Department of Anthropology, University of Iceland.

Vikufréttir. 1990. Fórnarlömb sifjaspella koma fram undir nafni: Ég drep þig ef þú segir mömmu. May 3.

Vološinov, V. N. 1973. *Marxism and the philosophy of language.* Tr. L. Matejka and I. R. Titunik. Cambridge, Mass.: Harvard University Press.

Vygotsky, L. S. 1978. *Mind in society: The development of higher psychological processes.* Ed. Michael Cole et al. Cambridge, Mass.: Harvard University Press.

Wallace, A. F. C. 1961. *Culture and personality.* New York: Random House.

Walsh, B. M. 1970. Marriage rates and population pressure: Ireland, 1871 and 1911. *Economic History Review* 23: 148–162.

Watson, (Captain) Paul. 1993. An open letter to Norwegians. Manuscript.

Whitehead, Þór. 1980. *Ófriður í aðsigi.* Reykjavík: Almenna bókafélagið.

———. 1985. *Stríð fyrir ströndum.* Reykjavík: Almenna bókafélagið.

Williams, Raymond. 1977. *Marxism and literature.* Oxford: Oxford University Press.

Wilson, James A., James M. Acheson, Mark Metcalfe, and Peter Kleban. 1994. Chaos, complexity and community management of fisheries. *Marine Policy* 18(4): 291–305.

Wolf, Eric R. 1957. Closed corporate peasant communities in Mesoamerica and Central Java. *Southwestern Journal of Anthropology* 13(1): 1–14.

———. 1966. *Peasants.* Englewood Cliffs: Prentice-Hall.

———. 1982. *Europe and the people without history.* Berkeley: University of California Press.

Wylie, Jonathan. 1987. *The Faroe Islands: Interpretations of history.* Lexington: University Press of Kentucky.

Yearley, Steven. 1993. Standing in for nature: The practicalities of environmental organisations' use of science. In *Environmentalism: The view from anthropology,* ed. Kay Milton, pp. 59–72. ASA Monograph 32. London: Routledge.

Young, K., C. Wolkowitz, and R. McCullagh. 1981. *Of marriage and the market: Women's subordination in international perspective.* London: CSE Books.

Young, M. D. 1992. *Sustainable investment and resource use: Equity, environmental integrity and economic efficiency.* Paris: UNESCO.

Þjóðin kýs. 1980. 1–4.

Þórarinsson, Jón. 1980. Alþingi þarfnast aðhalds. *Morgunblaðið*, June 27.

Þórarinsson, Sigurður. 1956. *The thousand years struggle against ice and fire.* Reykjavík: Bókaútgáfa Menningarsjóðs.

Þórarinsson, Þórarinn. 1993. Forseti Íslands og þjóðaratkvæði. *Tíminn*, January 20.

Þórðarson, Jóhann. 1993. Nokkur orð um gildi 26. gr. stjórnarskrárinnar. *Morgunblaðið*, January 23.

Ægir. 1926. 19(4): 53–54. Sýnið fánann.

INDEX

We follow international rather than Icelandic usage for listing names—surname or father's name first, given name second. We list authors only when they appear as subjects, not wherever they are cited.

masculinity, 70, 87, 88, 91, 97,
99, 107–109, 114, 119, 124
Mead, G. H., 7
media, Icelandic, 16, 27, 34, 35,
41, 42, 67, 111, 117, 128,
131, 132, 142–143, 182, 191,
195, 196, 198, 199–214, 226,
231
metaphors, for quota holders, 77,
78, 82
Milton, Kay, 59
Mintz, Sidney, 5, 12
mobbing, 131. *See also* violence
Mohanty, Chandra Talpade, 143,
144
morality, 152–170
Morris, William, 221
mothers and motherhood, 87–
105, 106–125, 127, 198; in
nationalist rhetoric, 11, 12,
106–125, 126–145. *See also*
independence, rhetoric of;
nationalism
Mountain Woman, 108–125, 132,
133, 229. *See also* femininity;
gender; presidents, Icelandic
Mullaney, Steven, 219
Murphy, Robert, 12

names, Icelandic, 134, 173, 174
nationalism, 2, 4, 7, 9, 10, 11,
14–16, 18, 25, 26, 28, 29, 35,
36, 39, 40, 44, 107–111, 115,
118, 119, 130–136, 169, 171–
190, 216, 217, 220, 227–235,
235n.3. *See also* identity, national; identity, individual; independence, Icelandic
nations, 2, 3, 8, 11, 14, 18, 19,
25, 28, 36, 37, 38, 108, 178

NATO base, 38, 45n.4, 114, 115,
117, 132, 211, 231
nature, 10, 11, 25, 26, 36, 39, 40,
41, 47, 48, 50, 54, 46, 107–
111, 120, 126, 147–235
newspapers. *See* media, Icelandic
Nordal, Jóhannes, 150
Nordal, Sigurður, 173, 220, 234–
235n.1

Odner, Knut, 14
Ólason, Vésteinn, 16
Olwig, K. F., 5
Ortner, Sherry, 186
ownership. *See* commons;
property

Pálsson, Gísli, ix, x, 4, 9, 10, 131,
145, 170, 172, 188, 190,
235n.3, 239
patriarchy, 126–145
Peacock, James L., 218
Pinson, Ann, 139
poetry, 109, 202, 222, 223
police, Icelandic, 136–138, 141
population records, 157–170
Posey, Darrell, 59
postmodernism, 17, 234
Povinelli, Elizabeth A., 143
practice and practices, 144, 180,
183, 185–214, 226
premarital sex, 151, 201. *See also*
demography
presidents, Icelandic, 12, 16, 21,
106–125, 231
privacy, 138, 140–142, 145,
227
property, 38, 41, 60, 65, 66, 71,
81, 83n.1, 152, 153. *See also*
boundaries; commons